Testimonies

of Jews who believe in Jesus

*If Jesus is the Messiah at all,
then he is the Messiah for all.*

Ruth Rosen, Editor

Published by
Purple Pomegranate Productions
San Francisco, California

97 98 99 00 10 9 8 7 6 5 4 3 2 1

Rosen, Ruth 1956-
Testimonies of Jews who believe in Jesus/Ruth Rosen, Editor—
Rev. 4th ed.

Library of Congress Cataloging-Publication Data
Testimonies of Jews who believe in Jesus

ISBN: 1-881022-31-5 (pbk.)
1. Jewish Christians—Religious life. 2. Christian life.
BV2623.A1J43 1997
289.9—dc20

Dedication

It's been over twenty years since I promised my mother, Ceil Rosen, I would someday dedicate "my first book" to her. I didn't know much about dedication then, but she did, and does, and so in part this book is for her.

As it turns out, this book really isn't mine to dedicate. It belongs to all the people who consented to tell me their stories. Many relived personal, sometimes painful memories to tell how Y'shua came into their lives. I think everyone whose testimony is told herein (including Ceil Rosen) would agree with me that this book is for Y'shua, to say thanks for all he's done for us--and for you, in hopes that you will know him, too.

Table of Contents

Introduction

Why don't Jews believe in Jesus? This is a question which perplexes many Christians. It seems to them that if anyone ought to believe in Jesus, it should be the Jewish people. After all, Jesus was a Jew and it was to the Jewish people that he presented himself.

Most Jewish people have a variety of reasons to explain about not believing in Jesus. Yet, as one listens to the many reasons given, two things become apparent. First, most Jewish people have never really, seriously contemplated whether or not Jesus might possibly be the Messiah. It is simply not an open question. And second, there seems to be a commitment to believe that he is NOT the Messiah. The reasons commonly given for the commitment to unbelief often sound like afterthoughts--justifications for a decision already made. That is because so many Jewish people see the commitment not to believe in Jesus as necessary to our survival.

The commitment not to believe in Jesus is a negative corollary to the commitment to maintaining one's Jewish identity, as if being Jewish and believing in Jesus are antithetical to one another. We Jews know who and what we are, we know our own history, and what our people have endured. We have plenty of good reasons for rejecting Christians (at least those reasons seem good to us).

Many Jewish people find it difficult to admit it's rejection of Christians and not Jesus himself that keeps us from believing. But who is it that is blamed for the Holocaust? The Pogroms? The Crusades?

The fact that the gentle Savior spoke against violence and against the persecution of any and all people should demonstrate that the perpetrators of such atrocities were not acting "Christianly." They were using religion to justify or excuse their blatantly "unchristian" conduct.

The commitment to Jewishness involves survival instincts which include the attraction of "our own" and the rejection and exclusion of those who are "not our own."

Buried beneath some rather esoteric theological reasons for not believing in Jesus is the pivotal fact: Jews don't believe in Jesus simply because we want to be Jews and we have been indoctrinated that the religion of Jesus belongs to "them" not to "us."

Because we have accepted that it is "their" religion, most of us have never listened or heard enough to realize that "they" discovered Jesus from the Jewish Bible. Therefore, out of a sense of loyalty most Jewish people simply haven't considered that Jesus IS for Jews.

It was not so in the beginning. The last in the lineage of Jewish prophets, Yochanon (John), preached repentance in Israel and gathered large crowds. It was this prophet who pointed to Jesus and called him "the Lamb of God." Two of John's followers determined to investigate the matter. After interviewing Jesus, they went out to tell others. Philip put it succinctly when he said, "We have found Him of whom Moses in the law and also the prophets wrote." This testimony of discovery was how knowledge and faith in Jesus was spread: from one Jewish person to another. Some were convinced by the miracles, others by his wisdom, and, to some, there were direct revelations from God himself.

A chance encounter Jesus had with a Samaritan woman had her running to tell the people of her city, "Come, see a Man who told me all things that ever I did. Could this be the Messiah?" After hearing her report, they came, they saw, they listened, and they told her, "Now we believe, not because of what you said, for we have heard him for ourselves and know that this is indeed the Messiah." That is the invitation of this book.

If you already know Jesus and believe in him, rejoice with those who want to tell you how they discovered him. If you don't yet believe, listen to what these people have to say, what they've discovered, and investigate for yourself the evidence that, indeed, Jesus is the promised One, for all people. He is not "for Gentiles only." *Jesus is for Jews.*

Moishe Rosen, Executive Director
Jews for Jesus

Preface: For Committed Unbelievers Only

In the mart of men with eyes shut tight, they call a blind man rich of light.   Genesis R.

He was as brilliant as he was black, only those two things, some supposed, were mutually exclusive in the Deep South of the 1920s. Still, he awoke that morning filled with hope for a new day--a day for him to seize opportunity, meet responsibility, exercise his right and register to vote. The black man was going to cast his ballot.

They thought he wouldn't be able to pay the poll tax. Either he wouldn't have the money or he'd prefer to spend it elsewhere--on wine and women--you know, the sort of things "those" people enjoy. The poll tax was their first checkpoint--their way of separating the men from "the boys," so to speak. They were a bit taken aback when the black man paid the poll tax.

They decided they had better test him to make sure he was literate enough to vote.   "Here," one of them said, thrusting a paper under his nose. "Read this." It was getting warm, but the black man did not care to loosen his tie or remove his suit coat. He cleared his throat.   His voice was deep and resonant as he read, "We hold these truths to be self-evident, that all men are created equal, that they are endowed by their Creator with certain unalienable Rights, that among these are Life..."

"Awright, that'll do jest fine." The redheaded one with the freckles grabbed the paper. "You read real nice. Real nice indeed."   They talked among themselves for a few moments. His reading was probably a fluke. Maybe someone taught him to recognize those words and he had memorized them.

They were prepared for that sort of thing. One of them opened a file folder and removed a sheet of paper. There were just a few sentences scribbled on it; they were in French. "Read this," challenged the skinny one with the suspenders.

The black man pronounced the sentences with a flawless accent that would have delighted any Frenchman.

"That's fine," said Skinny, who did not know that the black man was a professor of languages at the local Negro college. "Jest fine, but what does it mean?" Patiently, the black man translated the sentences.

They didn't know where he'd learned French, but what difference did it make? They made him read and translate sentence after sentence in German, Italian and Latin. They wouldn't have known if he was answering right or wrong, except a scholar had written the translations on a separate sheet of paper. The black man kept passing their tests. He was a tricky rascal, real devious; he had the knack of seeming brilliant, when everyone knew he really wasn't. He couldn't be. After all, he was colored, wasn't he?

Finally, the fat bald one handed him a piece of paper with some exotic symbols drawn on it. The black man recognized the characters as Chinese, but he couldn't decipher one of them. "Can you pronounce this?" the bald man asked.

"No sir, I can't," the black man replied.

"Well then son, can ya tell us what it means?"

"That I can, sir." Their eyes all narrowed to tiny slits as they awaited his translation.

"It means," the black man said, "that I can't vote in this state of the union."

Many such incidents have occurred and they continue to occur. They don't only happen between blacks and whites; they happen whenever and wherever people draw conclusions based on their assumptions rather than the evidence. They happen when people are on a "fact-finding" mission, where the only facts they find are those that suit them--the others are discarded and disregarded before the person accidentally catches a glimpse of what he or she is committed to not seeing. These incidents happen when people are more concerned with maintaining the status quo than they are with discovering the truth.

Prejudice enables people to reject reality. Some reject what is real, simply because the truth might demand action they are unwilling to take. Others armor themselves with prejudice for protection against thinking what might lower them in the eyes of their people. For whatever reason, folks can be quite adamant in demanding they shouldn't be told something they don't want to hear. Incidents of prejudice to maintain the status quo are not rare. They even happen when some Jews who don't believe in Jesus encounter other Jews who do.

The committed unbeliever's "Jewish approach" to Jesus is that he can't possibly be the Messiah; therefore any evidence that he is must be wrong, and other Jews who do believe in him are obviously defective in intelligence or integrity. They feel that they, too, would somehow appear defective if they allowed themselves to really listen to the claims of Jewish believers in Jesus. They'll listen to the case just long enough to distort the testimony of the already condemned "traitor," then drag that testimony into the chambers of their own minds where they act as judge, jury and prosecuting attorney.

I hope that is not your purpose in reading the following "testimonies." If you're only reading this book to pass judgment on Jewish believers in Jesus, why bother? The people who tell their stories here would be the first to tell you their shortcomings and frailties. The purpose of this book isn't to show them off as heroes. They are ordinary Jews representing their generations. They are not the giants of the messianic Jewish movement. Jesus is the only hero in this book. He is not breakfast cereal; the people you'll read about here don't advertise him as "the savior of champions."

If you really are committed to not believing Jesus' claims, this book is "small potatoes." He is the one whom you need to discredit. After all, the question is, is Jesus who he says he is? If he did what the "New Testament" Scriptures said he did, then who and what we are doesn't amount to much...a few toothpicks, not a tower beam of support. These testimonies are not to show how we support him, but how he supports us. The Bible itself is the main support and evidence that Jesus is the Messiah. And you'll not be able to discredit him by discounting the New Testament alone, for as Jesus said, "If you believed Moses and the prophets, you would believe me." Why not read the most comprehensive book ever written about him.

Read the "New Testament." No one is there to force it upon you or manipulate you into believing. Any shadow of doubt you could cast on the Bible would hold much more weight than the complaints you might have about this little book.

The following testimonies give eyewitness accounts of a few miracles and some answered prayers--even people returning from death's door. There are many voices in this book--voices of Jews who are eager to be heard. They're not selling because what they found is beyond price, and was given to them freely and fully by God. They are eager to tell their stories because they are Jews, and it is very Jewish to want to tell good news--especially to other Jews. They have chosen to make themselves vulnerable because they have dared to hope that if you knew what Jesus has done for them, you would want him, too.

They came to believe in Y'shua against all their natural and normal inclinations. Jesus--whose claims most Jews are either compelled to deplore, ashamed to explore or trained to ignore. How did they come to believe? If you really want to know, and you read this preface addressed to "Committed Unbelievers Only" more out of curiosity than unbelief, please, read on. Our ancestors had an awesome relationship with the God of Israel, and that relationship is still available--to you, today! You can examine the evidence for that relationship in the lives of these people, as told in the following pages.

You'll notice I said evidence, not proof. Whether or not it is proof depends on how you accept it into your own heart and mind. If you have impugned the integrity of the witnesses before they speak, they can say nothing to you. But if you read, you might recognize the ring of truth. Evidence is material, objective, whereas "proof" is almost entirely subjective. The black man gave evidence that he was qualified to vote. His evidence did not "prove" anything to his opponents, for they had judged his evidence as inadmissible in their court of prejudice.

If you are one of the "Committed Unbelievers" to whom this preface is addressed, and if you have judged the following evidence as inadmissable before even reading it, why waste your time? Squandering precious moments is the greatest tragedy of all, if this life is all we have.
--Ruth Rosen

And you will seek Me and find Me,
when you search for Me with all your heart.

Jeremiah 29:13

CEIL ROSEN

I was 16 years old, and it was the night of our school Christmas pageant. I was one of many Jewish girls who had sung the words to these songs without giving them a second thought. But now, as we glided across the stage in slow, dance-like rhythm, singing, "O come, O come Immanuel/And ransom captive Israel," *something stirred within me. I suddenly realized that Jesus was Jewish and it made me wonder for just a moment if he could be for us after all....*

I gave Dorothy the money and told her, "The last time I was in there, they were sixty-nine cents. That was just a couple of months ago, so I don't think they've raised the price. Go to the stationery section, you know, past the ledgers and the rolls of scotch tape and you'll see them right there on the shelf. Oh, and Dorothy..." I composed myself and hoped my voice would sound calmer than the frantic beating of my heart, "Make sure you get the whole Bible, you know, with both 'Old' and 'New' Testament." If my husband's cousin was shocked, she didn't show it. She didn't bat an eyelash or say anything to condemn me for wanting to read "the Christians' Bible"--a book which we Jews considered taboo.

I knew exactly what my new Bible would look like even before Dorothy handed it over. The cover was black with gold lettering. The pages inside were of cheap, flimsy paper--a small step above newsprint. It was a dimestore Bible and I wasn't supposed to read it but I did... and it turned my world upside down.

I was raised in an Orthodox Jewish home just outside of Boston. My natural mother died when my twin brother and I were infants. My foster mother prevailed upon my father to let her take care of me while he was still grieving. I discovered later that he didn't know the papers she coaxed him to sign were for my adoption. My foster parents, the Starrs, loved me and treated me as if I were their own.

My foster mother was strict about *kashrut* (the dietary laws). We had separate dishes for meat and milk which we washed with separate bars of soap and even dried with separate dish towels. We kept all the holidays and observed the Sabbath. I was forbidden to pick up a needle and thread, a pair of scissors, or even a pencil on Saturdays.

As observant as we were, I didn't hear much about God. I knew being Jewish meant knowing the real God. I knew he expected us to do things a certain way. I knew that unlike us, the *goyim* had very strange ideas about God and even dared to believe there was more than One.

When I was 4 years old, I expected God to care. I remember tearfully asking him to fix my red balloon, which had popped. My parents couldn't afford to buy games or dolls, and to me, that balloon was the most beautiful toy in the world. I was heartbroken when it burst and even more heartbroken when God didn't fix it. I think my hopes that God really cared for me burst along with that balloon. I didn't really love God; nobody had ever told me I should. I only knew I was supposed to obey him.

When I was 13 years old, we left New England. The doctor said my mother needed a warmer, drier climate, so we moved to Denver, Colorado. I was at the age when I was beginning to question authority. I chafed under the restrictions of my Orthodox upbringing. I was tired of all the "dos" and "don'ts." I'd had it with memorizing this and learning that, never knowing why...and where was this God of rules and regulations, anyway? I'd discovered that my parents were not especially right about everything, so it occurred to me that maybe they were wrong about God. Maybe God didn't even exist.

When I was 14 years old, I answered a knock at our door and found a boy named Moishe Rosen standing there. He was selling house numbers, the kind you post so people can read your address. I think they were supposed to glow in the dark. My mother didn't buy any numbers, but Moishe asked me out and I refused. I was really too shy. A year later he asked me again. We lived on the same city block, went to the same school, but until then we hadn't talked much. But at age 15, we went for a walk and from then on we began to "go steady."

Moishe's family was nominally Orthodox; they were members of an Orthodox synagogue, but his mother didn't keep kosher. I could go to his house and enjoy bacon for breakfast without feeling guilty.

I remember participating when the girls' chorus in our high school gave a Christmas pageant. We dressed up as Israeli women, with long, flowing gowns. As we glided across the stage in slow, dancelike rhythm, singing, "O come, O come Immanuel/And ransom captive Israel," something stirred within me. I suddenly realized that Jesus was Jewish and it made me wonder for just a moment if he could be for us after all. Then my attention returned to the singing and the pleasure of the performance.

Moishe and I were married at age 18--a year after I graduated from high school. The freedom was exhilarating! We would not have an Orthodox home; we would be modern American Jews without any hang-ups about religion. We were both proud of our heritage and knew certain ties and roots should be maintained. But the pressure to "be religious" was off.

When I was 19, we were expecting our first baby. I was so happy that I began saying prayers of thanksgiving to God. Now that I lived in the relaxed atmosphere of our own home, I felt freer to be myself and do as I pleased. The rebellion which had expressed itself in a denial of God's existence melted away. I wasn't sure what to believe about God, but I knew he was the giver of life, and I believed he was "at the controls."

Both Moishe and I loved going to the movies. One night we went to see "Quo Vadis" (whither goest thou), a film about the life of Christ. We didn't go out of a particular interest in Jesus. We went because this was an epic film in full color, which was something special in those days. And it was playing in a plush downtown theater, which was also a treat. The two of us slid down in the velvet seats, glued our eyes to the screen and ate our popcorn as though this was just any movie...and I think to Moishe, that's all it was. But the movie left a lasting impression on me. Something about Jesus captured my attention.

In December of 1951, Moishe bought me an album of Christmas carols. He knew I enjoyed the music and, to us, there was no religious significance in listening to these seasonal songs. But when I listened to the words to "O Little Town of Bethlehem," it was as though I was hearing them for the first time: "Yet in the dark street shineth/The everlasting Light." I remembered my high school Christmas pageant and the sudden realization that Jesus was Jewish. Just as suddenly, I prayed, "God, could it be possible that what these Christians are saying about Jesus is true? I'm ready to go back to Orthodox Judaism and keep all the laws if that is what you want--or I am willing to believe in Jesus if he is really our Messiah."

4

I forgot about that prayer until a week or so later. After all, I was a busy woman. I spent most of my time and energy caring for our baby daughter. But on New Year's Eve, I was startled into remembering my prayer. I was gazing at the sky from my pantry window when I caught sight of a bigger and brighter star than I had ever seen. As I stared, I found myself thinking, "Maybe that's what the Christmas star looked like."

How could such a question enter the mind of a Jewish woman? Was it possible that God really wanted me to believe in Jesus? I only knew that I wanted to find out the truth about Jesus and that I trusted God to show me. I began to wonder about the New Testament. I wanted to read it, but was afraid. It had been one thing to discard the dietary law; there were many Jews who had done likewise. But if I believed in Jesus, there was a good chance I would be ostracized by family and friends. I was happy; I did not want my life to be disrupted. I didn't want the disapproval of those I loved. Yet I was curious, so curious to read that book. I'd seen it in the Newberry's 5 & 10--I knew how much it cost, and I wanted it very badly.

Finally, I asked Cousin Dorothy to purchase the Bible for me--but I didn't show how eager I was to read it. As soon as she left, I opened to the beginning of the New Testament and began reading the Book of Matthew. Then I went on to read Mark, then Luke and John. After those four books I saw that the rest of the New Testament told what happened after Jesus went up to heaven. I promptly went back to Matthew and started all over again. I knew Jesus was real, and I just couldn't read enough about him.

It's hard to describe what I found so irresistible about Jesus. First of all, it was obvious that he was Jewish. The Book of Matthew begins with his genealogy and traces him back as a son of David. That set my mind at ease because I saw from the start that I wasn't reading about some foreign religion. But what really impressed me about Jesus was the way he talked. He was so practical, down-to-earth, I guess you could say--and at the same time, there was something unmistakably divine about him. He spoke with authority. He was compassionate, yet inspired respect and his commands were a call to righteousness. As I read, I knew he was not just a literary hero. He was real.

The "Sermon on the Mount" (found in Matthew, chapters five through seven) especially impressed me. I was deeply moved by the godliness of Jesus' message. I saw how he built his teachings upon the teachings of Moses; the section about doing good deeds in private rang true. If there had been an inward meaning to the many external activities we performed during my upbringing, it had never been explained to me. Jesus clarified the deeper significance of the Law of Moses.

There was another passage which left a big impression on me. It was a warning. Jesus said that whoever would confess him before men, he would also confess before the Father...and that anyone who denied him before men, he would deny before the Father. He warned that families would be divided over him, and that anyone who loved a family member more than him (Jesus) was not worthy of him. I know that some people have pointed to this passage as "proof" that Jesus came to destroy families. That interpretation never occurred to me. I did not see it as a threat, but as preparation.

Jesus knew that some would accept him while others would not. The issue of Jesus' messiahship cuts to the very quick of the human soul; contention over his identity would obviously cause rifts. If Jesus' claims were true, then to deny him for the sake of family would be to deny God. One thing I did learn in my Orthodox upbringing, and for which I am grateful, is that God deserves to be obeyed, whatever the cost. If Jesus was truly the Messiah (I was now convinced he was), I could not deny it, inconvenient to live with as it might be.

I wanted very badly to discuss these things with somebody, but I didn't know where to turn. I prayed that God would help me find someone who could help with my questions. The answer to my prayers arrived within a few weeks.

It was a snowy day in January 1953 when Mrs. Hannah Wago knocked on our door. She was a missionary. It seems that a Christian family, completely unaware of my search, had asked her to visit our home. I later discovered that this family had been praying for us three times a day, each and every day, for about four years. Their prayer was that Moishe and I would come to know Jesus as our Messiah. During those years of prayer, they had never felt moved to ask a missionary to visit our home...that is, not until I privately prayed that God would send someone. When Mrs. Wago smiled at me and explained why she had come, I was overwhelmed. I excused myself for a few minutes to go into the pantry where I had seen the star and resolved to learn the truth about Jesus. I brushed the tears from my eyes and thanked the Lord for answering my prayer.

Mrs. Wago began teaching me every week. She taught me mostly from the Prophets, using a special reference Bible. It showed how passages were interconnected and indicated how Jesus fulfilled prophecy. Mrs. Wago would come once a week when weather permitted, and when she couldn't come over, she would call so we could study over the phone. I soaked up the Bible like a sponge.

Moishe knew I was reading both the Old and New Testaments and when he saw my interest deepening rather than disappearing, he began to worry. He didn't want any part of it, and he didn't want me to tell anyone else about it either. I tried to show him some of the gospel tracts Hannah had left with me, but that only upset him. Finally, he told me she was not welcome in our home. We shifted all our studies to the telephone, and I continued eagerly, but with concern.

One day, Moishe came home and found me engaged in one of our telephone Bible studies. My husband, who ordinarily would not deny me anything, became so infuriated that he ripped the phone out of the wall! He did apologize and was embarrassed at his anger, but he took no steps to call a repairman. Though he didn't forbid me, I knew I had to be more careful in the way I studied the Bible. He particularly resented Hannah Wago, but in a mysterious way he also respected her as being a holy woman. Mrs. Wago and I continued our studies together, but after that we were careful to finish them by the time Moishe came home from work.

He once confronted me about my beliefs, and without hesitation, I told him, "Please don't make me choose between you and God. If it were anything else, you know I would choose you. But if you give me an ultimatum about this, I'll have to choose God." Moishe didn't pursue it any further because he knew I was serious. He didn't like what I believed, but he couldn't fault me for putting God first. I've seen families ripped apart when a husband or wife can't tolerate his or her spouse's belief in Jesus. I thank God that my husband's love for me outweighed his emotional reaction to my faith.

On Easter Sunday 1953, I walked into a church for the first time in my life. Mrs. Wago arranged for someone to pick me up, and my husband did not object to my going this once. He only warned that I shouldn't make a habit of it, or let anybody know I was going. His fears that my going to church could cause a scandal were not unfounded. If Jews who believe in Jesus are considered traitors in today's modern "free thinking" world, you can imagine the stigma it connoted in the '50s.

I was careful to honor his wishes. I hid my hat under my coat and didn't put it on until I got into the car. If my neighbors had seen me wearing a hat on Easter Sunday, they would have guessed where I was going. The church was decorated with a gardenful of flowers to celebrate Jesus' Resurrection. After the service, the minister invited anyone who wanted to make it known that they were hereby accepting Jesus as their Messiah to come forward. I went and prayed with the minister.

After that, I prayed for my husband every day, often weeping as I asked the Lord to show him the truth about Jesus. I didn't talk much about my faith, because I knew it would upset him terribly. But I did leave a little booklet about heaven lying on the table. My husband is naturally inquisitive and of course he read it. It was about seven weeks after I had prayed with the minister that Moishe said to me, "Heaven's not like that guy says." I was startled! "What guy?" I asked.

"The guy who wrote the pamphlet you left lying around." Moishe began telling me why he thought the pamphlet was wrong, and then he suddenly realized what he was saying. He had never realized that he believed heaven existed. Now he examined his thoughts honestly and faced what he recognized to be prejudice. My husband was an idealistic, if somewhat unambitious, young man. Though he had heard the gospel many years before, he had put it out of his mind--or so he thought. His feeling at the time was, "Though it seems to be true, that only shows how little I really know. The rabbis couldn't be wrong." When he saw my interest in Jesus, he began reading and could make quite a case against Christianity. He later said, "My arguments might have convinced other people, but they didn't convince me because I had the witness of God's spirit in my heart."

Apparently, God had been working on Moishe's heart without either of us realizing it. Even though he had only read about Jesus so that he could disprove my faith, the information had taken root. When he began contradicting the pamphlet about heaven, Moishe realized that he disagreed because he had some beliefs of his own that he hadn't admitted to himself--and those beliefs included Jesus. We were both surprised when he confessed his faith to me, and then asked, "Now what do I do?" We prayed together for him to accept Jesus as his Messiah that Saturday night. He told me he wanted to go to church the next day. We did, and he went forward at the minister's invitation just as I had on Easter Sunday.

Moishe had wanted me to keep quiet about my faith before, but now that he believed, he never doubted for a moment that we should tell our family and friends. To him, not believing in Jesus had been a misunderstanding. He was confident that once our parents understood why we believed, they would understand and accept Jesus too. As far as he was concerned, he had discovered the answer to all the questions of existence, and it never occurred to him that our families wouldn't want to hear or believe. Not only did they not understand and accept Jesus, but they could not understand or accept us, for believing in him.

We told Moishe's family first, and they quickly contacted my parents. My mother responded by telling me in Yiddish, "I hear you've become a goy." I tried to explain to her, "No Ma, I'm still Jewish. But I believe that the New Testament is true and that Jesus is our Messiah." She wouldn't hear a word of it. My father was a little calmer. "Will you at least go talk to the rabbi?" he asked. I agreed to see the rabbi because I wanted my parents to know that believing in Jesus did not mean I would disregard all their wishes. But I warned them that the rabbi would not change my faith.

Moishe and I went to the rabbi together. He asked us to explain our beliefs, and when we did, he asked for our reasons. I quoted from the 53rd chapter of Isaiah about the Messiah dying for our sins, and I also quoted from Jeremiah 31 about the New Covenant God promised. I quoted some other prophecies besides, but the rabbi would not discuss them with us. He told us that he didn't have his commentaries with him and therefore could not discuss it that day. Perhaps another day would be better.

My parents were present. I could see that my father was interested in the prophecies and disappointed when the rabbi did not give us answers. He wanted us to go back to the rabbi, but I felt I had done what I should to show them I cared about their feelings. I realized that no amount of visits to the rabbi would satisfy my parents as long as I believed in Jesus. I did not want to mislead them into thinking that I would change my mind. When they saw that I did not intend to go back to the rabbi, they told me they would forget I was their daughter. I don't think parents can really forget about their children, but they did leave town and we never saw them or heard from them again. Somebody told us they moved to Israel, but we could never find a trace of them.

As for my in-laws, they threatened to disown us at first, but did not cut us out of their lives for more than a year or so. We went back East so Moishe could attend Bible school, and in the process, I was reunited with my natural father. He was so happy to see us and his new grandchildren that he did not mind our belief in Jesus.

Years later our younger daughter visited with my dad and my stepmother for a week and a half. During her visit, my father went to the *shul* each morning to pray. This led to some discussion of religion, but when she talked to my dad about why we believe in Jesus, she was met with the usual smile and "That's all right dear, but when you get to be my age, you'll know better." But she challenged my father to go to God and ask him the truth about Jesus. In the end, my father promised to ask God to show him whether or not he should believe in Jesus. Being a man of his word, he kept that promise. We didn't speak to him about the matter again. About a year passed, and my father accepted Jesus as his Messiah.

When I began praying that Moishe would accept Jesus as his Messiah, I had no idea what I was asking! Once my husband committed his life to Y'shua (Jesus), he could not bear to stand idly by while the majority of our people went on believing that Jesus is only for Gentiles. Moishe completed his theological training and devoted himself to proclaiming Y'shua as the Jewish Messiah. My husband eventually became the founder and executive director of Jews for Jesus, a team of people who have challenged literally millions to think about Jesus.

ANDREW BARRON

I was a scientist, an engineer. The only God I could bring myself to believe in was far too busy coordinating the clockwork of the cosmos to concern himself with me, and I saw little reason why I should concern myself with him. Faith in a God

who actually cared would be intellectual suicide. Unless, of course, God was not who Spinoza and Einstein made him out to be....

Sometimes people walk up to me--people I don't even know--and say,"Why don't you get a *real* job?" I'm not a panhandler, I'm not on welfare; I'm not even a starving artist. The fact is, I'm a fairly well-fed, decently-dressed working man. The question of my employment isn't really a question; it's a comment on the fact that some people don't think too highly of my occupation. They might be surprised to know that I left my "real job" working on the space shuttle program at Martin Marietta to work with Jews for Jesus. So how did a nice Jewish boy like me end up becoming a missionary?

My name is Andrew Mark Barron. My parents were born and raised in New York City. I spent the first year of my life (1959) in that bastion of Jewish civilization known as Brooklyn; then my family moved to Queens and there we stayed until I was 11.

Our Conservative synagogue in Queens both puzzled and fascinated me. While it seemed to me that the velvet-lined pews were not meant for something so mundane as sitting, they lent a certain elegance to worship. The first thing one saw upon entering our synagogue was a huge golden plaque engraved with a list of names of people's dead relatives. I silently wondered why people paid to write their loved ones' names on that big brass list, and why, on special days, a lamp next to the plaque was lit. Once inside the sanctuary, I was momentarily awed by the majestic altar, the very size and beauty of which seemed to command admiration and respect.

Then the service would begin. Almost mechanically, I would stand up for certain parts and then sit down again. My mind wandered and I wondered--wondered about things like why God cared if we sat or stood. And why did we have to whisper in the sanctuary? Perhaps these rituals had something to do with keeping away evil spirits. It didn't occur to me to ask; it seemed natural for "religious" things to be mysterious. Though there was much I did not understand, I developed an early awareness of God and the fact that things pertaining to him were to be somehow set apart from the ordinary.

The first person who told me about loving God was

my Hebrew school teacher. I was 10 years old when I began attending *cheder* after school. We had a class of about 25 boys and girls which met twice a week. Our teacher was also the synagogue cantor. I don't remember his name but I do remember that he told us he loved God. He also explained how he did many things to please God. I hadn't ever thought of God as someone to be loved.

I never forgot my teacher's explanation of why he prayed when he awoke each morning. He told us that when we sleep, our bodies are close to death. To wake each morning was a miracle, and a sign of God's ownership and watchful care over our bodies. He thanked God each morning for letting him awake instead of leaving him to sleep forever.

I rode my bicycle two and a half miles to Hebrew school in the winter and was pleased to think that, like my teacher, I was doing something to make God happy. I remembered hearing how Abraham Lincoln walked for miles in the dead of winter to return a book. Maybe I would become the first Jewish President and people would tell stories about how I'd ridden to Hebrew school in the freezing cold!

Everyone in New York City was Jewish, or at least it seemed like it. But when I was 11 years old, we moved to Monroe, in upstate New York, and I discovered that I was in a minority. My mother explained that being Jewish was special. We were obligated to have higher morals and stricter intellectual standards than others. She often pointed out that many of the world's greatest achievers were Jewish: people like Albert Einstein and Jonas Salk. Their great accomplishments, she explained, were due to the fact that they were Jews.

I enjoyed knowing that I was different from the others, and that I was destined for greatness. My mother probably intended that I develop just enough pride to hold fast to my Jewish identity in the midst of a Gentile society. She succeeded, but I may have gotten a bit of an ethnic "superiority complex" in the process.

Childhood memories of Jewish life snap into focus when I recall the aromas which seemed to herald most of our holiday observances. Our nostrils twitched as the

14

pungent sting of ammonia signalled the coming of Passover. Then there was the must and dust of my yearly trek into the attic to retrieve our Passover dishes. And, finally, there were the fragrances of chicken soup, *tzimmus*, brisket *and* chicken. My grandmother's deft hands separated the egg whites from the yolks as she prepared her famous desert and when she put it in the oven to bake, the whole house was filled with the sweet aroma of "the-most-delicious-spongecake-you-ever-tasted."

I loved to breathe in the scent of fresh-cut wood when it came time to build the huts for *Sukkot*. And *Purim* was great for the fresh-baked smell of *hamantaschen*, not to mention the delicious taste! But even more than the holiday cookies, I enjoyed raising the ruckus which was only permitted in the synagogue on that one incredible night of the year. As we cheered Mordecai and booed wicked Haman throughout the reading of the *megilla*, I think my voice was loudest of all!

My ideas of God changed as I grew older. When I was 14 years old, I watched my grandmother die a slow and painful death which resulted from hardening of the arteries in her brain. She had been an altruist all her life. Where had it gotten her? What good had it done her to keep all the religious rituals so faithfully? In 1974, Grandma Jenny's name was added to the brass plaque in our synagogue in Monroe. I thought bitterly that if such was her reward, it left much to be desired. The thought of a loving God seemed absurd.

I began to wonder about the distinctions between Jews and Gentiles, and why we were separated. One day I was playing basketball with some friends when a man came to join us. As he approached the court, one of the boys mumbled to me that he was a priest and asked me if I was allowed to play with him!

I considered my friend's question. Once I had visited a Catholic church and wondered if being there would somehow make me dirty. Now in high school, I wasn't sure if I was supposed to worry about being contaminated by this basketball-playing priest or vice versa. But the court was a far cry from a Catholic church, so I decided it wouldn't hurt me to play ball with him. If he had a problem about playing with me, well, what he didn't know wouldn't hurt him.

Thoughts of Jesus were few and far between. I assumed he was Catholic. I figured the Gentiles were looking for a way to be more like Jews, so they built a religion around a Jew who was Catholic. I might have realized how silly that was had I given it more thought, but I saw no reason to bother about it.

After high school, I saw myself as a sophisticated college student...which meant I had no tolerance for superstition and no need for God.

In college, I became friends with Dr. Cissy Petty. Cissy was the director of student activities and my boss. I did part-time office work to earn a little extra pocket money. One day, she told me that Jesus was my Savior. At first I thought she was crazy, but then I realized she probably just didn't know who I was. Therefore, I informed her that I was Jewish, expecting that she would immediately realize her mistake. But she still thought Jesus was my Savior. In addition, she asked what being Jewish meant to me. I wasn't certain how to answer. To me, being Jewish was sort of a birthright to success. After all, I was following in the footsteps of Albert Einstein and Jonas Salk!

I shrugged off the fact that Cissy thought being Jewish shouldn't keep me from believing in Jesus. But I could not shrug off the fact that she lived differently from everyone else I knew. She acted as though God was actually watching. She had a morality that seemed to be more than a social standard. C.S. Lewis described it when he wrote: "There is something above and beyond the ordinary facts of men's behavior, and yet quite definitely real--a real law, which none of us made--but which we find pressing on us." (C.S. Lewis, *Mere Christianity*, Macmillan Publishing Co., 30.) It was amazing to observe God's reality in Dr. Petty's life. She gave me a Bible toward the end of my senior year; the inscription was dated May 20, 1981. I accepted it only to avoid hurting her feelings.

Cissy Petty was just one of many reasons for me to begin thinking about God again. A book called *God and the Astronomers*, written by a famous astrophysicist named

Robert Jastrow piqued my interest. Jastrow was convinced that the creation account was backed by science. Even though he wrote as an agnostic, there was something in his conclusion that jolted me into thinking more seriously about God. Jastrow wrote, "For the scientist who has lived by his faith in the Power of Reason, the story ends like a bad dream. He has scaled the mountains of ignorance; he is about to conquer the final peak; as he pulls himself over the final rock, he is greeted by a band of theologians who have been sitting there for centuries." (Robert Jastrow, *God and the Astronomer*, New York: W.W. Norton & Co. Inc., 1978, 116.)

I majored in space science at the Florida Institute of Technology, so I spent hours and hours up in the observatory. Sometimes I paused from observing the stars and planets to wonder if I, too, was being observed. It was the strangest feeling, but studying the vastness of the universe just naturally led me to think about God. One night a friend and I watched a spectacular meteor shower. As we counted the "shooting stars," he mused over the thought of planet Earth as a mere experiment in someone's gigantic petri dish--in which case he said all our striving and the meaning we attribute to life would be a ridiculous joke. I was not given to such cynicism, but I did wonder how a God who was busy making the sun shine and keeping the planets with all their moons in orbit could possibly care about me. I believed God existed because of the phenomenal order to the universe; yet I felt human beings were far too miniscule for his notice.

Upon graduation I moved to Denver, Colorado, to take a job with Martin Marietta. They paid me quite well considering I was "fresh out of college." I wasn't surprised that my dreams of success were becoming a reality, but I still could not resolve the spiritual questions I had begun to ponder in college. I had expected my knowledge of science to supersede my belief in God. Instead, it seemed to point to his existence, to insist upon it in a way that I could not ignore.

It came time for a vacation and I went back to Florida. While there, I visited my friend Cissy. She gave me a Jews for Jesus pamphlet and I addressed a note requesting more information to their headquarters in San Francisco. I don't remember much of what that pamphlet said except the title, "Hospital *Tsuris*," and frankly, I forgot about writing the note until three or four months later, when the response came.

One of their staff, Mitch Glaser, ended up with my letter just before a trip he had scheduled in Denver. I was surprised when he called and introduced himself over the telephone, but I agreed to meet with him. Mitch and I had a good rapport, and he was able to answer some of my questions about how a person could be Jewish and believe in Jesus. Still, I wasn't quite ready to believe. I'd had oral surgery the day before and had taken plenty of Percodan to kill the pain. I knew I wasn't quite myself, so I told Mitch I was probably crazy to even be thinking about Jesus.

I felt much better the next night, so I went with Mitch to watch him do a presentation about Passover. He talked about the Jewish roots of Christianity and explained how Jesus' death and resurrection were in keeping with God's plans for redeeming our people even as far back as Moses. Before he left, Mitch put me in contact with Eliezer, who worked with the American Board of Missions to the Jews. Eliezer is an older Jewish believer in Jesus whom Mitch knew to be a wise and godly man.

From the first time I walked into his home, it reminded me of my grandmother's house. First there was the familiar smell of moth balls in the closet when I went to hang up my jacket and then the aroma of chicken soup wafting in from the kitchen--I felt at home instantly! Eliezer and his wife, Sarah, might believe in Jesus, but they were *mishpochah*, they were Jews.

I spent time with Eliezer and observed the people who came to his home for Bible studies. I was impressed by the way they related to God, especially in prayer. It was incredible to hear people praying for daily concerns, not needing a liturgy to approach the Maker of the Universe.

Eliezer and I read the Bible together. We studied messianic prophecies, and we read from the Gospels so I could see for myself who Jesus was and what he taught. "The

Sermon on the Mount" from the Book of Matthew really took me by surprise. I saw that people can be clean on the outside, and still be dirty on the inside. I realized that one didn't have to be a criminal by society's standards in order to be a sinner in God's sight.

I had grown in my reverence for God. I knew he was real, and that he was holy. I knew I was separated from him because I couldn't measure up to his standards. I wanted to be a part of the people he called his own.

The biggest obstacle between me and Jesus was my pride. I was a scientist, an engineer. Until now, the only God I could bring myself to believe in was far too busy coordinating the clockwork of the cosmos to concern himself with me, and I'd seen little reason why I should concern myself with him. I had a couple of words to describe faith in a God who actually cared--intellectual suicide.

No one could explain to me why the Creator of the Universe should care about his people, but after confronting Scripture, I knew God is not who Spinoza and Einstein had made him out to be. He is not some impersonal force. He is a personal Creator who made us because he wants to be involved in our lives. He constructed us with souls that can be fed only by his own hand. I concluded that believing God cares is not intellectual suicide; believing that he doesn't care is spiritual starvation.

I came to faith in Jesus as my Messiah on May 20, 1982. I went home that night to read the Bible Cissy had given me. I was astounded to see her simple inscription: From Cissy Petty to Andrew Barron, May 20, 1981. It had taken exactly one year from the time she gave me that Bible to the time when I finally read it...as a believer in Y'shua.

Cissy had challenged me to think about spiritual matters. But somehow, it took other Jews who believed in Jesus to help me overcome my prejudices. When I realized I could be helping my people discover the Messiah, building space shuttles, exciting as it was, no longer seemed like the career for me. I can't be angry with people who tell me to get a "real job." If they'd just look to God with an open mind, they'd know that the job of proclaiming his Messiah is very real.

NORMAN • BUSKIN •

From timid, to tough, to telling about Jesus; that's the story of Norman Buskin. Read how a Jewish cop came to believe that only Jesus can protect us from the evil in the world, and from the evil in ourselves....

My friends from the motorcycle gang had drifted away and most of my Jewish buddies from the old street gang were becoming respectable businessmen. It seemed like the right time to choose a career, so at age 21 I became a rookie police officer. It was a profession which would satisfy my craving for action as well as my obsession with protecting the innocent against the bullies of the world.

I was the youngest graduate at the police academy, a rookie eager for adventure and ready to take on the world. However, the glamour of being "in uniform" wore off at about five o'clock in the morning as I finished the first shift of my beat in the wind, snow, and sub-zero degree temperature of the Detroit ghetto.

Detroit is a tough town. I was born there in 1936 in a predominantly Jewish neighborhood. We were not especially religious, but on the high holidays my grandfather took me to the synagogue. I can recall the singing and the solemnity of the services, though I did not understand what was being sung or said. My memories of Detroit are mostly of a cold gray place that held little comfort, beauty or charm.

My great-grandfather on my mother's side was the last in a long line of rabbis in the city of Bobruisk, Russia. My paternal great-grandfather is reputed to have been the chief rabbi in Moscow, although I cannot document this with the same certainty as on my mother's side of the family. With such *yichus* one might think my parents would have been strict adherents of Judaism, but this was not the case. All our relatives who remained in Russia perished during World War II. Those who left were fiercely loyal to the Jewish people, but not particularly to the religion.

My grandfather watched out for me and helped mold my character because my father was seldom at home. Dad was a big man with a loud laugh and a quick temper, a habitual gambler who "lost it all" to the horses. So my mother's dad acted as my father and protector. I called him "Pa."

He and his brother-in-law came to Montreal hoping to leave the persecution of the old country behind. The anti-Semitism they encountered in Canada was mild compared

21

to the pogroms of Russia, but it kept my grandfather alert and constantly ready to defend himself. Pa was a tough man and could knock out an ox if he had to, but he wasn't one to go looking for trouble. He was a "no-nonsense" type of guy who liked to be left alone to do his job in peace. His name was Pete. He seldom smiled, and the old photos I have of him remind me of Buster Keaton.

Pete worked for the Canadian Railroad. Some loud-mouthed workers on the railroad made the mistake of starting in on the muscular man with steel-gray eyes whom they referred to as "Pete the Jew." My grandfather did not find their pranks amusing, and when the men persisted, he landed several of them in the hospital. Thereafter they called him "the crazy Jew" and stayed out of his way. Pa maintained his reputation as a man not to be trifled with long after he moved to Detroit.

My family left Detroit and moved to Los Angeles when I was about 4 years old. It was to be the first of several moves between Detroit and Los Angeles, due to my father's pendular lifestyle. I was always "the new kid on the block," and as such, received plenty of attention from local bullies. I remember running home from school with a bloody nose; my "offense" had been the mere fact that I was timid. I was a boy of medium height and marginal courage, in continual dread of being pushed around and humiliated. I soon became acquainted with the term "dirty Jew." It was a popular expression, so I heard it often; it confused and upset me.

One day a kid named Larry who lived across the street accused me of killing "his Lord." I knew he was referring to a plaster statue of a dead man which hung on a cross in his church. I'd seen the statue through the open doors of the church. How could I have killed that man? I was never even in the church! I asked my mother about it and she told me the fellow on the cross was Jewish. That really confused me. Why would my "good Christian neighbors" talk about dirty Jews and then go into their church every Sunday and bow down to one? My first impression of "Christianity" was not very favorable!

22

I was 9 or 10 years old when we returned to Detroit for good. It was still cold and still gray. My father had not changed. He was still gambling and living away from home. My mother divorced him. No more Los Angeles for us!

As I approached my 13th birthday, a local rabbi gave me a two-month crash course so that I could become *bar mitzvah*. His dedication was commendable and he was very patient with me. However, it seemed apparent to me even at that age that his zeal was for tradition rather than the Word of God. I rarely saw a Bible, and regrettably, never felt close to God.

Whatever or whoever was responsible for comforting troubled souls remained unseen and unknown in my neighborhood. It would have been nice knowing God. I assumed that to do so one had to take extensive religious training, read Hebrew fluently and wear special clothing. My knowledge was meager and I accepted the fact that I would not excel in either religion or righteousness. After my bar mitzvah, my thoughts, like those of most boys, were not of God but of doing my own thing.

There was a small gang of teens--the bad boys of our school--who made life miserable for those of us who were not well-connected. I grew tired of being a life-sized punching bag and a perpetual loser, so I asked Pa to teach me his methods of taking people apart. He taught me. Did he ever! I walked up to the gang's "head moron" during a class change and punched him out in front of everyone. Life was wonderful! The satisfaction of winning fights can best be appreciated by one accustomed to losing. That was the last time anyone dared to demean the Jews in my presence. And it was the beginning of my reputation as a guy most people wouldn't care to cross.

I was growing bigger, taller and more aggressive. When I was 17 years old, I became "president" of a large Jewish street gang called the "Eldorados." We'd named ourselves after a local singing group. Youth gangs in the '50s were not like the gangs of today; there was little crime, and lots of good times together. We would hang around drive-in restaurants in our customized cars, including my souped-up 1954 black Ford convertible. Our activities consisted mainly of chasing girls and making a lot of macho bluster.

There were a few street battles but those were the exception. One night during the summer of 1954, four of us were attacked on Davison Avenue by a gang of 30 to 40 fellows from 12th Street. They were looking for another gang, but they figured we would do instead. A skinny guy wearing a big hat took three swings at me with a butcher knife. Unbelievably, he missed. The police arrived before anyone was killed, namely me, and we ran! That night was the first of many times I was spared from a violent death.

By the time I graduated from high school I was six feet two, weighed over 220 pounds and had developed a mean streak. I seldom ran from trouble anymore; I would usually punch first and ask questions later. After years of being victimized by bullies, I didn't have to fear the "bad boys" anymore. I maintained a disgust for those who tormented the weak and reserved my wrath for the tough guys I felt needed a lesson.

High school was over, the gang had dissolved, and life was becoming dull. My future was uncertain, but I was not ready to settle down. During the winter of 1956, I was introduced to a wild guy named Bob. Bob rode with a motorcycle club called the "Highwaymen," who were well-known and feared throughout the Detroit area. I found the club very exciting. What action, what adventure--this was for me! I think it was the number of riders that alarmed people, and the fact that many of us were "big guys." I rode with the Highwaymen until 1960, looking like a creature from outer space in my black leather jacket, Levi jeans and Mickey Mouse cap.

The Detroit Police Department made me give up the gang when I joined the force. How did I get from a motorcycle gang to the police force? I had run with some bizarre people and was certainly no sweetheart, but I kept my nose clean, my record clear and my references respectable. As I approached my 21st birthday, I thought about career options. Law enforcement interested me because I thrived on action and any opportunity to defend those who were being bullied. The Detroit Police Department was looking for tough guys like me, but they did not have room on the force for Highwaymen--so I made a career commitment and sold my beloved Triumph motorcycle. My seven years of service with the Detroit Police Department began in 1960.

I quickly discovered that things were turning ugly in Detroit. My sergeant was shot to death with his own pistol on the Edsel Ford Freeway in 1963. Two other friends on the force were shot to death and another was run over and killed by a drunk. I had my share of dangerous encounters as well.

One winter night I caught a burglar in a dark first precinct alley. He attacked me, and as we struggled, he attempted to shoot me with my pistol. He lost, and we were both taken to a receiving hospital--the burglar for a bullet in his arm and myself for swallowing a piece of my own cigar! I also managed to survive a motorcycle crash and a few other incidents, including dragging a drunk out of a burning apartment. It was a seven-year nightmare, but there was one event which brought a little light into that dark period.

My partner and I had just transported an injured prisoner to the police prisoner cell at a Detroit receiving hospital. The officer who guarded the small holding cell was permanently assigned there--exiled, really--to keep him off the streets. His name was Ray and he had a reputation as an anti-social cop who was dangerous when aroused. Ray was built like a bull, with a large round head and small beady eyes. Very few people would talk to him. Even fellow officers avoided Ray.

I was startled when he approached me out of the blue and began speaking. I saw him coming and thought, "Mmm hmm, here comes trouble." But when he opened his mouth, I was amazed by his soft spoken and humble demeanor. He said, "I was a violent man, but I found Jesus and he changed me." I was impressed. What could make a man with such a frightening reputation say a thing like that? It was the first time I witnessed a person whose life had been changed by religion, and by Christianity in particular. Somehow that made me feel good. I did not pursue this avenue, however, for it didn't seem to have any bearing on my own life. It was 14 years before anyone else spoke to me about God.

The '60s saw a mass exodus of young policemen-- myself included--who felt Detroit was just too hazardous to our health. In 1966 I moved to Southfield, a large suburb north of Detroit. This might well have increased my life span; however, there were still incidents of extreme danger.

One night a man with a hunting knife tried to finish me off during a scuffle in traffic. He was an ex-convict who had just abducted a girl; I'd been pursuing him in a high-speed chase. He abandoned the car and I was pursuing him on foot through traffic when he turned on me with the hunting knife. I managed to knock him down and drag him away. The city awarded me the first medal of bravery, but I was just glad to have walked away uninjured.

William P. Kemper was my partner and friend during most of my years in Southfield. Many people thought we were brothers. We both stood six feet two, weighed about 240 pounds and had dark hair, dark eyes and similar mannerisms. We were considered "outsiders" because we did not socialize much with "the guys." Most of our contemporaries were perpetually broke, but Bill and I tended to be "tightwads" and were subsequently able to build large homes and live a little more comfortably than the others.

Bill and I had our share of bad moments on the street, but we did our job well and didn't get into too much trouble. The tough guys always addressed us respectfully. Some of the more aggressive chaps developed sudden headaches when we were around. I'm sure this had something to do with a memorable incident which took place at about two o'clock one morning. Four assaultive drunks decided to take on Bill and me behind a hamburger stand on 8 Mile Road. The most aggressive drunk laughed and pushed me. He was promptly conveyed to the emergency ward at Botsford Hospital with a major skull disorder. Amazingly, the other three became quite sober. This caused something of a sensation among the night crowd, and it altered the behavior of some of our local troublemakers. It was also a typical example of my behavior, which was that of hot-headed and hard-fisted cop.

1976 was a turning point in Bill's life as well as mine. I began noticing strange changes in Bill, like the green hard-cover Bible he began to carry. He also stopped smoking cheap cigars and began to "clean up his act." I wondered what had gotten into him.

Bill had never mentioned the arthritis in his hand. He did not tell me of his agony, or the fact that his despair over the pain had led him to look for help which doctors could not provide. A Christian police officer invited Bill to a prayer breakfast at a delicatessen, and Bill, not exactly a religious type of guy, accepted.

Several people prayed for Bill at that breakfast, and he was healed on the spot. Bill became a follower of Jesus and changed, much to my annoyance. His language was suddenly more respectable, his temper more even--was he getting soft, or what? Bill was reluctant to tell me his story because he assumed that as a Jew, I would not be interested in Jesus. Yet, strange things were occurring in my own life while Bill was undergoing these changes.

If you could somehow "preview" your own death as you slept, and if you were to see the face of Satan, you might wake up screaming. That is exactly what happened to me at about four o'clock in the morning during Passover 1976. I had a strange nightmare which was somehow more than a dream. I was immersed in darkness and I knew that I had died. Satan appeared in the darkness. His face was aglow with an eerie light. He had no eyes. He smiled at me and it was not a pleasant smile. A cloaked figure with a double-edged sword appeared to fight for me. I felt my body begin to float.

I awoke, screaming. I lay in the dark, big man that I was, with my pistol in hand, too terrified to even switch on the lights. I had never experienced anything like this in my life. I was overwhelmed with horror and disbelief. This sort of thing was for grade B movies; how could it happen to me? In the light of day it seemed even more unbelievable, yet I could not wipe the memory of that nightmare from my mind. Try as I would to forget it, I kept remembering the evil grin on that hideous face.

The next few months were topsy-turvy. I was promoted to sergeant, which should have made me happy, but it didn't. My wife and I divorced. To top it off, one day I was showing off, curling a 100-pound barbell, and something seemed to snap in my right arm. The pain was immediate and intense. The injury did not heal and I remained in constant pain for weeks. Nothing was making any sense. I could not seem to forget my horrible dream. I was not seeking any spiritual significance to all this--I just wished things would settle down.

That October the media was filled with news of the Billy Graham Crusade which was coming to the Pontiac Silverdome Stadium. Bill Kemper was supervising the volunteer security detail. He called and asked if I would volunteer my time at the crusade. Why not? I had volunteered for Richard Nixon, Gerald Ford, Lyndon Johnson, Martin Luther King, and Abba Eban, among others!

The final night of the crusade found us guarding Johnny Cash and Senator Robert Dole as we awaited the arrival of Billy Graham. My arm was killing me. The throbbing pain from the weight-lifting injury was excruciating. I could not take medication for the pain as that might have dulled my reflexes.

Billy Graham arrived, and my partner, Bill, introduced us. I heard myself saying, "Doctor Graham, I am Jewish and I admire the work that you are doing." I was thereby letting him know that although his work had nothing to do with me, I respected him for what he was doing among "his own" people. Billy Graham smiled, gripped my hand, and said, "God bless you." God did.

As Bill walked away with Dr. Graham, Johnny Cash and Senator Dole, I remained, rooted to the spot. The pain in my arm had suddenly and completely disappeared. All I could think was, "Oh God, the pain is gone! What happened to me? This only happens to Gentiles. What should I do? Who can I talk to? God, I need an answer...I need to talk to someone." That "someone" turned out to be Dale Gross.

I did not know Dale; however, I knew about him. Dale is a handsome man, a martial arts expert, a police sergeant...and a minister. As I was telling God I needed someone to talk to, I saw Dale standing against a wall, alone and looking in my direction. So I approached him and after an awkward moment of hesitation, explained what I had just experienced in my right arm. "What is happening to me?" I asked.

Dale looked me straight in the eye and calmly spoke words which tore at my soul. He said, "Norm, I know you are Jewish and I want to tell you that Jesus is *your* Messiah. He is coming again for his Jewish people. Don't let Satan rob you of what the Lord did for you today. God is revealing himself to you." Then he gave me his phone number, asked me to call him if I felt like talking, and walked away. I remained, overcome with emotion.

I walked into the Detroit Lions' locker room and began to cry. I cannot remember the last time I had wept. God was dealing with me, allowing me to realize that I did not belong to him. I knew I had committed wrongs against man and against God. Suddenly, I saw how those wrongdoings had caused an ever-widening separation between God and me. How could I possibly come into his presence? I did not want to be left on the side of the evil which had been manifested in my dream.

The reality of God's existence hit me that night in the locker room. God cared about me. He had taken notice of the pain in my arm and had healed me when I never would have thought to ask him. I remembered Ray, the once violent officer whose life had been completely changed by Jesus. Maybe the changes in Bill's lifestyle had only seemed annoying because I'd never known the peace of God in my own life. I suddenly found myself believing that Jesus was the Messiah, as Dale had suggested, and I wanted to know more.

I told my partner what had happened, and he loaned me a Bible. I drove home in tears and with one thought on my mind: Jesus! Jesus was the Jewish Messiah and I was determined to investigate what that should mean to me.

The following evening I opened that Bible to the Gospel of John, as my buddy, Bill, had suggested. "Well, here it comes," I thought, "...swell stories about popes, assorted saints and Roman burial sites." I was amazed to find that all the main characters in this book were Jewish. When I reached the 49th verse of the first chapter of John, the words seemed to leap from the page: "Rabbi, You are the Son of God! You are the King of Israel!"

What a revelation it was to learn that Jesus was not the personal property of the Vatican. He is ours, too, a Jew of Jews! This added a whole new dimension to my Jewish identity. Being Jewish was more than using my fists to defend my honor and the honor of my people. After all, the Bible was about Jews and about the Jewish Messiah, Jesus. Further, it was written by Jews and *for* Jews...and that included me. *The Scriptures said that I could be a part of God's kingdom and that was the best news I had ever heard.* My life as an outsider was nearly over.

A few days later on November 16, 1976, I awoke at 4 a.m. for no apparent reason. The room was very dark, but in the midst of the darkness I visualized a dazzling image of a man dressed in white. He smiled at me as he raised his hands. Once again, I wept. I did not understand exactly what was happening; I knew that Jesus was making himself real to me in a very unique way, but why?

The following evening I called Dale Gross and he met with me the next day. We talked about the spiritual occurrences I'd experienced during the past months. Dale discussed these things in light of certain Bible passages.

Psalm 18:4-17 gives a striking account of King David's description of God's deliverance--which bore a certain resemblance to my dream. The Jewish prophet Joel told how God's spirit can cause dreams whereby the Lord reveals himself (Joel 2:28). I'm not saying this is an everyday experience, and I don't think it's how God reveals himself to most people, but it showed me that this was not an un-Jewish or unheard-of phenomena. When I told Dale of the figure holding the double-edged sword in my first dream, he showed me that that was how Jesus appeared in Revela-

30

tion 2:12. I realized that my former life was about to become history.

Dale opened his Bible to Romans 3:23 and read, "For all have sinned and fall short of the glory of God." That included me. My reputation for violence and chasing women was well known. Next, Dale turned to Romans 6:23: "For the wages of sin is death, but the gift of God is eternal life in Jesus the Messiah our Lord."

Death and hell are poor choices, and they certainly did not appeal to me. Jesus, the Messiah who gives life, is a good choice. I'd made plenty of mistakes, but unlike my dad, I've never been a gambler. I knew that if Jesus was calling me, now was the time to answer. Dale and I prayed and I accepted Jesus as my Messiah and my Lord on November 17, 1976. He is the Holy One of Israel. He is magnificent. He came to me when I did not know him and in his mercy he forgave me.

The Lord immediately placed other godly men in my life. Other Jewish believers in Y'shua taught me much when I knew so little. Al Brickner was one such man; he was instrumental in my mother placing her trust in Jesus. Al explained the Jewishness of Jesus in a way she could understand. My mother's sister accepted Jesus soon after.

In 1978 I left the Detroit area and moved to southern Florida. Within four months, I had a new home west of Fort Lauderdale. One of my first friends in Florida was Baruch Goldstein who, at the time, was the leader of the Miami branch of Jews for Jesus. Al Brickner had given me Baruch's phone number and suggested I call him when I got to Florida.

Baruch helped me move into my new house and invited me to Bible studies in his home. I discovered that one of my old buddies from the Jewish gang I belonged to in high school was living in the area. I invited Bernie and his wife (also Jewish) to the Jews for Jesus Bible study in Miami. They came, and afterward, Bernie's wife, Rita prayed with Baruch and me to receive Jesus as her Messiah. Bernie came to faith in Y'shua about four months later.

A few months after I'd moved to Florida, a policeman I met at a law enforcement refresher course told me about the town of Davie, Florida. Davie is a fast growing western-style town with plenty of cowboys and even more horses. It was a town which, unlike the places of my youth, had a great deal of beauty and charm. Moreover, it was a town closer to my home than the one where I had been serving. There were no less than 500 officers being tested for eight openings on the Davie Police Department. I handed in my application and resume and was told not to hold my breath. One week later I was first on the eligibility list and the following week, I was a Davie officer. It had certainly seemed unlikely that I would be chosen, and I couldn't help but wonder what would happen next.

I discovered that Davie is not behind the times, despite its old-time western charm. It is a community with a large Jewish population and a spirit of progress. I was also pleasantly surprised by the large ratio of Jewish police officers there. The senior sergeant was Harry Rose, a highly-decorated combat veteran of two wars. Harry was also a Jewish believer in Jesus. Two Jewish believers on the same department--I figured it must be some kind of a record! If it was a record, it was about to be broken.

Howard Rausch, a Jewish veteran officer of 11 years, was dying. He had cystic fibrosis, and his affliction had turned him into an ill-tempered recluse. I felt sorry for the guy. As mean as he was, one could not look at his wasted body without feeling sympathetic. The night I told Howard that Jesus was his Lord, I expected him to really tear into me, verbally, that is. Instead, he burst into tears and asked if Jesus had suffered like he did. This man wanted God so badly and nobody had ever told him about the Messiah. He had difficulty saying the name of Jesus because of training he'd received as a child. When I told him that "Y'shua" is the Jewish way to say Jesus, he burst into tears once again and accepted Jesus right there in my automobile. Jesus brought Howard the comfort he had longed for during his years of physical agony. He was able to share his story with many before he died, a peaceful man who knew he was going home to his Messiah. Howard was the third Jewish officer in Davie to trust in Jesus as his Messiah.

Stan Perlmutter retired from the New York Police Department after 20 years as a detective in Harlem. After moving to south Florida, Stan took a position with the Davie Police Department. He had a desire to know more about the Bible and his Jewish roots, so he investigated the Scriptures. After doing so, Stan concluded that Jesus was the Messiah of Israel. On June 17, 1981, Stan and I prayed together and he accepted Jesus as his Messiah. Stan Perlmutter was the fourth Jewish officer in Davie to receive Jesus.

Richard Rein (now Sergeant Rein), left the Davie Police Department in 1979 to take a position with another law enforcement agency. He returned to Davie a few years later as a detective and a follower of Jesus. Richard Rein was the fifth Jewish law enforcement officer of Davie to accept Jesus as the promised Messiah of our people. I believe there will be others, because God is revealing himself to our people. Davie is but one area where Jewish people are recognizing the Messiah.

I am still active in law enforcement, but God has taken away my desire to teach tough guys a lesson with my fists. Instead, he has given me both the desire and the opportunity to teach my fellow officers lessons from the Bible...lessons of love, about the Jewish Messiah.

HENRY AND JANET FEINBERG

This story of "lost and found love" may sound like a soap opera--the episodes of adventure and disappointment that brought Henry and Janet together, split them apart, and led them on a torturous quest for truth which lasted for nearly two decades are that dramatic.

Soap operas, silly and unrealistic as they may be, are based on the real and perplexing problems of love, loneliness and learning to make the right choices. But Henry and Janet's story is real...and unlike a soap opera, there is, finally, a resolution.

Henry Feinberg: My parents' faces were lined with tension as they listened intently to the radio reports of fighting between Arabs and Jews. It was 1956 and there was a war in the Sinai.

God was seldom a topic of conversation in our home, but now he was being discussed almost by default. My parents were saying that God might not intervene, that we couldn't count on his help. Israel might be destroyed. We had no way of knowing that all the early reports were from the "other side" and that stories of Israel's impending doom were largely propaganda. As far as we knew, the reports were true, the situation desperate.

At 12 years of age, I pondered the possibility of Israel's destruction. The thought seemed to drop from my head right down to the pit of my stomach where it lay as a nauseating fear. Israel destroyed! I felt that if the life were crushed out of our tiny state, I too, would be crushed; I would perish along with my people. While I had never been anywhere near Israel (I was born in Brooklyn; we moved to Scarsdale when I was 10), I believed my destiny was somehow tied up with that distant country.

Mrs. Bernstein probably had a lot to do with how I felt--how I still feel--about Israel. She was my Hebrew school teacher. I remember her as a very strong woman, not physically large but an outspoken woman. She had an air of authority that commanded the respect of all her students. Mrs. Bernstein was very much a Zionist and instilled in us a tremendous love and loyalty for Israel.

I went to cheder at Temple Israel in White Plains for two and a half years. My bar mitzvah marked the end of the religious training I received while growing up. My bar mitzvah was a matter of tradition and Jewish identity. It was important to be Jewish, but religion and God were peripheral.

Mom and Dad explained our roots to me; they told how my grandparents immigrated to the United States at the turn of the century, fleeing the pogroms of Russia and Eastern Europe. They made it very clear that as a Jew, I could expect persecution from Gentiles. I was supposed to be suspicious. The bits of anti-Semitism I experienced, mostly in the form of jokes and snide comments in high school, reinforced my parents' teaching and kept me apart from Gentiles. I remember one incident which particularly emphasized the feeling of separation.

It was Passover, I was 16 years old, and my mom was ill. My sisters were grown and I was the only child left at home. Dad dutifully stepped into Mom's shoes and brown-bagged my lunch for me. When I opened the bag at lunchtime and saw that he had made a *matzoh* sandwich, I quickly glanced around the cafeteria table. There were mostly Gentiles and my few Jewish friends, none of whom had matzoh sandwiches. A hot flush spread from my face down to my neck as the kids made snide remarks, and I could barely taste the lunch my father had prepared for me. I don't know how, but even childish persecution somehow deepens our Jewish identity. I know it did mine.

It wasn't belief in God, but just the fact of being Jewish that motivated my father to bring out the Haggadah each Passover. He would spend an hour to an hour and a half going through it. Then, of course, we'd have a wonderful Passover meal. And my dad was faithful, as he still is at 77 years of age, to attend synagogue during Rosh Hashanah and Yom Kippur.

As I was growing up, my parents had aspirations of a medical career for me, but I did not share those aspirations. I graduated from the Scarsdale public school system without any particular academic distinction--though as a pitcher, I did letter in baseball.

In 1962 I enrolled at Syracuse University in upstate New York. I joined a Jewish fraternity, and while I had Gentile friends, my close friends were Jewish. My closest friend of all turned out to be Janet Rothman.

I met Janet in November of my senior year. It was the night of the famous 1965 electrical blackout. East Coasters still occasionally ask each other, "Where were you when the lights went out?" Well, I was a cook's helper at a sorority house, and I was washing dishes when the lights went out. One of the sorority sisters came to the kitchen with a candle. She walked toward me slowly, so as not to stumble in the dark. The candlelight played upon her face giving it the soft, warm glow that makes candlelight so romantic. I know it sounds trite, but I was smitten at first sight. She left the candle at the sink so I could finish washing the dishes, and she walked out of the room...but certainly not out of my life. That was Janet.

We began dating, and even discussed the possibility of marriage. I was crazy about Janet, not just because she was pretty, but because we seemed to have so much in common and it was just good to be with her.

After we'd been dating for about eight months Janet became pregnant. Abortions were illegal at that time--but we went that route anyway. It turned out to be devastating to us both, and it put a tremendous strain on our relationship. I should have been supportive of Janet and tried to ride out the rough time we were experiencing, but I couldn't see past it. I only knew our relationship had gone awry. It had been spoiled and I didn't think it could ever be fresh and good again. And I was frightened of commitment, determined not to be "trapped" in an unhappy relationship.

As I was pondering a "way out," I remembered an advertisement my dad had sent me just a few weeks before graduation. He'd clipped it from the *New York Times* classified section. United Airlines was expanding rapidly during the mid-'60s and they were looking for pilots. With the Vietnam War heating up, the government was keeping a tight rein on all the military pilots. So the airlines decided to hire college graduates with commercial pilots' licenses.

I was more concerned with myself than anything or anyone else at the time, and flying seemed like a wonderfully adventuresome idea. I ended my relationship with Janet--just dropped her--and went off to Oklahoma. I attended flying school there, got my pilot's license and went to work for United Airlines.

The thrill of flying was all-encompassing. Imagine a little boy who has just unwrapped the most marvelous toy in the world. I was totally involved and excited with the sheer joy of operating this most marvelous toy when I was flying a jet airplane. The power and thrust at one's command, and the ability to lift a huge mass of metal off the ground provide an incredible thrill. I think some people almost have a love affair with airplanes because they free us from earthly confines. The tremendous feeling of release and liberty is exhilarating, if only temporary.

I worked my way up from flight engineer to copilot. Large jets generally have three pilots. The flight engineer is in charge of maintaining all the systems, including air pressure, air conditioning, hydraulics, etc. The position is sometimes referred to as "second officer." Flight engineers "preflight" planes, making sure the equipment is functioning properly before passengers board. Once in the air, the flight engineer watches a control panel and flips switches to ensure that all systems continue operating smoothly. Between the pilot and the copilot (also referred to as the captain and first officer), one flies while the other speaks to the ground control people, and together, they navigate.

I travelled all over the world for a few years, bought new cars frequently and dated lots of women. It seemed as though the world was my oyster. But after a while, I grew discontented.

I began to realize how others were suffering while I enjoyed good fortune. Something inside me insisted that there must be more to life than the materialism in which I was immersing myself. One might wonder what kind of suffering a kid from Scarsdale could see, but there was plenty.

In 1969 I was a flight engineer for DC-8s. We flew passengers from Los Angeles to Honolulu, had an overnight layover and flew a cargo-configuration (all freight, no passengers) back to L.A. the next morning. One morning I was preflighting the plane and I saw the ground personnel loading on boxes of a size and shape I'd never seen before.

I walked over to one of the employees and asked, "What are you loading?" He told me that these were caskets of dead soldiers from Vietnam to be flown to the mainland for burial. Corpses as cargo? It couldn't be--but it was--an entire planeful. Many of those soldiers were probably my age. It shook me to the core to think of young men dying in a war which, from my perspective, only older men seemed to understand. I began to sense the injustice in the world.

A few years later I spent a brief time in the employ of an extremely wealthy Israeli. At that time, few Israelis even owned a car; yet this man owned a Boeing 707. We flew him all over the world in his private jet, the interior of which he had spent eight million dollars to refurbish. That's some interior decorating! And, of course, wherever we landed, we stayed in the finest hotels.

I found this opulence somehow repugnant. We spent a few days in the Philippines, and my reaction to our fine accommodations was to ask a cab driver to take me to the worst section of the city. We were in Manila and the worst section was pretty bad. There were homeless people starving in the streets. There were a lot of them!

I was distressed. I was agitated. I had to know, does God exist? If so, why did he set up a world that is so unjust? Over and over I would ask myself, are money, power, food and sex all that human beings desire? Isn't there more to life than gratifying the senses? And what is this bitterness, this grief in the heart of man which plays itself out in terrible famines and wars?

My restlessness and discontent were exacerbated when in 1971, due to economic difficulties, United Airlines lost a great deal of money and had to furlough about 500 pilots. I didn't lose my job, but I lost my seniority and had to step down from copilot to flight engineer. It was a big disappointment and I didn't take it well.

I was drinking quite a bit then. While I was never physically dependent (I was too much the athlete for that, with lots of running, swimming, bike riding and long walks), I was emotionally dependent on alcohol. I drank when things got too uncomfortable; it seemed to make life more bearable.

During this time of disillusionment and discontent, I took a short trip to Palm Springs. I was based in Los Angeles at the time and decided to leave the smog and enjoy some sunshine for a few days. I drove to Palm Springs and rented a motel room; I was sunning myself by the pool when a very beautiful woman began speaking to me.

She said she was an actress, and I think she said she was in her early thirties. After she told me, I did recognize her, but I don't remember her name. She poured out her heart to me, saying how miserable and depressed she was because as far as Hollywood was concerned, she was "past her prime." She'd had a successful but brief career and although she certainly didn't look "past her prime" to me, she was having difficulty finding acting jobs because of her age.

I thought what a shame it was for our culture to be so youth and beauty oriented and I felt bad for this woman, but there was nothing I could say to console her. I just listened sympathetically; I didn't know what else to do.

Within a week of my return to Los Angeles, I heard on the news that the same Hollywood actress had committed suicide. The reality of death, when I had just seen this woman alive and physically well, was a tremendous jolt. I was angry about the crazy, senseless values which had led to her despair. I was grieved over her death. But what shook me the most was fear. I, too, was severely depressed and questioning the meaning of life. I realized I had better guard well my will to live if I expected to survive.

I spent the next two years as flight engineer, yearning to be back in the copilot's seat the whole time. Something inside me felt as though it would burst if I didn't give vent to the frustration which was building. I didn't want to quit my job, so I asked for a leave of absence. I was unable to persuade my supervisor to grant me the leave, so, being the selfish, manipulative kind of guy I was, I found another way to get what I wanted.

I began to let my hair grow. As it got long and curly (not too long, but a far cry from the crew cut I'd been wearing), my supervisor took notice. He told me to get a haircut and I refused. Eventually, I was fired for insubordination: refusing an order from a flight manager. I suspected, however, that our union would be powerful enough to get my job back since the firing had nothing to do with my performance on the job. As far as I was concerned, I was simply taking my leave of absence.

I went to Hawaii, bent on taking Timothy Leary's

advice to "turn on, tune in and drop out." I hear the phrase now and it strikes me as gibberish. So many young people, including me, gave up opportunities and careers to grow hair, grow beards, and take drugs because we thought that was how to find God. Now I see it as a terrible waste of time and talent.

Anyway, I was looking for a simpler lifestyle than what I'd had as an airline pilot. I wanted to free myself of unnecessary material entrapments and "get back to the earth." I worked at a restaurant and did apprentice carpentry to earn enough for necessities. I met others who were on a "quest for spiritual awareness," and discussed the meaning of life with them. The whole experience was pretty much what I expected, except I wasn't finding a solution to the gnawing hunger inside me. I spent three months in this fashion. As I continued to ponder how I might find God, I developed an idea that I would discover the answers in my Jewish heritage.

My enthusiasm to search out my Jewish roots took form in a consuming desire to go to Israel. I was enjoying Hawaii, but I could not resist the attraction, the pull I felt toward Israel during this time of questioning. Surely I would discover my destiny and the answers I was seeking there. The Israel connection from my childhood remained strong.

I can still recall the excitement and anticipation I felt as I boarded the plane. I expected to have all sorts of incredible revelations from God; I would finally understand who he is and where my piece of existence fit into the puzzle of the universe.

My actual experience knocked the feet right out from under those expectations. I'd imagined an entire country filled with religious, "spiritually aware" people. I thought their lives would somehow be governed by what they knew about God, and a mystical understanding of his will.

Instead, I found a largely secular majority forced (much to their chagrin) by a religious minority to observe certain ordinances regarding the Sabbath and other matters of Jewish law. If this minority possessed the "spiritual awareness" I craved, I saw no evidence of it--and neither, it seemed, did the non-religious Israelis I met. I stayed for three months on Kibbutz Nachal Oz, and what I learned there can best be described in a conversation I had with one of the kibbutzniks. One day as I was drying some huge pots in the kitchen, I asked one of the cooks, "Is there a God?"

She answered, "How could there be a God when evidence of the Holocaust stands as a testimony of man's inhumanity to man?" I'm not sure what man's inhumanity says about the existence of God, but she continued, "No, I don't believe in God. I believe in the state of Israel and the right to defend her with a weapon till death."

And so it was, not only with this woman, but with most Israelis I met. Life's real simple there--you fight or die. The fighting isn't just in the military, it's an everyday struggle against an oppressive economy. And there seems to be very little room for God.

If expectancy and excitement had brought me to Israel, then dejection and despair were my ticket home. If we Jews weren't believing in God, weren't pursuing him, who was? I'm not sure how I arrived at the conclusion that standards of spirituality would be so high in Israel. It was probably a combination of Mrs. Bernstein's influence in molding my love for Israel and the fact that none of my Jewish family and friends back home seemed to think much about God.

I made subsequent visits to Israel; I stayed at Hatzor for a while and then later at Kibbutz Erev. Altogether, I lived on various kibbutzim for about a year. These visits continued because as a Jew, I identify with Israel--not because I was finding any answers.

When I did settle back into life in the U.S., I was able to go back to work for United Airlines. After my first flight, however, I realized that I no longer wanted the job and the lifestyle it would afford me, so I resigned.

I wanted adventure, and with nothing and no one to tie me down, I indulged in the spirit of wanderlust. One night I was talking with a friend over a couple of beers and we decided we'd head for Alaska. We drove through Canada, travelling up about 1500 miles of Alaska highway. We camped along the way on some of the most beautiful coun tryside I've ever seen. There were shining lakes by day and shining stars by night, and it was a wonderful time of discovery.

When we got to Alaska I took a job as a copilot on a twin-engine turbo-prop. We flew supplies into pipeline camps that were dotted from Fairbanks all the way up to the Arctic Circle. The vastness of the magnificent Alaskan landscape was awesome and it was exciting to fly over places where practically "no man had gone before."

I stayed in Alaska for two months. The little outfit I was flying for had expected to land some government contracts; when the contracts didn't come through, the company had to lay off eight or nine of us. I was one of the last pilots hired, so I was one of the first to go. And I was happy enough to head back to Hawaii, having briefly sojourned in Alaska.

My next adventure was sailing the South Seas. I was looking for paradise on earth, and the most exquisite place I'd seen when flying with United Airlines was Tahiti. I inquired about making an extended visit there, but the visa restrictions were tight. The French administrator of Tahiti did not want Americans making themselves too much at home and so I contented myself with crewing on a sailboat-- a 46-foot yacht--throughout the South Seas.

Tahiti was breathtakingly beautiful and exotic. The islands were still relatively unspoiled by tourism. I drank in their beauty and savored a little bit of what I imagined paradise must be. Gazing out on the crystal sea in the daylight, I would occasionally be startled by the lush greenery of an island looming up on the horizon. At night, the dolphins would leap across our bow in the moonlight, playfully crisscrossing one over the other.

Despite scenes which frequently filled me with wonder and longing, there were constant reminders that I was a far cry from paradise. The owner of the boat and the captain were constantly bickering. Even if they weren't exchanging harsh words, there was a heaviness, a tension in the air. We were surrounded by beauty, but it was as though a dark cloud was hovering over our boat. We were supposed to set sail from Tahiti back to Hawaii, but there was such a squabble between the owner and the captain that it never happened. I flew back to Hawaii and renewed my quest for God.

Friends began lending me books about Hinduism, Buddhism and all sorts of other "isms." Soon I was checking such books out of the library on my own, and next I was buying them and lending them out myself. I found New Age libraries and looked for weekend retreats with this guru or that one. I read endless stacks of books as I searched for some path to God, some way to know him.

All the books seemed to say the same thing, namely, that there is a certain amount of divinity in all of us, and through reincarnation, we will live forever and eventually be one with God. That seemed to be the core of the "New Age" philosophy, which is not new, but actually quite ancient--as old as the pantheism of Eastern religions.

Now and then I met a particularly articulate guru and became excited over his or her teachings. But my enthusiasm always waned when I saw that I wasn't getting any closer to God. This idea of "God is in you, me, and every living thing" was getting old. It seemed hollow, even ludicrous in light of, or maybe I should say "in dark of" life's grim realities. Still, I had a hunger for spiritual truth that kept me searching.

Occasionally, I'd hike down into Haleakala (the crater of an inactive volcano on the island of Maui) and I'd take LSD. Such trips were infrequent; during the whole span of my "hippie" days I don't think I took LSD more than five or six times.

Every couple of years or so, I'd be in touch with Janet. We always had some mutual friend who could tell one of us where the other was. And I just didn't want to lose touch with her; something about Janet was, I don't know, like a lighthouse. I'd wander and I'd roam, but I'd always find myself looking back in her direction.

In 1980, fourteen years after breaking off our relationship, I asked Janet to marry me. I'd asked her once before, in 1978, but she wasn't convinced we could make a go of it. This time, she accepted.

I proposed to Janet from the Polarity Institute at Orcas Island (one of the San Juan Islands). I'd taken an eight-week self-improvement course and had experienced what I believed was a major breakthrough.

I'd just come from a session that was typical of a certain kind of therapy. A person sits down across from an empty chair. He or she imagines someone with whom they need to work out a problem sitting in the empty seat. Usually it would be someone very close: a parent, sibling or spouse. The person begins speaking to whomever they've imagined in the chair in an effort to understand and work out the problem. They voice their own feelings as well as trying to imagine how the other person thinks and feels.

I imagined Janet Rothman in that chair; I had many unresolved feelings toward her and still considered her a significant person in my life. I felt remorse over letting her down. I missed her terribly. By the time the hour was over, I was on bended knee, proposing to the empty chair! As soon as the session was over, I called Janet and asked her to be my wife. To my relief and delight, she accepted.

Janet was living in Mount Shasta at the time. We married in California, then went off to New York to visit our families. After that, we flew to Hawaii for our honeymoon. Janet had visited Hawaii before and strongly preferred California, so before we married, I decided to sell my home and move to Mount Shasta. The honeymoon stretched into six weeks, and two things were becoming increasingly clear to me. I did not want to leave Hawaii. I did not want to be married.

In retrospect, I failed in marriage because I didn't want the responsibility, I was afraid of the commitment, and I was unwilling to make healthy compromises. At the time, I only knew I was miserable, and being single suddenly seemed very desirable. I didn't want other women. I didn't want to lose Janet. It's just that more than anything, I didn't want to be married.

Janet was a midwife and two of the babies she'd committed to delivering in Mount Shasta were almost due. The plan was for me to finalize the sale of my house, which was already underway, wrap up loose ends in Hawaii, and meet my wife in California. Instead, two weeks after Janet left, I wrote a letter telling her that I had made a terrible mistake and wanted out. Our marriage lasted six months on paper; in actuality, we never got past the "honeymoon."

Getting divorced was like being yanked in front of a mirror. I finally saw who I really was. I'd been on a quest for spiritual awareness for years, and considered myself a basically nice guy with a hunger to know God. I was, so I thought, tuned into spiritual things. Now I saw that I was not such a nice guy after all. I was extremely selfish and my actions had devastated another human being.

I took stock of my life and concluded that this spiritual quest of mine was bogus. There was nothing to it. I had found absolutely no lasting peace. None of my experiences could prevent my failure in marriage, or even provide comfort when it was over. And what kind of a person was I, that I should put on airs of spirituality? Who was I to be running here and there on a search for God? I was a hypocrite, that's who. I resolved that I would stop chasing after gurus, philosophies and consciousness-raising groups. I would give up my quest and just go about my life.

Giving up my search was not so simple. Despite the hypocrisy I'd seen in myself, I still had a hunger in my soul. I really wanted God. I felt that only he could remove the confusion and loneliness, the sense of futility I felt about life. I wanted peace of mind, and no person, place or thing in all my array of experiences had been able to provide it.

The conflict between my hunger for God and my decision to stop searching literally kept me awake at night. I would lie in bed tossing and turning, the hours would drag by, and still I could not rest. I began each day feeling tired and worn out.

It might sound strange, but my solution to the fatigue was to train for the Hawaiian triathlon (a running, swimming and biking event). I figured if I pushed my body to the limit all day long, I would be able to sleep at night. It worked. After training six to eight hours a day, six days a week, I was able to sleep at night with no problem.

Still during waking hours, as I was running, bicycling, whatever, my concentration would turn to the unresolved question of God. And I would spontaneously call out, "God, if you're real, please reveal yourself to me. If you're in my heart, as the Hindus say, or if you're out in the cosmos as Judeo-Christian philosophers believe, please show me. Give me some sign. I want to know you."

I never considered this calling out to God a violation of my resolve to stop searching for him. These prayers (although at the time, I never thought of calling out to God as prayer) were a complete break from the search I'd been conducting. I'd practiced spiritual gymnastics for years in an attempt to find God. Now, in desperation, I had abandoned my efforts. If I could not come to God, perhaps he would come to me.

I went on in this way for about three months. Then, one day while jogging, I met a woman named Mary. We struck up a friendship; she was very friendly and outgoing and I was glad enough for the company.

Mary and I had been friends for several weeks when I asked if she would come with me to the other side of the island. I had set aside one day a week to take care of odds and ends, and it was time to file income taxes. My accountant lived in Hilo, 120 miles away. It was usually an all-day event to get there, take care of business and get back. I thought it would be nice to have a friend along for company.

Mary and I set off for Hilo. I was just making conversation, and asked her what she felt was important in life. Mary told me that she was a "born-again Christian." She hadn't been a Christian for long, less than a year. She was very excited about her Jesus and tried to tell me about him, but I quickly cut her off. I simply said I wasn't interested in discussing Christianity. She respected my wishes and didn't bring it up again.

We got to Hilo and I worked out everything with my accountant. Mary and I were sitting in my van drinking a couple of sodas before the ride back, when she opened her Bible and began reading to me. I listened for a minute, then said, "Look, you don't even know me that well. Your Bible seems to give you a lot of peace and joy, but to me it's just another book, and believe me, I've read plenty. You have no idea how many paths I've taken searching for God. As far as I'm concerned, this is just another intellectual trip about religion and I'm not interested. If that Bible could speak to my heart rather than my head, I might believe. But I've already been through too many head trips and I don't want to go through another." Once again, Mary complied with my desire to drop the subject. But, as she later told me, she began silently praying that God would bring people into my life who would tell me about Jesus.

With that, we began the drive back to the other side of the island. We were half an hour into our ride when Mary asked if I would stop at a nearby junkyard. She needed a part for her car, a horn, to bring it up to safety regulation. And she happened to know the son of the man who owned this junkyard.

The junkyard was at the top of some sugar cane fields on a forest reserve; it was a beautiful area. I pulled into the driveway--the junkyard was adjacent to a private home. There were all sorts of cars and pieces of scrap lying around. The junkyard owner came out of the house, and Mary asked if his son was at home.

He said no.

Mary seemed disappointed and ready to leave. But then this man turned to me. He was a stocky man, short, but powerfully built. He struck me as being a very robust, strong person. He didn't introduce himself, but he made a comment about the weather, something about the torrential rains we'd been having. I assumed he was making small talk, but before I could reply, he continued with, "this is one more reason why I believe that the Lord Jesus is going to return soon, because of the peculiar weather patterns we've been having."

Talk about peculiar, I thought this guy was pretty peculiar! I stood there, nonplussed, while he started quoting to me from the Bible. I'm not even sure how I knew it was from the Bible, but I did. And I was angry. Mary was amazed. She hadn't expected God to answer her prayer so quickly, and she certainly hadn't planned this!

I listened to this man pouring out words which he had obviously memorized, and I didn't want to hear what he had to say. I tried to intimidate him by looking into his eyes, I intended to stare him down and put an end to this

Bible quoting. I was surprised to see a quality of softness there. Not soft in an effeminate way, there was just a warmth that seemed to radiate from him. And his eyes were a bit teary, as though something about me made him sad.

I could not imagine why this man would care about me, but it disarmed me. I decided to hear what he had to say. Once I decided that, his words seemed completely different. I don't remember exactly what part of the Bible he was quoting, but the passages dealt with sin and redemption. The words seemed to go straight to my heart. As I drank them in, they reached the empty spot I had been aching to fill.

God was finally speaking to me...and when I least expected it! I hadn't meditated, hadn't taken any drug, hadn't read a book, hadn't engaged in a deep philosophical discussion. Yet, the realization that God exists and that he had something to say to me was almost overpowering. No, this man's voice didn't suddenly take on a strange, eerie quality; he wasn't possessed uncontrollably by some spiritual power. I simply felt that what he was saying was the truth, that it was from God. I'd heard so many others quote "holy books"--friends or gurus--people with whom I had established relationships. I would've been much more likely to believe them than this stranger. Yet these words gripped me in a way that the others hadn't.

I feared I might break down in tears, but I didn't. I just stood and listened. After he finished, he turned and walked away--no comment, no question--he didn't even ask why we had come. He just went back into his house. I was stunned. I turned to Mary and said, "Only half an hour ago I told you that if your Bible could speak to my heart, I might believe. I know that man was sent to tell me those words."

I got into my Volkswagen van and backed out of the driveway. We started down the road, but before long, I burst into tears. I pulled over to the side of the road and wept, not even caring what Mary might think.

When I stopped crying, Mary started reading to me once again. It was as though I had different ears than I'd had the first time. I knew I was hearing words that had been conceived in the mind of God. And I thought to myself, "How can God speak to people through a book?" I said, "Let me see that book!" My suspicions were confirmed: it was the Bible.

I told Mary, "This is what I've been searching for. I've longed to hear from God for over ten years, and what I wanted was here in this book the whole time." I thought of all the books I'd read, all the gurus I'd listened to, all the retreats I'd participated in, all the everything I'd done except this one thing...I'd never read the Bible. Someone gave me one as a gift back in 1976, and I'd opened and shut it after reading only the first page. I'd been so close, and never even knew it! I felt, as we used to say, "ripped off" for so much time and energy. All those years, it seemed, were wasted. I didn't even know what to do about this incredible discovery, but I told Mary I wanted to go home and spend some time alone to think it over.

I drove back down the sugar cane road and just before turning onto the main highway, picked up a hitchhiker. He turned out to be a friend of Mary's who'd become a Christian about the same time she had. He climbed into the back of my van and the next thing I knew, he'd pulled a little black book out of his backpack and began reading to me. He didn't ask, "Hey, can I read to you from my little black book?" He just started right in. I'd picked up hitchhikers many times before and this had never happened. As I listened to what he was reading, I knew that for the fourth time that day, I was hearing the Bible. I could not understand what was happening. He stayed with us for about half an hour before he asked to be dropped off. Then he walked around to the driver's side and told me, "I feel in my heart that you are ready to accept Jesus as your Lord and Savior."

I didn't even know what that meant, but oddly enough, something inside me agreed that I was ready to do this thing, whatever it was. I didn't tell him that; I just told him goodbye. I drove Mary home, and then finally arrived back at my own house, exhausted. But something was stirring deep inside me. I went to bed, but didn't sleep well.

When I awoke the next morning, I looked on my training schedule to see what I had planned for the day. It was a long bike ride, so I did my warm-up exercises and put on my funny little outfit, the kind bike racers wear. I loaded my bicycle into the van, as was my usual practice before lengthy rides. I lived at the top of a huge hill, but near the bottom was a superhighway where all the triathletes trained. I used to park my van at the bottom of the hill and ride up and down this superhighway.

I got into my van and turned on the radio. The first words I heard were the lyrics, "Pick up the good book now, son, it's the gospel, it's the truth." It was from a song Cat Stevens had recorded during a time when I think he was considering becoming a Christian.

When I heard the line of that song, once again, I burst into tears. I parked my van and was still crying when I became aware of a tremendous weight on my shoulders. Not a physical weight, and not literally on my shoulders, but I don't know how else to describe it. I felt an incredible heaviness and it was something very dreadful; I wanted desperately to be rid of it. Almost immediately, it flashed in my mind that this weight was sin.

That was the first time the word "sin" had meaning to me. The day before, when the junkyard man had spoken so lovingly to me about sin and redemption, I believed he had the truth, but I wasn't sure what it meant. I had experienced feelings of guilt in my life, but sin? I'd never thought about it until now. I think God was very gracious to allow me to perceive the weight of my sin in this way. It was an oppressive burden, and I'd never recognized I'd been carrying it all my life. I reflected on the idea of "sin," and began to make the connection between this experience and the junkyard man's words the day before. He'd said that Jesus could forgive me of my sin, that the result of sin was death, and Jesus had paid that penalty so we could have a new life. Now that the concept of sin was real to me, I wanted that forgiveness and that new life.

I rolled down my window and reached out toward the sky with my left hand; my right hand was touching the roof of the van. It's not that I thought God was up in the air somewhere, but it was the only way I knew to reach out to him. I shut my eyes to squeeze back the tears and I said, "Jesus, please come into my life and take away this sin. I don't want it and I don't want to run my life anymore. I want you to run my life. I want you in my heart. Please forgive me for the things I've done."

I began to recall many ugly things I had done over the years: selfish behavior, taking advantage of others. I asked forgiveness for one incident after another. I had only just become aware of the crushing weight of my sin and now it was lifted. I felt so much lighter!

I got out of my van and went on my bike ride. As I rode, I thanked Jesus for forgiving me. I had taken what God offered, and it was good. It didn't even occur to me that I had become a "Christian."

When I returned home, I called Mary to tell her what had happened. She said, "Stay right there, I want to come over to your house." She came over and told me that I had been born again; she gave me her Bible and told me to read the Gospel according to John. Then out the door she went.

There I was, alone in my house with this Bible. I opened it with trembling hands, trembling mostly with excitement and anticipation because I was eager to hear more from God and learn about my new life. But I was a little nervous as well. I remembered what my parents had told me years ago about Christians and the "Christian Bible." What if I discovered that the "New Testament" really was anti-Semitic? Being a Christian was one thing, but I wasn't prepared to start hating my own people! I felt no conflict with my Jewish identity when I called out to Jesus to forgive me, but now that I was about to delve into this forbidden book, I was afraid of what I might find.

To my relief, the Gospels were about a very Jewish person named Y'shua (Jesus). It seemed plausible to me that he was God incarnate--that God would come to earth to accomplish a specific task. It struck a chord that I'd never heard in all my readings about all people being divine, reincarnating, and eventually merging with God. It made far more sense to me that God was separate and holy. For him to come to earth and accomplish what man could not do for himself seemed logical just by virtue of who people are and who God is. Three days after I finished reading the Gospel of John, I went to the little church Mary attended and made known the fact that I believed in Jesus and had committed my life to him.

I was no longer tormented by sleepless nights. Instead of training six to eight hours a day to develop my physical stamina, I spent my time devouring the Bible to build up spiritual strength. I still participated in the triathlon, but instead of entering the "Iron Man" triathlon which I had begun training for, I entered the Maui "Tin Man" triathlon.[1] I placed twentieth out of eighty participants. But the best thing about the triathlon was the fact that God had used it to bring me into contact with the people who told me about Jesus.

I met people at the church who told me how powerful prayer can be, and offered to pray for any matters that might be troubling me. First, I wanted to get rid of alcohol; I'd been drinking regularly since I was a teenager, with very little respite. As I said, it never caused physical problems, but I was emotionally dependent on it. Some people from the church prayed with me, and to my amazement, my desire for alcohol simply ceased. It was a few years before I even had wine at a Passover celebration.

I was so impressed with how God answered that prayer that I began earnestly praying for my ex-wife, Janet. She and I had taken similar but different paths, seeking God through gurus, New Age philosophy and all sorts of teachings that were mostly connected with Eastern religions. It may be hard to believe that I really cared for Janet, considering how I had treated her, yet I did care.

After I came to faith in Y'shua, I was able to care more. I had a new concern for Janet which was not based on what I wanted *from* her, but what I wanted *for* her. And what I wanted for Janet was the relationship with God I'd received, a relationship that could not come through gurus or reincarnation or seminars, but only through the Messiah, Jesus.

Shortly after my decision to believe in Jesus, I spent time on the mainland, doing carpentry work for some Jewish believers in Jesus who lived in Minnesota. Friends in Hawaii had told me about different groups of Jewish believers and I was excited to meet them. I wasn't uncomfortable with the Gentile Christians I knew, but I felt that fellow Jews would understand and know how to explain how my faith in Jesus fit together with my Jewish heritage.

I stayed in Minnesota for three months. I thought about visiting Janet in Mount Shasta on my way back to Hawaii, but realized it would not be wise for me to do so impulsively. I had learned to seek God's guidance for important decisions, so I prayed; I asked God if he wanted me to go to Mount Shasta and speak to Janet about Jesus. The answer was no, I should go back to Hawaii—and so I did.

A few weeks after I arrived home, I was spending Thanksgiving Day with some friends. It was nearly time to eat when the phone rang. A woman was responding to the ad my friends had put in the paper to sell their old Toyota station wagon. They told her we were leaving to go to dinner soon; if she wanted to see the car, she would need to come right away. Well, the woman said she would hurry over, and sure enough, the doorbell rang soon after. My host went outside to show this lady the car, and I stayed in the kitchen talking to his wife and children. I finished the cup of tea I was drinking and went to the sink to rinse out my cup. As I looked out the kitchen window, I saw my friend talking to this potential buyer...who was none other than Janet Rothman.

I could not believe my eyes. I just could not believe it. I remembered that my prayer for the past three months had been, "God, please send someone to talk to Janet about Y'shua." This was the unique time and place God had chosen to answer my prayer.

Janet's Story

Janet Feinberg: I was utterly amazed to see Henry; he was the last person on earth I expected to run into. We hadn't had any contact with one another since a visit the previous January. A mutual friend of ours had told me that Henry was in Minnesota. Yet oddly, I was very happy to see him.

After listening to him talk for a few minutes, I realized there was something very different about Henry, something I'd never seen in the entire 17 years we'd known one another. I'll need to backtrack in order to set the scene and tell my story.

Both Henry and I are Jewish New Yorkers whose families moved out to the suburbs as soon as they were able. My family moved from the Bronx to Monsey when I was 7. One year later, when Henry was 10, his family moved from Brooklyn to Scarsdale--just half an hour away from us! So we grew up very near one another, though we didn't meet till years later in Syracuse.

I went to Sunday school at Temple Beth El in Spring Valley, where I had classes in Jewish history, art and music. Like the Feinbergs, our family's Jewish identity was grounded in loyalty to our culture and our people rather than specific beliefs about God. I knew, for example, that it was very important to my parents that I marry a Jewish man. That's what being Jewish was about; that, and of course the traditional weddings and bar mitzvahs we attended, the foods we enjoyed, and the expressions we used. I remember once trying to tell a Gentile friend what it meant to be Jewish and it was very difficult. Being Jewish was something that was just part of you; it was very hard to put into words, especially to someone who wasn't Jewish.

I don't remember hearing much about God, but somehow, I always believed he existed. When I was 11 years old I began a before-bed-time ritual of getting down on my knees and praying. It was nothing profound, just, "Now I lay me down to sleep, I pray the Lord my soul to keep. If I should die before I wake, I pray the Lord my soul to take." I don't know where I heard that prayer or whatever made me repeat it, but I did, for a little over a year.

The first spontaneous prayer I recall was when I was in the eighth grade. My teacher had lent me a book which I accidentally left on the school bus, and oh, I was so afraid of losing that book! I remember praying that it would be there in the morning. When I saw it lying on the school bus seat the next day, I felt that someone had heard and answered my prayer. That was the extent of my God-consciousness.

After high school, I studied liberal arts at Syracuse University and majored in physical education. Henry and I met when he was a senior and I a sophomore.

Henry was hard to resist from the beginning. Of course, meeting by candlelight during the blackout set the stage for a very romantic relationship. Unfortunately, that romantic aspect was not enough to keep us together. Yet, strangely there was something that prevented us from severing our relationship entirely. Maybe our differences, combined with the things we had in common, kept us interested as well as comfortable with one another over the years. On the one hand, I found Henry very exciting and different. On the other hand, we came from similar backgrounds, we enjoyed many of the same things, such as athletics, and we felt very much at home with one another.

Henry and I were so much in love, or at least we thought we were, that I quit school so I could be with him after he graduated. We each went home to our parents that summer, and every night Henry would drive from Scarsdale to Monsey to see me. But his visits became more and more dutiful. I was having difficulty coping with the fact that we had terminated my pregnancy. It seemed like the reasonable thing to do at the time; we had no idea of the emotional havoc it would wreak. The security, tenderness and joy that had once characterized our relationship were overshadowed by confusion, pain, and resentment. I expected us to ride out the storm together--we would see one another through and, as they say, love would triumph. That was not to be.

I was devastated when Henry announced that he wanted to go to Oklahoma--alone. I had dropped everything to be with this man, and now he wanted to start a new life--one that did not include me. My heart was more than broken, it was shattered.

It took a while, but I realized I had better pull my life together and start making some plans of my own. Many of the classes I'd taken for my physical education major at Syracuse were also requirements for nursing, and I found the idea of being a registered nurse appealing. So the next fall, I entered nursing school.

I was constantly studying and preparing for exams, so thankfully, my rigorous schedule left little time for regrets or self-pity regarding Henry. I graduated in 1969 and moved to Boston, where I took a nursing job at Massachusetts General Hospital.

Boston was the beginning of more than my nursing career. I met people there who were into "alternative lifestyles," and I quickly developed an interest in yoga and natural foods. Next, I began smoking marijuana and taking psychedelic drugs. My experiences with the latter convinced me that there was a spiritual dimension of life to be explored.

I do not advocate the use of drugs; in fact, I am strongly opposed to drug use. It so happens that in my case, a "trip" on drugs first sparked my desire to learn about God. I later discovered the dangerous and deceptive nature of drugs. They can create the illusion that the user is having true spiritual experiences, but in order to continue having these experiences, he or she must keep coming back for more drugs. Even "non-addictive" drugs can cause emotional and mental dependency, because users come to feel that normal (non-drug enhanced) reality isn't okay anymore. Drugs become necessary in order to enjoy life.

Drugs are also dangerous because they can perpetuate the lie that "everything is God" and that people can create their own reality as divine beings, co-creators with God. Certain substances can also be physically harmful. Some can cause brain damage; others leave psychological scars. I actually did permanent damage to my eyes by looking at the sun while high on psychedelics. Someone had told me that the energy of the sun could be taken through my eyes and used to awaken my "chakras." [2]

I continued in this counterculture because I thought it was the way to learn who I was, why I was alive and what part God had in it all. These questions were typical of the '60s and '70s. It was common to find whole communities of people asking the same questions--sharing books, philosophies and experiences in an attempt to find answers.

I left Boston after a year to continue my "quest for

God" in Northern California. I attended endless classes on meditation and yoga, including pre-natal yoga classes which I used in the pre-natal care I was giving as a lay midwife. The midwifery provided some income, and I also had used savings to purchase a home in Mount Shasta, which had two rental units which provided income as well. So I was able to pursue my lifestyle without too much worry over how to pay the bills.

During this time (beginning in 1971), I involved myself with a group called the "Sufis." Their approach to God is very eclectic; they believe that all paths lead to God. They stress unity by seeing truth in all religions. I found this very appealing. If there was one thing we all wanted during the days of the Vietnam War, it was peace and unity. What better way than to respect one another and agree that anyone who wanted peace, love, and God was right? No one was wrong. It didn't matter what you believed, as long as you were sincere and you didn't hurt anyone.

I studied Sufism for about five years. I attended numerous classes in Eastern mysticism. In addition, I was getting astrological readings and tarot readings and just about any kind of readings I could find in my attempt to gain understanding of God, the universe and myself.

I became quite religious, in my own way. I say "in my own way" because I viewed spiritual truth as sort of a giant smorgasbord, a cosmic cafeteria. I simply selected teachings and philosophies which appealed to me and left behind the ones which were not so appetizing. I wouldn't purposely turn my back on truth, it's just that what I perceived as true was often a matter of personal taste.

Eventually, I made my home into a "New Age Center." "New Age" is a spiritual approach which is basically pantheistic; it teaches that God dwells within everything. People can realize that they are divine through meditation, yoga, and various other spiritual pursuits. The end result is enlightenment--a state of "God-consciousness."

I sang with a New Age band called "Planetary Peace," whose other members eventually became my new tenants. We gave regular concerts at my home; on full moons, equinoxes, and solstices, I would have big community gatherings. We shared a potluck dinner, after which I would lead Sufi-dancing.

I scheduled, advertised, and opened my home and my land to all sorts of New Age classes, concerts and events. I was sort of a New Age organizer and I was satisfied that I possessed a great deal of spiritual maturity and understanding. I considered myself a "spiritually evolved" woman and was certain that I was well on my way to merging with God. I was already having temporary experiences of my supposed deity through intense yogic activities combined with drugs.

During these experiences, I felt incredibly powerful and aware. The "high" was like going up and up and up in an elevator and not stopping when you reached the top floor. It was like going through the roof, so to speak, and floating for a time, high above everything and everyone. Of course, I would always come back down. But I felt it was only a matter of time before I would perfect this God-consciousness, and through my own efforts, achieve a permanent state of enlightenment.

There was a steady stream of religious philosophers and teachers passing through my home. I remember one in particular, a British man by the name of Benjamin Creme. He was a highly articulate, personable man who managed to attract quite a following.

Creme would speak of "the Christ" in the context of a "spiritual hierarchy." "The Christ" as he put it, was just an office in this chain of command, to be held by different enlightened people throughout the ages. According to Creme, the office is currently being held by a man named Maitreya. Benjamin Creme also predicted the return of "the Christ." He even gave a date--April of 1982, I think. Well, the date passed and "the Christ" did not appear, yet there are still people who are faithful followers of Mr. Creme's teachings.

As Henry stated, we were in contact with one another every couple of years. It is interesting to me that one such "connection" was during the time that I was hosting Benjamin Creme in Mount Shasta. After one of Mr. Creme's lectures, we had a question and answer session. I distinctly remember the question that Henry asked; he wanted to know, "What did Jesus mean when he said 'I am the way, the truth, and the life. No man comes to the Father but by Me'?"

You have to understand, Henry was not a Christian when he asked that question; in fact, he did not even realize that he was quoting the Bible! Like me, he had been heavily involved in Eastern mysticism and had listened to various "gurus." These teachers of Eastern religion freely quote passages from the Bible, but they quote them out of context in order to support their own teachings. Henry was not trying to prove a point or set a trap when he asked that question; he'd heard the verse somewhere or another and it made an impression on him. He was genuinely curious about it.

I remember Creme's answer just as clearly as I remember Henry's question. He said that Jesus was in a position of authority, very close to "the Lord of the Universe." (It sounded as though Jesus was his secretary!) During Jesus' time, the "Lord of the Universe" was an "ascended master" (someone who had realized his divinity and achieved oneness with God) named Sanat Kumara. In order to get to Sanat Kumara, one had to go through Jesus.

Neither Henry nor I knew enough about the Bible or about Jesus to realize how ludicrous Creme's explanation was. Years later, I learned that the unique unity Y'shua claimed to have with the unchanging, eternal God is a far cry from the pantheistic interpretations of a man who taught that God is whoever happens to be in the office of "Lord of the Universe" at a given time. But I am getting ahead of myself....

The fact that Henry was in Mount Shasta during Benjamin Creme's visit was not too unusual. In fact, in 1978, Henry sold his home in Hawaii and moved in with me in Mount Shasta. We talked about marriage, but it became obvious that Henry was still too restless to settle down. He ended up moving back to Hawaii where he bought another piece of land and built another home.

As Henry described, he proposed to me from the Polarity Institute on Orcas Island in 1980. I was 34 years old, had never been married, and was sick and tired of the relationships I'd had with various men. I wanted to settle down and raise a family, so I joyfully accepted Henry's proposal.

Henry was very inspired and enthused about the institution of marriage when he proposed. The Polarity Institute offers some very positive teachings in that area; they believe the way to a better society is through healthy families and strong marriages. They even teach some biblical principles, including abstinence from extramarital sex. All this was very appealing to Henry and he was eager to put what he had learned into practice. I think I knew deep down that an eight-week course is not enough to make a marriage work, but I brushed aside any reservations I may have had. Henry and I loved each other, and I wanted to believe that would be enough to overcome whatever obstacles we might face.

Again, I was wrong. Marriage was much more workable as an institution to be studied in the classroom than as a day-to-day process in real life. No theory or ideology was going to change whatever it was in Henry that could not face being married. The Polarity Institute had given him food for thought; it had stimulated him intellectually, but it could not change the deep distress that held his heart captive.

Henry had already found a buyer for his house when I left Hawaii to keep my birthing commitments in Mount Shasta. Two weeks later, January 30, 1981, I was on my way to a tarot reading. I stopped at the post office and read Henry's letter announcing that he did not want to be married.

There wasn't much time to let the implications sink in. While I was at my tarot reading, one of my patients called to announce that she was in labor. I had to leave the reading and rush over to perform her delivery. Childbirth takes every ounce of concentration a person can muster, whether you're the one actually giving birth or the one assisting. Any personal problems must be left outside the door. The labor lasted several hours and by the time the delivery was over, I was exhausted.

I finally allowed myself to think about Henry's letter. Could it be that our marriage was really over before we'd even begun? Had I been crazy to think things would ever work out between us? I couldn't believe all this was happening. It was like a bad script for a soap opera. Only the sharp reality of pain made it believable.

Henry called me a few times; at first, he was very distant, but then in March he flew over to visit me in Mount Shasta. During that visit, he realized he still loved me and wanted to try to make the marriage work. He asked me to move to Hawaii and be with him there. Once he returned to the island we realized, through subsequent phone conversations, that neither of us was willing to move. That's when Henry initiated divorce proceedings.

I was of the heart to wait and see if things would change, but we are both willful people, and it's unlikely that either of us would have compromised. I don't know, maybe if I had been truly convinced that the relationship could work, I might have agreed to leave Mount Shasta and begin a new life in Hawaii. Maybe I felt a need to protect myself from being left "high and dry" the way I had been after quitting school in Syracuse to be with Henry so many years before. At any rate, after six months of marriage (about half of which was spent apart), I signed our divorce papers.

Months later I heard that Henry was in Minnesota. I decided that I was not going to spend another cold winter in Mount Shasta. During the cold season, there is very little happening as far as concerts, lectures, etc., so there was really no reason for me to stay. I rented my home to a couple who agreed to take care of the land and the house, and off I went to Hawaii, planning to return in a few months.

I arrived in Hawaii in October and found a place to live without much difficulty. By November I was pretty well settled, except I needed a car. I didn't have much money, so I was keeping an eye on the classified ads, hoping to find a good deal on a used car.

On Thanksgiving Day, I was scheduled to have a "crystal chakra cleansing" (a New Age-type healing) as well as a meditation session and an astrological reading. Quite a full day! All this was to take place in Hawi, which was about two hours from where I was living. A friend had offered to drive me there.

As we rode along, I was scouting out the classified section of the newspaper hoping to spot a good deal on a car. An advertisement for an old Toyota station wagon caught my interest. My friend asked me to read him the phone number, and when I did, he said the owners lived close to our day's destination. I called and asked them if I could come by to see the car, and that just about brings us up to where Henry left off....

As I said, there was something remarkably different about Henry. Though he'd hurt me many times, I still felt an affection toward him and probably always would. But it was more than that. Henry seemed happy and very peaceful, and he was extremely enthusiastic about telling me what had transpired in his life. There was an inner strength and stability that contrasted dramatically with the restless man I knew. Henry told me he had found what he was searching for all those years...he had found God at last.

We got together a few days later in Hilo, and Henry gave me the expanded version of how he had come to faith in Y'shua. My first inclination was to smile condescendingly, because Jesus was nothing new to me. I even considered him one of my many mentors. But as I listened to Henry, I realized two things. First, the Jesus Henry had experienced was not the "borrowed" Jesus I knew, whose words had been lifted out of the Bible and dropped into the Hindu teachings I had come to believe. And second, Henry was more spiritually "together" than I was.

That second realization came as quite a shock. I'd always felt I was ahead of Henry when it came to spiritual awareness and the quest for God. I was the "nurturer," the more mature one, the more spiritually developed. I was the one who had experienced my "kundalini rising" (see footnote 2) and I was the organizer of all sorts of New Age activities. Each time Henry and I were reunited over the years, I advised him and explained whatever the latest shortcut to enlightenment might be. He was sort of the untamed wanderer, the adventurer; I was the stable one. Or so it had always seemed.

But this "new Henry" was explaining his experience of God to me, not in a condescending way, but in an earnest, openhearted manner. He seemed spiritually centered, yet he had both feet planted firmly on the ground. In addition to "seeming" different, there were some measurable differences in his lifestyle.

Henry was no longer running all over the world looking for God. He was no longer drinking--at all. That was a new one. And his joy in seeing me had no romantic undertones. He made no attempts to rekindle our physical relationship, nor was he sleeping with any other women. He related in a very straightforward manner how Jesus had changed his life.

As I was driving home from our meeting, I had an experience that was somewhat similar to Henry's. I saw my life for what it truly was and saw, for the first time, that there was an enormous amount of sin in my life. My first reaction was amazement that, for years, I had seen myself as being such a spiritual woman. I had believed a lie about myself and the deception had been truly grand.

I had grown accustomed to calling wrong behavior right. The way I had deceived myself in regard to my own actions, it is no wonder that I was so deceived in spiritual matters.

For example, I had rationalized an adulterous relationship I was involved in, convincing myself that, in this case, it was okay to be with a married man. Over the years I had grown hardened to the guilt I first felt over sexual sin. What I thought was a loss of inhibition was actually a loss of morality.

I had also rationalized cashing several of Henry's checks after he left. He had interest accruing from an investment and the checks just kept coming to my address. I never heard a word about it from Henry, and I figured, "He hasn't even written to ask about this money. I don't think he cares. If he needed the money, he'd ask me for it. And after the way he's treated me, I'm entitled to something." I collected the checks for a few months, then cashed them (about $2,000) and bought a hot tub I'd been wanting. I honestly thought I hadn't done anything wrong. I was genuinely amazed when Henry wanted his money back!

Those were just a few things that were typical of the way I had rationalized the sin in my life. Now, as I saw the sin for what it was, I repented. Once I saw that I was a sinner, I also saw that I needed a "savior." This was a concept which had always seemed too archaic and unsophisticated to take seriously. I broke down in tears and said, "Jesus, I need you. I need you as my Savior. Please take my life and show me how you want me to live." That was what was going on in my heart; in my head, I remember vaguely wondering, "Does this mean I've become a Christian?"

An atypical thing happened when I asked Jesus into my life. I don't know whether to say I "heard" or "experienced" a voice, but in any case, the message was, "I'll never leave you or forsake you," which I later found out is a promise in the Bible.[3] And there was one other sentence: "I'll never hurt you as men have hurt you."

I can't tell you how overjoyed I was to hear this. I had been hurt in many relationships and so this came as glorious news. I never doubted that these were God's promises to me. Not everyone has this sort of experience when they come to faith in Jesus, but God knew just how to touch my heart.

This was a completely new experience for me; it was not anything that I was capable of bringing about by my own efforts. I realized that I was not divine. I was not the creator, but the created. Moreover, God was perfect; I was not. There was a world of difference between us! When I had looked for God within myself, my "spiritual experiences" had to be induced either by chemicals or by altering my breathing. Now I saw that God was very much outside the world of drugs and meditation and all the other practices which I thought had put him at my beck and call.

When I got home, I called Henry to tell him what had happened. He was as excited as I was, and a little surprised that it had all happened so quickly.

As the reality of my decision sank in, I began a tremendous struggle which lasted about a month. The vague thought, "Does this mean I've become a Christian?" snapped into focus, and it made me very uncomfortable. I had a certain image of Christians as very stuffy, conservative, big-black-Bible toters garbed in polyester suits. Frankly, I saw myself as being entirely too cool to identify with "that" crowd. I thought, "Well, I'll continue believing in Jesus but I won't tell anyone."

Having separated myself from other believers in this way, it wasn't long before I was having serious doubts about my decision. The woman who had done my astrological reading on Thanksgiving Day left me with a paper that warned about "blocks to spiritual growth." One of the blocks to guard against was "dogmatic beliefs or heavy religious programs that block inner awareness." I began to fear that I had embraced a system which would limit my spiritual growth. Most of my friends seemed to feel that way. They encouraged me not to abandon the lifestyle in which I had become so firmly entrenched. Did I really want to give up smoking marijuana, and join the ranks of the "uncool"?

I had devoted over a decade of my life to the New Age teachings which had become central in my life. Could I turn my back on all that? What about the meaning of all my kundalini experiences? (See footnote 2.) And what about all the beautiful, loving people I knew who didn't believe in Jesus? How could I be so narrow as to think that they didn't also have the truth?

Had my thinking been limited to these questions, I would not be a believer in Jesus today. It would have been much more convenient and in keeping with the life I had chosen to simply consider my experience with Jesus one of a number of spiritual truths I'd found along life's way. But there was another question that gnawed at me. The question was, "Is it true?" I wanted so much to know, is Jesus really the Messiah, the one who saves us from our sin--or was it possible for me to get to God through my New Age thinking? In my heart, I realized if it were true about Jesus, everything would fall into place. Despite my pride, I knew that finding the truth was more important than protecting my image or my lifestyle. I continued to ask God to reveal his truth to me, and I was willing to accept whatever that might be.

During this time of confusion, Henry became a very dear friend to me. He related to me in a way he had never done in all the 17 years we had known one another. We made an agreement that this time, we would not become romantically involved with one another. This was important, because I can look back and know my decision was not brought about in the context of an emotional entanglement.

It was apparent that Henry's concern for me was genuinely motivated by a desire to see me find the truth. He was already friendly and accepting of me as a person regardless of my beliefs; there was nothing further to win from him by believing in Jesus. After a month of calling, visiting and encouraging me to read the Bible, Henry gave me a book entitled *The Death of a Guru*, by Rabindranath Maharaj and Dave Hunt.

This book gave me a clear understanding of the difference between the Eastern/Hindu philosophies I had been practicing and the biblical beliefs I was now coming to understand. I realized that I had been deceived for years, and it was the most humbling experience of my life. Once again, I repented of my sin, and this time, when I asked Jesus to come into my life, I was prepared to begin following him, and him alone.

I'd like to say a little more about *The Death of a Guru*, because it made a real impression on me. Rabindranath Maharaj was from a family of gurus; his father before him had attained Samadhi, which is the term used in Eastern philosophy to mean "God-consciousness." Rabindranath himself was being worshipped as God, which meant people were bringing him money and food and sitting at his feet, waiting to hear whatever wisdom might fall from his lips. One day, he heard a voice that told him, loud and clear, "You are not God." That was one of many incidents in his life that eventually brought Rabindranath to Jesus. I remember how moved I was at his conversion, knowing that for this man to follow Jesus meant giving up far more

67

than the piddly lifestyle I was concerned with losing. He was not only rejected by friends and family (which often does happen with believers in Jesus, especially those of us who are Jewish), but he lost his position of status as a Brahman Hindu guru. He gave up the worship, adulation and honor that so many misguided people had been perfectly willing to bestow upon him. What a life-wrenching decision! Yet, this man was willing to sacrifice everything for the truth.

It would take an entire volume to outline the differences between what the Bible teaches and what Eastern religions teach, but I can give sort of a "nutshell" explanation of the ones that were especially significant to me.

Eastern philosophies are basically pantheistic; they teach God is in everything and we are one with all of God's creation. God dwells within every part of creation, but humans are set apart because we can realize our divinity, and thus be enlightened. Reincarnation is a central teaching; it supposedly gives us opportunities to learn our lessons and work out our karma. "Karma" basically means the result of our actions. For example, the karma for a child-beater in this life might be that he or she will be beaten in the next life. Eventually, as we work out the karma and learn the lessons, we will be enlightened, merge back into the oneness of God, and no longer have to reincarnate. That is what Eastern religions teach.

The Bible teaches that God is a being separate from his creation; God cannot be added to nor diminished. He is not scattered in particles throughout the universe in the form of creation, although he has used creation to reveal himself to us. God is everywhere but not everything is God. Regarding the human race, the Bible teaches that man has only one life to live on this earth, after which comes judgment. We cannot merge with God through our own efforts, but we can have an everlasting relationship with him based on faith in his provision of atonement for our sins.

In addition, the Bible has much to say about the kind of pantheistic teachings Eastern religions offer. You can read about people who thought it possible to be divine in the third chapter of Genesis. It describes how sin entered the world because people wanted to be God instead of obeying God. That is really the root of the "New Age" philosophies and the Eastern religions. There is something in people's hearts which is so jealous of the "otherness" of God that we delude ourselves into thinking we can share God's divinity. Some do this in a rather unstructured way. They don't consider themselves religious; they simply ignore the Creator and make their own standards of right and wrong as though they were God. Others actually follow a system of beliefs that teach the divinity of man. They even quote Bible passages which talk about God's unique majesty and twist them into proclaiming the exact opposite. For example, Psalm 46 is a description of God's power and glory. One verse says, "Be still and know that I am God." I have read more than one New Age book which uses this to claim that if one quiets one's mind through meditation, he or she will realize his or her own divinity. Read the Book of Psalms, and you will find that none of the Psalms even hint at the majesty of man, apart from being God's creation. They ascribe glory only to God. Yet that interpretation is typical of the deception that is woven throughout pantheistic philosophies and religions.

The Bible teaches that God loves us, wants fellowship with us, and promises to provide power and strength for daily living when we submit to him. But the Bible has a word for the practice of blurring the distinction between the Creator and his creation. It's called idolatry. It's called sin. To me, that is the most important distinction between the Bible and the New Age Hindu-based teachings I once held. We can either choose to worship God or we can worship ourselves.

Once I came to terms with the "otherness" of God, I was able to address the matters that had troubled me. Among them were the "spiritual" experiences I'd had with drugs, many of which seemed to corroborate the mystic teachings I now had to set aside.

As I thought about these experiences, I realized a few things. First, by altering my consciousness I was, indeed, opening myself to spiritual experiences, but not necessarily the spirit of God. If there are spirits which are evil and hostile to God, it stands to reason that any experience they might involve themselves in would pull a person away from worshipping God. It made perfect sense for these drug-induced experiences to fall hand in hand with the false teachings I had been reading.

Second, the more I thought about it, the less profound these experiences were. Often, while on drugs, I would feel I had grasped some matter of earth-shaking importance. Yet, the next morning, the experience would be forgotten. I would not remember what it was that had seemed so all-important; I felt that I had been enlightened, yet there was no evidence of any enlightenment.

Drugs, meditation and yoga make everything seem crystal clear while you are high on them. Once you come "down" to day-to-day living, the memory of these experiences is often blurred beyond any sort of significance. Yet the user retains the feeling of having understood some great truth, a truth which usually doesn't translate very well into coherent speech.

As for my fears of becoming narrow-minded, I suppose in a way I have. I do believe that Jesus is the only way to God--that's what he said, and I believe it. But anyone who is truly committed to anything is, in a sense, narrow-minded. If a woman wants to be true to her husband, she has to be very narrow-minded about not having sex with other men. That doesn't mean she has to hate every man except her husband. I don't hate people who don't believe in Jesus, but I cannot accept their beliefs as true.

Our society lauds the quality known as "open-mindedness." The way to be "nice" is to be open-minded and say that everyone is right. But if there were six supposed cures for cancer, and each appeared to work while only one was truly a permanent cure, would it be "nice," would it be "open-minded" to tell a cancer patient it didn't matter which one he chose, so long as he was sincere? If that's being nice, I'd rather be narrow-minded! And that's how I feel when it comes to telling people about Jesus.

So many exciting things began to happen after I came to faith in Y'shua. Once I made my real commitment (which was about a month after I'd first asked him to come into my life), things began to change dramatically. First, I felt differently about drugs. For years I had thought they were a great asset to carry along on my spiritual journey. After I became a believer, I realized that those drugs were harmful in many ways...and even more, I realized I didn't need or want them. My desire for psychedelics completely fell away. This gave me a tremendous feeling of freedom. However, I did still have a desire to smoke marijuana, and I knew I would need God's help to quit. I asked Christian friends to pray for me and, amazingly enough, I lost my desire for marijuana, too! I tried it one more time after that, but it really brought me down--it wasn't a "high" for me like it used to be. I believe that was God's intervention and, oh, I'm so thankful for it.

The next thing was the change that began to occur between Henry and me.

It was frightening for both of us when we once again began to feel a romantic attraction to one another. Every previous attempt to work out a relationship had been so short-lived and had caused so much pain; we each had strong reservations about trying again. The big difference this time was that we both had something to consider besides our own fears and desires. We had a personal relationship with God; we had each learned that he is concerned with the details of our lives. And so we prayed and trusted him to provide guidance in the matter of our relationship.

Henry and I both concluded that God wanted to heal our marriage. With Jesus in our lives, there was hope. Our relationship with him changed how we viewed our relationship to one another. That doesn't mean that when we realized God wanted to heal our marriage, everything came together in an instant. I guess God could have done that if he'd wanted to, but that's not what happened. It was hard for me to release the past and relate to Henry in the present. We allowed the process to unfold slowly; it wasn't easy to let past hurts heal.

I sensed the deep and intense connection Henry and I shared; I was afraid of it, yet longed for it at the same time. When I told Henry that I was ready to try to put our marriage back together, he agreed with me that we would need help. We contacted some Christian counselors and spent about three months working with them. In April of 1983, we were rejoined in matrimony.

God has truly blessed our union this time, because we have built it on a rock-solid foundation--Jesus. It's still hard work to be a good husband and wife, but as we grow closer to God, he strengthens us both as individuals, and as a couple. And Henry and I are both very grateful for the healthy baby girl who was born to us on April 5, 1986. Her name is Hannah Grace, and though Mom had her a little later than most (I was 39 when she was born) Hannah has proved to be one of our greatest joys.

Another thing which has happened to us since believing in Jesus is the deepening of our Jewish identities. During all my years of searching and seeking, I never understood what it meant to be Jewish. Oh, I knew what it meant culturally, but I wanted to know how being Jewish related to my quest for God. I asked people about the spiritual significance of my Jewishness, and they gave me the most ridiculous answers. One said that I had karma from a previous life that had to be worked out with my father. Since he was Jewish and I was supposed to work out this karma as his daughter, I too, would naturally be Jewish. Someone else told me that I was born Jewish because I was the reincarnation of some Middle Eastern someone or other. Honestly!

After I came to faith in Jesus, I began digging into the Bible. I had been so ignorant about my ancestors! I read about Abraham and Sarah, Isaac and Rebekah, Jacob and Rachel, and was filled with wonder at the richness of my heritage. It was so good to read God's Word and get a glimpse of how he dealt with my people in the past and will continue to deal with us in the future. And as I read further in the Prophets and on to the Gospels, I saw how very Jewish Jesus was and how beautifully God's plan of salvation fit together. It was a thrill to realize that I am a part of the people God has chosen to make that plan known to the world.

Henry: I feel the same way. And appreciating our Jewish heritage goes beyond the mere excitement of reading about our own people in the Bible. Janet and I feel that as Jewish believers, we have a special responsibility to talk to fellow Jews about Jesus. That is the main reason why we have made our lives an "open book." We hope that by doing so, some will see how Y'shua, the Jewish Messiah, can transform lives.

ENDNOTES

1 The "Iron Man" triathlon includes a 2.4-mile swim, 112-mile bike ride and a 26-mile run. The Maui "Tin Man" is a 1.2-mile swim, 56-mile bike ride and a 13-mile run.

2 "Chakras," in Hindu teachings, are seven energy centers in the human body. The "kundalini," which is believed to be the "spiritual reality of the human body," is supposedly coiled at the base of the spine. As it is awakened by spiritual practices or with drugs, it ascends up the spine through these chakras. When the kundalini passes through the crown of the head, a person is said to experience "merging with God."

3 Hebrews 13:5, "Let your conduct be without covetousness, and be content with such things as you have. For He Himself has said, 'I will never leave you nor forsake you.'"

JERRY
KARABENSH

I didn't run out to join the Jews for Jesus staff nor did I give up my business to begin handing out gospel leaflets. But I am not ashamed to tell anyone who is interested that I am a Jew who believes that Jesus is the Messiah. It is true that Jews who believe in Jesus are often misunderstood and misjudged by our closest family and friends. But a person has to do what he thinks is right.

I wasn't looking for something to believe. I pretty much believed in me. I was a successful businessman, the owner of a marketing and publishing company in the field of health care. My work was not only lucrative but meaningful; my company provides information and services for pharmaceutical companies as they relate to the medical community. I had my work, I was content with my wife and family. I was not particularly religious, though I identified strongly as a Jew.

Then a Catholic woman, who was probably no more religious as a Catholic than I was as a Jew, asked me a question. It was more like a casual comment than a question, but it made me stop and think. She said something to the effect of, "You don't really believe those stories are true, do you?" She was referring to "the stories" in the Bible, and the "Old Testament" in particular. I realized I had no answer because I didn't know if I believed "those stories" or not. I realized that the "Old Testament" was the Gentile designation for the Jewish Bible. I decided at that moment that I ought to find out whether or not I believed in it.

I was born in Milwaukee, Wisconsin, on December 10, 1934, the oldest child of Fred and Blanche Karabensh. My parents were also from Milwaukee, but their folks came here from Europe. My mother is Jewish, from a family of Russian immigrants, the Shavzin family. Like Tevya and his friends from "Fiddler on the Roof," they had to flee the pogroms in the early part of the 20th century. My father's family came to Milwaukee from a village in what is now Rumania. But the Karabenshes, unlike the Shavzins, were not fleeing the pogroms. They were Catholics who came to America hoping to improve their economic situation.

My mother and father were both amateur actors. They met and fell in love at a community theater organization in Milwaukee. They eloped in 1933, thereby demonstrating their flair for drama.

I was an only child for 9 years...and then rather suddenly (I thought), my parents presented me with a baby sister. A few years later there was another baby sister...and then another! But when I think back to family ties, what influenced me the most was not the arrival of three little sisters, but the close relationship I had with Grandma and Grandpa Shavzin.

Grandma was an arthritic invalid and Mom wanted to live as close to her as possible--so we took a duplex where my grandparents could live downstairs. Mom was thus able to stay close to Grandma, and I received a very Jewish upbringing in what otherwise would have been a "half and half" situation. Grandma kept a kosher kitchen, and since my mother worked, I usually ate downstairs. So I pretty much had a kosher upbringing. Sometimes I'd tease Grandma by waving one of her *fleishedik* knives in the air pretending I was about to thrust it into the butter, but I never would have done such a disrespectful thing. I learned the *aleph-bet* at my grandfather's knee. In many ways, having Grandma and Grandpa downstairs was like having a second set of parents. After school, if I wasn't out playing with friends, I'd be with my grandparents.

We celebrated the Jewish holidays in great style. At Passover my grandmother would have the house thoroughly scrubbed from top to bottom. We'd bring in separate sets of pots and pans for those eight days. There was no such thing as Kosher-for-Passover milk products back then, so we ate only meat dishes during Pesach. We even spread chicken *schmaltz* on our matzoh instead of butter. Only after Passover ended could we eat our matzoh with butter.

We weren't members of one particular synagogue, so on holidays and Sabbaths when my grandfather and I did go, we would choose a synagogue at random. This worked well, but when it came to the High Holidays, I would go to one of the larger synagogues in town with my friends. Since one needed to buy tickets to be seated, those of us who didn't purchase them would take turns with friends whose families were members. One of us would sit in the service for a couple of hours while the others were outside playing ball. Then whoever had the ticket would come outside and switch places with one of the players. It may sound irreverent, but few of us boys were willing to spend the entire day in the synagogue, so taking turns sitting in services was our way of showing that being Jewish did matter to us.

My kosher upbringing, "Folk Schula" (the cheder I attended) and holiday celebrations are clearly etched memories. But what about my father's background? How did Catholicism fit into our household?

In essense, it didn't. Whatever I learned about Catholicism came, not from my father, but from my paternal grandmother. Who knows, had we been living with my father's parents instead of my mother's, perhaps I would have considered myself Catholic instead of Jewish. But even if I had been more under their influence, it's hard for me to imagine that could ever have been the case. My paternal grandmother may have been a devout Catholic, but my paternal grandfather had little use for religion and regarded church merely as an appropriate location for weddings and funerals. My father seemed to feel the same way, though he never said much about it. Certainly, no one ever gave me the impression that being Catholic had much to do with God.

On the other hand, no one conveyed to me the impression that being Jewish had much to do with God--not in Hebrew school, nor in the synagogue, not in my grandmother's kosher kitchen or by my grandfather's easy chair. Being Jewish was mainly a matter of culture and tradition to those who taught me. My Jewish school-pals didn't seem to think any more about God than I did, so I doubt if it had anything to do with my parents' mixed marriage. God was simply not much of an issue throughout my childhood, adolescence and young adulthood.

I earned my pharmacy degree in Madison, at the University of Wisconsin and remained there to earn my Masters of Business Administration. That's when I met a nurse named Delores (Del). I had pretty much decided that this was not the time for me to get married. My roommate fixed me up with Del and I figured that her being Gentile would prevent a serious relationship from developing. It would be "safe" to make a date with her now and then until I finished my degree, then we would part friends. I would establish myself in the business world and settle down with a nice Jewish girl.

Well, you know what they say about the best laid plans of mice and men...I ended up falling in love with Del and we married in May of 1960.

Del was Catholic, but I was already "immunized" to that from the little bit I'd learned from my paternal grandmother. I'd been to church with Grandma Karabensh a few times and it hadn't made much of an impression on me. As far as I was concerned, being Jewish was all that was necessary. I just accepted that since my wife was Catholic she believed in God and Jesus, and since I was Jewish I believed only in God.

The church was not only central to Del's religion, but an important part of her social life as well. I was quite secure in what I didn't believe, so I was amenable to socializing with Del's "church friends." There were about six of us couples who met bi-weekly for discussions and social events, such as tennis games and gourmet dinners.

That little group was where I happened to meet Arlene Yaley, the woman who asked the question I mentioned earlier, "You don't really believe all those stories, do you?" We were discussing the Bible that night, but since I wasn't sure what she had in mind, I asked, "Well, what stories are you talking about?"

"Oh, you know," she replied, "Noah, Jonah--the flood that covered the earth, the whale--that sort of stuff."

I have my faults, but I'm basically an honest man, so there was really only one thing I could tell her. And that was, "Actually, I've never thought about it."

Until then, I'd never accepted or rejected the Bible. The thought that it somehow belonged to me because I am a Jew hung in the back of my mind like an inherited suit might hang in the back of my closet. Such a suit might be mine, it might have meaning because of the previous owner, but I could go for years without feeling the need to either wear it or give it away. There was plenty of room for such a suit to hang there unnoticed until an occasion arose to try it on.

Arlene's question was an occasion that made me want to pull out the Jewish Bible and try it on for size. Did I believe all those stories? Should I believe them? Were those people real? These Bible stories were part of the Old Testament that Jews are supposed to believe. But what was the Old Testament? Oh, I had used it as a textbook for a course in college, a Hebrew literature class. We viewed the Bible from a strictly stylistic point of view, analyzing various elements of its poetry and so on. But what about the Bible from a religious point of view? It had never been an issue till now.

I found myself thinking, "Hey, I'm the resident Jew in this group, and in the land of the blind, the one-eyed man is king. If I'm supposed to be the expert, I better do a little research."

So my curiosity and sense of Jewish pride motivated me to begin reading the Old Testament. That interest in learning about the Bible was a turning point for me. Meanwhile, my wife was in the process of reaching her own turning point.

Through a particular priest and a number of lay people involved in a special movement within her church, Del began thinking that it wasn't all the church rituals that mattered--it was knowing Jesus. She began to evaluate her belief in him based on the Old and New Testaments rather than certain traditions which had no basis in the Bible. Her faith was no longer in a religion, but in her personal relationship with God. That relationship was based on Del's faith in Jesus. In short, my wife became a true Christian.

Del was secretly delighted when I decided to investigate the Jewish Bible, because she had begun to pray that I, too, would come to faith in Jesus. Surprising as it may sound, she knew the best way for me to meet Jesus would be by starting in the Old Testament. She realized I would not be looking for a religion that was not Jewish, and by now, she also realized that her own Christian faith was rooted in the Jewish Bible.

Del was right. I began reading the Old Testament to find out more about my Jewish background, and I got more than I bargained for. First, I discovered that I believed this Bible of mine was true. I also discovered statements in my Bible about someone who was supposed to come in the future. I vaguely remembered references to such a person called "the Messiah" mentioned in synagogue prayers.

Oddly enough, the Old Testament descriptions of the Messiah and what he was supposed to do reminded me of this Jesus person I'd heard about now and then. That was unexpected...and interesting. I decided to continue investigating the Bible until I could reach a conclusion about Jesus and whether he had anything to do with my Bible and my Judaism.

My wife knew better than to push. She kept praying and she told a church leader (the one who was instrumental in her becoming a Christian) about me. He offered me a book called *The Promise*, by Hal Lindsay. It had prophecies from the Old Testament on one side of the page, and passages which were supposed to be fulfillments from the New Testament on the other.

The book did not convince me to believe in Jesus, but it did substantiate my hunch that he was not some idea the Gentiles had fabricated from thin air. It looked as though who he was and what he supposedly accomplished could all be traced to the Jewish Bible. How could this be true in light of the fact that it is Gentiles, not Jews, who believe in Jesus?

At the urging of one of her new friends, Del told me about a Jewish Christian named Paul Yates who might be able to answer the questions which had begun to well up within me. I said I didn't mind if Paul wanted to talk to me about Jesus, so one day he came to call at my office. We talked for a while and then he confronted me with the question, "Are you a sinner?" I'd never thought about it before, yet it didn't take me long to answer, "Yes."

Paul was surprised. Few people answer him that way. I guess most figure that "sinners" are all locked away somewhere for committing their special crimes. Well, there was no doubt in my mind that I had done some things which were displeasing to God. That didn't make me a criminal in a court of law, but I knew instinctively that it did make me a sinner.

Paul went on to explain that there must be an atonement, or covering for sin in order for people to have a relationship with God. He noted that an important role of the

Messiah was to provide that atonement. He showed how Jesus' death and resurrection made sense, not only in light of the prophecies, but in light of the principles of sacrificial atonement found in the *Tanach* (Leviticus 17:11).

I concluded that if Jesus wasn't the Jewish Messiah, we might as well forget the whole messianic promise. No one else was going to fit the description more closely than he. I accepted the fact that Jesus was *the* Messiah, but now the question remained, was he *my* Messiah? Why should I let him into my life?

I forestalled my decision, not because I was having a hard time believing, but because I was having a hard time reconciling it with my Jewish identity. I didn't know many Jews who believed in Jesus. People who believed in him were Christian--Gentiles. Not that I had anything against Gentiles, but I was very satisfied with the Jewish culture and identity with which I had been raised. I was not willing to exchange it.

I was annoyed with God. I felt it was too much for him to ask a Jew to become a Christian. How could he expect us to give up the very identity he had given us in the first place? If the Gentiles hadn't accepted Jesus, well, maybe things would have been different. On the other hand, I had to admit that if I really believed this was true, Jesus deserved my allegiance regardless of what I would have to give up. I continued to wrestle with the issue.

On April 23, 1976 (my wife's birthday), we went to Los Gatos Christian Church to hear a concert by The Liberated Wailing Wall, Jews for Jesus' music group. I'd been given a tape of their music and liked it so my wife called their office to find out where we could see the group. I never expected to hear anything like their program that night. Here were about half a dozen Jewish people who believed in Jesus and they had certainly not traded in their Jewish identity!

I listened to their songs and watched their drama, and I realized that my reluctance to commit my life to Jesus was based on a lie. If he was the Jewish Messiah, as I now believed, how would admitting it make me less of a Jew? It might make me less of a Jew in the eyes of some of my family and friends, but what about in God's eyes? He created the Jewish people. Wasn't it more important what he thought? If he had sent Jesus to be the Jewish Messiah, and I knew it, did I have the right to refuse this truth?

Everything fit into place. Even if nobody except other Jewish believers in Jesus understood that I was still Jewish, believing in the Messiah was not going to mean sacrificing my Jewishness. At about 9 p.m. that night, Tuvya Zaretsky, who was the leader of the Liberated Wailing Wall at that time, asked if anyone wanted to accept Jesus as his or her Messiah. I raised my hand.

I didn't run out to join the Jews for Jesus staff nor did I give up my business to begin handing out gospel leaflets. But I am not ashamed to tell anyone who is interested that I am a Jew who believes that Jesus is the Messiah. It is true that Jews who believe in Jesus are often misunderstood and misjudged by our closest family and friends. But a person has to do what he or she thinks is right.

My mother has also come to faith in Jesus. She, too, worried about how the family would respond. Maybe it was a little easier for her, knowing that I believed and had not turned my back on my Jewish identity. But to us, the final question was not whether it would be easy or hard to face people as a Jew who believes in Jesus. Eventually, we had to ask, is it right to believe? It is!!

Being born in a Christian home... doesn't make you a Christian any more than being born in a bakery makes you a bagel!

STAN TELCHIN

With persistence, I would certainly find what I needed to win Judy back. I had always stood up for Jewish causes. What Jewish cause could be more important than my Jewish daughter?
I *had* to disprove her belief in Jesus!

The subway car bumped and jerked like an urban bronco. Our feet were firmly planted, our knees slightly bent. Balance was the key to collecting coins instead of bumps and bruises. The rumble and roar of the train was not conducive to speech-making so we kept our spiel brief. "Please give to the Jewish National Fund," I'd shout, then I'd hold out the little blue and white can which we referred to as a *"pushka."* Occasionally I'd shake it because the clatter of coins made me glad: glad that people cared about us Jews having a homeland, and glad that I was doing my part to help.

We worked the train all the way from the Fort Hamilton Parkway Station in Brooklyn to Coney Island, the end of the line. Then we'd work the train all the way back to the other end of the line, which was Times Square. From Times Square we would take the train home. All for a nickel! The whole ride cost five cents!

Most of the people were happy to see us, but then most of the people were Jewish! And even among those who weren't there was a growing compassion for the Jewish people, especially as more and more was known about the peril of the Jewish people in Europe. There wasn't much money—nickels and dimes—but after all, this was still the Depression and if you collected three bucks a night it was better than a punch in the nose.

Anyway, the main thing wasn't the amount we collected for the Jewish National Fund. It was the fact that we were out there trying, and we had a sense of participation and identification with the Jewish people beyond the confines of our own neighborhood. Nobody had to tell me how important that was. I just knew.

In those days, being Jewish wasn't something that one had to prove or define. One learned to be Jewish from other Jewish people, or from circumstances. I grew up believing in Jewish values, Jewish causes, Jewish community, even Jewish rituals now and then, but the Jewish God? No. My feeling was that the God of Israel (if he existed) had been unresponsive enough to our pain to show that he wasn't interested in us anymore (if he ever had been). I hadn't made a study of it, but experience seemed to indicate that either God didn't exist or he didn't care. Let me tell you why I felt that way.

When I was seven years old, some of us boys were playing on a lot where construction workers had left a bucket of hot tar unattended. Imagine the worst that could happen with a gang of boys and a bucket of hot tar, and then picture that happening all over my feet. I called (actually screamed) out to God as a spontaneous reaction to the excruciating pain and terror. There was no answer and no comfort. There was only pain.

Somewhere I heard that God was created by human beings. I never came right out and said "There is no God," but for me it was enough to be Jewish and to work at those things that would ensure survival for our people.

A Jewish homeland was one of the things we desperately needed to survive. That was a lesson I learned in depth at Ha Shomer Ha Tzair, a neighborhood Zionist youth group I attended from the age of 12 through 15. I joined in the dancing and singing with gusto and I listened intently as guest speakers talked about what it means to be a Jew. And as I was growing up in the '30s the need for a Jewish homeland was a topic under continual discussion.

Thirteenth Avenue was our public platform, a New York version of "Speaker's Corner." We used to gather there in the evenings to listen to the soapbox orators. This was way before TV, even before everybody had a radio. Thirteenth Avenue was, in many ways, the hub of the Jewish community in our neighborhood.

It was a wide street, and from 39th Street to 42nd it was filled almost wall to wall with pushcarts. That section of 13th Avenue was actually an outdoor market such as you still can see on the lower east side of Manhattan today. Up around 43rd through 47th or so, there were "regular businesses" including Orloff Opticians (where I got my glasses) and a father-and-son shoe store (where I got my first pair of boots when I was 10 years old).

Anyway, the best broadcasting system in Boro Park Brooklyn was the way people who were concerned about an issue would get up on a soapbox and "let it rip." My friends and I often gathered to hear the Jewish activists. This is where I received much of my Jewish education and identity. These speeches stretched my understanding beyond what I knew about Jewish life in our neighborhood. They helped me understand what it meant to be a part of world Jewry. I learned about the centuries of persecution and came to understand our desperate need for a Jewish homeland. Remember, this was in the late '30s and the later we got into the '30s, the more conversations there were about what was happening in Nazi Germany, and how it impacted Jews all over the world.

Though I received the bulk of my Jewish education at home, from street corners, and at meetings of Ha Shomer Ha Tzair, I also received the customary religious training and was bar mitzvah toward the end of the summer of 1937.

My grandfather, who was a very *frum* man, gave me some training and then sent me to a synagogue, a Talmud-Torah. I lasted there for several months and then the rabbi hit me—with a stick—I think because I did not recite as quickly as he would have liked. My response, which I would not want to see in print, got me kicked out of the Talmud-Torah.

So I had to have a *lerner* come and he would "lern" me (he would teach me) on a private basis. But I didn't have to learn how to be a Jew. It was a given; you breathe as a Jew, you walk to the subway as a Jew, you put a nickel in the slot as a Jew, you push through the turnstyle and get on the subway as a Jew. So you prepare for a bar mitzvah and you follow through as a Jew. That is what we all did. My bar mitzvah was slightly different from most. We had a small ceremony with family and friends at a mid-week service in the synagogue. I was disappointed because all my friends were bar mitzvah on Saturday. Later on I understood that in the middle of the Depression we just didn't have the money for a fancier weekend celebration.

Not too long after my bar mitzvah I began dating, but there wasn't much money for that, either. So what we used to do was invite the girls out to a movie, or we'd go to what we called a "gathering" at someone's house. Then later all us guys would meet over at Skilowitz's Deli for "the usual." The usual was two hot dogs, some french fries and a Coke—all of which cost a quarter. We couldn't afford to take the girls out for a movie *and* a bite to eat, so our going out to eat without them had to remain a well-kept secret.

When World War II broke out, I was among those inducted. Because I played a pretty good trumpet, I was placed in the Signal Corps of the United States Air Force. We musicians were especially able with Morse code. Unfortunately, because I'm very hard of hearing in my right ear, I was getting terrible headaches from my headset. To solve the problem, I applied for a transfer to the 764th Army Air Force Band in Waycross, GA. I was down there for nine months before we went up to Fort Dix, NJ for assignment overseas. On the last night of my last three-day pass, I dropped by to visit an old friend named Helen. It was at her home that I again met Ethel David. Ethel and I had gone all through Montauk Junior High School together, yet she had refused to invite me to her Sweet 16 party. That really hurt me. But I crashed the party anyway. And now, three years later, to my surprise we hit it off. I offered to walk Ethel home from Helen's house. As we were saying goodbye, she asked if I wanted her to write to me while I was overseas. I gladly accepted her offer. And what a terrific correspondent she turned out to be! Her letters were a real lifeline while I was away from all that was familiar, and we became fast friends.

I left the States on January 5, 1945 and landed at Le Havre on January 15, 1945. After getting established, our band would rehearse a concert and then go out on the road for a month at a time, playing at different bases. Our dance band even alternated with the Glenn Miller band for a month in Paris. We crossed the Rhine on April 3, 1945 and came back to Luxembourg City, Luxembourg just in time for VE Day. I'll never forget it; we played parades all day long. Nine months later, I was finally eligible to return to the States.

On the trip home I heard there was an opening for a ship's announcer and disk jockey. As a lark, I applied, auditioned, got the job...and it was fun! I used to play Glenn Miller, Gene Kroupa, Charlie Barnett, Jimmy Dorsey, Stan Kenton and all the really great bands.

After my discharge and return home, one of the first things I wanted to do was see Ethel. We began to date seriously, even as I was thinking about what to do with my future. While I wanted to stay in music, I knew that I really had to get an education.

Because of the post-war enrollment crunch, getting into college wasn't easy. Nevertheless, I managed to be admitted to the George Washington University in Washington, D.C.

My roommate at G.W. was also a Jewish kid from Brooklyn and we hit it off very well. In October 1946, he tried out for a part in a play called "Winterset" and encouraged me to do likewise. I'd discovered a bit of a dramatic flair as a DJ on board ship, so I thought I'd give it a try. And I got a part! It was a bit part to be sure, the role of an Irish cop, but it was enough. I fell in love with "show biz."

Meanwhile, I did not lose sight of the fact that I'd come to get an education. I started out in engineering. My oldest brother Charlie was an architect, 18 years older than I, with three sons and two daughters. He thought it would be a good idea to make his firm "Telchin and Telchin" when I graduated. I could study to become either an architect or an engineer and he would take me into the business. The plan was that by the time Charlie was ready to retire, his sons would be ready to enter the business and I would take them in. I would head up the firm as their mentor and do for them what Charlie was going to do for me. Then when I retired, they would take over and presumably, by then, they would have children of their own to take into the business.

I really looked up to my brothers. Charlie was an architect, Joe was an attorney, and Sam was an accountant. It was very important to me to have their respect, and so I wanted to do very well in school. I hadn't been thinking a great deal about the field of engineering, but then I hadn't been thinking about anything except music for the previous three and a half years. Charlie's offer was too generous to ignore.

I began with courses like trigonometry, basic economics, freshman English—customary first semester courses. I was determined to do well; nothing but straight A's would do. I knocked myself out and I did get an A in every single class...but I also got sick as soon as the semester ended. I was ill through the entire winter break and worse, after the break I missed the first week of classes.

The second semester included a wonderful course called Differential Equations. I walked into the fourth class which was, for me, the first class. I took one look at the blackboard, and before I even sat down I said, "Oh my, am I in the wrong place! Where does an alien go to register around here?" That day, I went out and I dropped all of my engineering courses. I loved my brother Charlie but I would find other ways to show it.

After dropping my math and pre-engineering courses, I went to the Veterans' Administration for a series of aptitude tests. After what seemed like 16 hours of testing, and six weeks to tabulate the results, they told me: "Mr. Telchin, we don't know what you should do in life, but there are several things we can suggest that you not do: anything involving visual perception or spatial relationships." At least I hadn't missed my calling when I dropped all my engineering courses!

I was taking some liberal arts courses, and I began taking speech and drama courses as well. I tried out for the next play and continued to do well in that area. I kept trying out for more plays and the directors kept giving me more important roles. This provided a freedom of expression and an outlet that was totally new. Young Stan Telchin had not done much talking. All the other Telchins who were older and wiser did most of the talking as I was growing up. My trumpet had been my voice in those years. Suddenly, I was coming forth as a character actor with all sorts of voices that people wanted to hear. It was a terrific feeling.

In addition to the theater, from 1947 to 1949 I worked with Harry Brager and Larry Frommer on a wonderful radio program called "The Jewish Life Hour." It was a weekly, half-hour program utilizing drama, poetry and special guest interviews to cover topics of interest to Jewish people. Our focus was exactly what the name of the show indicated: Jewish life. We highlighted Jewish holidays, history, and various issues, such as our concern for Israel. Brager was the host, Frommer wrote, produced and directed, and I did the poetry, the dramatic readings and whatever else was needed for a touch of Yiddishkeit. Every other week or so I'd read from a series of shtetl stories, "The Wise Men of Chelm." We used a lot of Sholom Aleichem and Isaac Bashevis Singer stories. Occasionally I even read from Scripture, usually a Psalm.

This was a quality show on WGMS, and for me it was just a marvelous opportunity to do two things which were very satisfying: to exercise my growing interest in the art of drama, and to make a contribution to the Jewish community. At that time, Harry Brager was the national membership director for the B'nai Brith. He had some wonderful connections, which meant that I often came in contact with people whom I greatly admired. Harry was a close personal friend of Abba Eban who, as I recall, came to do one of our guest interviews. Abram Sacher, the founder and original president of Brandeis, did a guest interview and the president of B'nai B'rith came—all sorts of Jewish community heroes. But what I valued most about the experience was that Larry, Harry and I had a great working relationship and we developed a friendship despite the fact that they were much older than I.

Before I knew it, the time came to declare a major. I chose Speech and Drama. Ed Mangum, the head of the Drama Department, became a great friend and encourager. His dream was to establish a repertory company in Washington, D.C., and I hoped some day to have a part in it.

Meanwhile, my courtship with Ethel had progressed to an engagement, and we were married at the end of my junior year on May 26, 1948.

After finishing my undergraduate degree at George Washington University, I decided to go on for a master's degree in drama. Catholic University, Yale and Carnegie Tech were three of the top drama schools in the East at the time. In fact, I had seriously considered transferring to C.U. for my undergraduate degree, because of the quality of the work they were doing and the size of the department. Going to C.U. for my master's degree would have another plus: it would not take us away from Washington and Ethel could keep her job as a buyer at Lansburgh's Department Store.

In April 1949 I went to see Father Hartke, who was the head of the Drama Department at C.U. We had met a year and a half before when he advised me to finish my undergraduate work at George Washington rather than transfer to Catholic University. Knowing that I was Jewish, he wanted to spare me from having to take all of the religion and philosophy courses at C.U. In graduate school I would only have to take one religion course: The Moral Aspects of Art and Literature. We both agreed that I could handle that.

C.U. was an amazing experience. While G.W. provided the nuts and bolts, C.U. gave me a tremendous perspective. The variety of roles I played there was just unbelievable. About three months before I received my M.A., Father Hartke called me to his office and offered me a part in the touring company of "Players Incorporated," which was the graduate touring company of Catholic University. They were going to do *Macbeth, Much Ado About Nothing*, and *Arms and the Man*: two Shakespearean plays and one by George Bernard Shaw.

They offered me the part of Macbeth in *Macbeth* and Leonato in *Much Ado About Nothing*. To compensate for those two heavy roles, I would work backstage doing sound on *Arms and the Man*. Ethel would be the wardrobe mistress and stage manager for *Macbeth*, and they would give us $50 a week each, out of which we would have to pay our hotel and food! I would also have the great honor of driving a nine-passenger Desoto Suburban station wagon. Ethel and I discussed what we should do and she, being an adventurous soul, was agreeable to the tour. It was a fantastic experience. Few people have a chance to take a role like Macbeth and play it for nine months. It was a tremendous time of learning to take a role apart, to take language apart, and begin to understand what the playwright was really trying to communicate to the audience.

We returned to Washington and I called Ed Mangum. In my absence, Arena Stage, the company we dreamed of starting, had been born. I had hoped that there would be a place for me in the company but they were already staffed. The timing was a bit of bad luck for me as I came back too late to find a niche and help Ed and Zelda Fichandler make the company successful.

Because there seemed no place else for me to go as an actor, Ethel and I returned to New York at the end of May 1951. I tried to work wherever I could: doing summer stock, TV, whatever I could find. Alan Schneider (now deceased), who had directed me in *Macbeth*, was one of the hottest directors around. He had a place in New York and was doing a lot of work on and off Broadway. Just about the time Ethel and I moved back to New York, Alan was getting ready to go to London for the Fulbright Scholarship. He offered us his apartment on 21st Street. It was a godsend.

Ethel got a job as a buyer in Stern's Department Store on 42nd Street in Manhattan, and I started making my "rounds." It was horrible. It was nothing but heartbreak. I'd never been so rejected in my entire life. Whereas I had been a hot property in the Washington community and was quite well known, in New York I was just another guy making rounds.

Here's a quick picture of what I experienced: I went to see a man one time and waited about two hours to get into his office. Finally I got in and here's this little man sitting behind a big desk with his hands clenched—didn't even get up to shake hands or welcome me—just motioned me to the chair. I gave him my resume and my pictures. He looked at them for a moment or two and then said:

"How's your health?"

I said "Fine." I thought he had a job for me.

He said, "How are your finances?"

I looked at him and said, "They're okay."

He said, "Well, you'll need them both in New York. Good afternoon."

After waiting for two hours!

Meanwhile, Alan Schneider came back so we needed to find another apartment. We moved to Brooklyn. Every morning I would get on the subway with Ethel. I'd push her ahead of me to get her into the subway doors. We'd ride to Times Square, get off, and I'd walk her to work. Then I'd go to a bank and trade a five dollar bill for 50 dimes.

I'd wait till 10 o'clock, and then I'd make my 50 telephone calls to 50 different agents to let them know I was alive and to ask "Do you have anything for me?" When I ran out of money I started walking. And I walked and walked and walked and knocked on doors and went to see people until it was time to pick up Ethel and go home. I think I went to one movie during that entire period. One day I just couldn't stand it any more and I chickened out. But every other day I was out there as systematic and organized as could be, drumming away, trying to find a way to break through.

I was becoming very frustrated and very angry. A sympathetic friend who was seeing a psychiatrist told me, "Look, I talked to my doctor about you and he's willing to see you for a few visits. It will be for occupational therapy, not psychoanalysis. And I'll pay for it. Will you go?" What could I say?

I went to see Dr. Fox and after the first hour he said, "Mr. Telchin, I want to give you some homework to do. I want you to make a list of all of the 'things' that you want out of life. Be very specific. You're married. Do you want a family? Do you want a house? Do you want a car? Do you want two cars? Do you want to be able to send your kids to school? Do you want them to go to summer camp? Do you want to be able to retire? Come back next week and give me a detailed list of all the things that you want out of life."

I came back the next week with my list and we went over each item. At the end of the hour Dr. Fox said, "For next week I want you to do another piece of homework. I want you to make a list of all of the occupations which our society values enough to make the things that you want available." In other words, it would take a certain amount of dollars to do and have the things on my list. What were the fields of endeavor which would pay the kind of money I'd need to do the things I wanted to do?

I came back the following week and no place, no place on my list was music or theater or teaching, which were the three things I thought I wanted to do. It became clear that if I really wanted the things I said I wanted, I would have to change my career goals. Talk about having to face reality! This was a real crisis for me. What do I do now? How will I be able to support my family? What am I going to do with the rest of my life?

November came and I had to have a job. I saw an ad for the Custom Shop, which was across the street from the Waldorf Astoria. It was a job selling ties. I applied for the position and got it: $25 a week and they would teach me how to sell ties. I worked there from November of 1951 until the end of January 1952. After three months, I felt I had to leave. I couldn't stand it; I hated it.

I hated not caring. I hated not having a relationship with people. I hated that my value was measured by how many ties I sold. It is not my nature not to care, and that brought conflict. There was a place not far from our store called the Cardinal Shop, where they used to sell ties for a dollar apiece. One poor lady came into our store and she only had five dollars. I showed her a tie for three and a half dollars. Crestfallen, she told me, "It's Christmas and I need five ties, but I only have five dollars."

I said, "Lady, the Cardinal Shop is two blocks up and around the corner. You can buy five ties there for five dollars." She thanked me profusely and I felt good.

As I was thinking about leaving the Custom Shop, I saw an ad in the paper for a writer in a public relations department of the United Jewish Appeal. I said, "Hey, that's me!" Since I had minored in English and wrote fairly well, getting the job was not a problem.

I used to write letters for the field men. They would come back to the office after a meeting and, often in broken English, tell me what they wanted to say. Having grown up in Boro Park Brooklyn, and with the concerns of the United Jewish Appeal rather close to my heart, it was easy for me to understand these men. I was able to hear their hearts beneath the heavy accent, but even more, I shared what they thought and felt. I enjoyed transforming their thoughts into some rather highbrow English prose.

I worked for the United Jewish Appeal of Greater New York from February until May 1952. The precipitating factor for me to leave was some advice from my Aunt Fanny. Aunt Fanny could see that I was very unhappy, although my job with the United Jewish Appeal was certainly more fulfilling than selling ties. One day she said to me quite simply, "You seemed to be so happy in

Washington. If you were happy in Washington and you're not happy in New York, why don't you go back to Washington?" I looked at her in amazement and said, "You've got a very good point."

Ethel and I discussed it and decided that I would make a trip down to Washington to test the waters. I called Harry Brager and Larry Frommer, my old friends from the Jewish Life radio show. Larry couldn't see me but Harry, who had become the city manager for the State of Israel Bond Organization, could. We were having lunch, and I was telling him about life in New York when, all of a sudden, I could see by his glazed eyes that he was not listening to me. I stopped talking and waited. And Harry said,

"Hey, I've got it!"

I said, "What?"

He said, "Come back to Washington and work for me."

I said, "What are you talking about? Doing what?"

He said, "Come and join my staff. Be my business manager for the State of Israel Bond Organization in Washington, D. C. I'll pay you $100 a week."

That was all the encouragement I needed. It was May. Ethel and I moved back to Washington, D. C. and settled into an apartment in time for me to begin working with Harry in June 1952, right after our fourth wedding anniversary.

After about two months Harry said, "I'll tell you what. I need you in public relations. Come to work with me in the PR department and help me set up meetings." So I transferred over to the PR staff and began to work even more closely with Harry.

After about six months or so, Harry decided he was going to go into business for himself. He left the State of Israel Bond Organization and formed Harry E. Brager Associates, Fund Raising and Public Relations. Then six months later, he came to me and said, "Hey Stan, I've got more work than I can handle by myself. Come and be an account executive for me. I'll pay you $125 a week." That was a pretty good raise so I said, "Yes."

My first assignment involved fundraising for B'nai B'rith. We were to help raise the first $500,000 for what is now the major headquarters for the B'nai B'rith in the United States. I went all over the country setting up meetings for Harry. I was his advance man, setting things up and going on to the next city.

Later, we went to work for Brandeis University. Dr. Sacher

had been on our radio broadcast a few times back in the late '40s, and he knew of Harry's ability to raise money. Harry and I traveled quite a bit, arranging meetings to benefit Brandeis University. I was away from home more than I wanted to be, but I was earning a good living and again was making a contribution to a Jewish cause. The trouble was, I was out three nights and four days a week.

The pending birth of our first baby made being away from home even more difficult, (though I did manage to be at home when our daughter Judy was born on September 18, 1953). Then there was the time when Ethel was sick and Judy had roseola. I wanted to be with them to take care of them...but I had to work down in New Orleans. I was miserable. Another time, when Ethel needed a gall bladder operation, Harry asked me if she could postpone it until after the next campaign!

By this time we'd bought our first house and I was earning $7,500 a year! But I still felt empty. I knew that being a husband and a father involved more than just providing material things for my family. I wanted to be with them.

So after two years on the road, I told Harry that I would have to quit unless he could find work for me that would keep me in Washington. If he had other work for me, work that wouldn't keep me out on the road so much, I'd stay. But his reply was, "Stan, if there was work to be done in Washington, I would do it myself. The nature of this business is to be on the road."

I really loved the work and didn't want to leave the firm. Harry Brager was a kingmaker and it was exciting to work alongside him. Harry changed people's lives by writing speeches for them, getting them invited to important meetings...he was a power broker. And I was his right-hand man. But after two years I did not feel I could continue to be away from home no matter how good the job. I told Harry I would stay until he found someone to replace me and then I would have to leave. I left feeling shaken, for although I had decided beforehand that this was the right thing to do, I was still worried about how I would support my family.

The very day I quit, as I was coming down from our office, I ran into Robert R. Nathan, the world famous economist from whom we rented office space. Bob saw how upset I was and asked me what was wrong.

I told him, "I just quit."

He said, "You didn't."

I said, "I did."

He said, "Come with me." And he took me back to his office. We talked for about an hour and then he said, "I don't blame you, Stan. I think you did the right thing. I think that what you have to do is change your career. You might want to think about the life insurance business. It's a growth industry."

I said "Are you kidding?" I was picturing the little guy with the big black bag from Metropolitan Life who used to come knocking on the doors of our apartment building in Brooklyn. This did not fit the image I had of myself. "Are you kidding? With my education? No way!"

He said, "It's a growth industry; I think you'd do well."

"No way!"

Well, to make a long story short, I answered some blind ads, and one turned out to be for the Massachusetts Mutual Life Insurance company in Washington, D.C. Chet Jones, the general agent, introduced me to a field called "estate planning." As he helped me to consider my own situation, I saw how vital insurance planning was for my family's security. Chet Jones had come to tell me about a career in insurance and I ended up buying a policy! As he was leaving, I said, "I don't know if I can sell insurance, but I can do for other people what you did for me tonight."

He replied, "I'll tell you what. If you can do that, then you'll be very successful." And so on July 23, 1955, I went to work in the insurance business. I told Chet Jones, "If you'll be the mold, I'll be the clay. I must succeed and I will succeed. All I need to know is how and to be given an opportunity."

He replied, "Well, I can't succeed for you, but I sure can teach you how." Chet Jones poured himself into me for the next year and a half, and I became very good at what I did. I began to sell substantial amounts of insurance and was moving forward in my new career.

I also understood the importance of additional education: I took my Chartered Life Underwriter courses, which are to the insurance business what CPA courses are to accounting. I did the five year program in three years and received my C.L.U. designation. Then I taught C.L.U. classes for an additional three or four years. I specialized in the areas of wills, trusts and taxation and developed a tremendous clientele, wonderful people.

In 1959 I qualified for the Million Dollar Round Table for the first time. The M.D.R.T. represents the elite in the insurance industry. It is made up of top producers from all over the world. I was a member of the Table for some 22 or 23 consecutive years. Then I was also a member of "the Top of the Table." Qualification for the Top of the Table is based upon the production of the top 300 agents in the world. Any M.D.R.T. member who has equalled the volume of the 300th top man can join. It's the cream of the crop, the most successful insurance people in the world.

I never would have guessed how much I could love working in the insurance business. It enabled me to support my family in better style than I ever could have dreamed, and at the same time it allowed me to really help my clients. When you talk to people about money—their financial goals and what they want for their family—you learn a great deal about them, and about how to help them. Sometimes men in mid-life crisis would break down weeping at my conference table about situations in their lives, and I was able to help. An additional plus was that 85% of the people I worked with were Jewish, so I was constantly coming into contact with people who were eager for my involvement in Jewish causes.

Frank Selwin was one such contact. He was a wonderful friend and a great accountant. Frank was very much involved and active in the Hebrew Home for the Aged and he was promoting me to move on into a leadership position with that organization. I became involved, and was elected to the board of the Hebrew Home. A couple of years later I was elected to be a trustee of the United Jewish Appeal. I made time for these and other activities because of my concern for a homeland for our people: for the right of Jews to survive and be free to live like Jews. These issues would always be of the utmost importance to me.

Occasionally I found myself bothered by the competitive pressure that was built into my career. I felt I had to become a super achiever in order to accomplish what I wanted to accomplish for myself and my family. Success was not just something to "try for." As far as I was concerned, it was mandatory. And not just ordinary success—I went at everything I did with an energy and intensity that would get me to the top. In the insurance business they do cruel things on December 31st each year. They erase the blackboard. Here's what I mean: some place off in some room there is a blackboard which lists the production of every single agent in the house. And when you come in, you hang up your coat, you look at the blackboard and you see where you stand in relation to everybody else. I worked hard to stay in one of the top three slots in that agency for over 20 years. Each December when they cleaned that slate, everybody was on equal ground. We would have to race up the mountain all over again.

For the most part, I enjoyed it. I really enjoy accomplishing things. It's part of my life, to meet goals, check things off lists, get things done. As I made more money, moved into a larger house, to a larger community, a bigger car, air conditioning, swimming pool, country club...I always needed more to "keep up." And of course the agency's objective was to get us to want more and more because the more we wanted, the harder we worked. They drove us like thoroughbreds in a horse race.

Now and again, I'd feel a twinge of dissatisfaction. In 1953 a movie called "The Robe" was released, and in 1960, there was one called "Spartacus." These were epic films. "Spartacus" starred Kirk Douglas as a slave of the Roman Empire who gave his life attempting to lead an army of slaves to freedom. It won three Academy Awards and I think I saw it three times. It made me feel...just...wow! "The Robe" was about a Roman centurion who became a Christian, and what a radical difference it made in his life.

The characters in these movies had something we didn't have. We had each other and we had our history, and don't get me wrong, that was very precious to me. But it all had to do with survival, and both these films showed people who seemed to be centered on something beyond that. They were willing to die for what they believed. I was impressed by the joy that was on the inside, and the confidence. These people seemed to have answers to questions I hadn't even articulated. I found myself longing for something that would compare to what they had.

I wouldn't say that my life was characterized by this kind of longing, but it wasn't something that was restricted to a movie theater. One year we had a company convention in Canada, up at Lake Louise in Banff. It was beautiful up there in the mountains. I took the cable car up to the top of one particular mountain and drank in the breathtaking 360-degree view of this gorgeous landscape. As I looked around me, there were other mountains, some of which were even higher than the one upon which I stood.

I remember thinking, "This is like my life. All I do is climb mountains. Every year I climb a different mountain, I get to the top of the mountain, I look around and what do I see? More mountains. There's got to be more to life than this." And I felt a pang in my heart, a keen awareness that I was missing something. I wanted, I didn't know what. Something bigger than me. Something deeper, higher: something I couldn't name.

Meanwhile, business just kept getting better and better. Since I had so many professional clients, doctors and lawyers, I became very active in the professional corporation field and helped form the company called Professional Corporations Limited. I enjoyed the corporation, because while I was competitive, I also felt the need to both contribute to and receive from others.

Everything was as it should be as far as I was concerned. The risk I had taken in leaving Harry Brager had paid off. Not only was there more time for my family, there was more money. The goals I had set in that vocational counselling session years before in New York had been far exceeded. Judy was a healthy, happy girl and when her sister, Ann, arrived, our family was complete.

Our daughters had their share of squabbles, but for the most part Ethel and I were pleased at how well they got along. They were four years apart. Despite the age difference, by the time they were both in high school, they were best of friends.

Then our daughter Judy dropped the bomb.

She was a junior at Boston University when she called us that Sunday night early in 1975. Judy had always only given us reasons to be proud of her. Yet the moment I heard her voice on the telephone, I knew something was wrong. Words and phrases like "something to tell you," and "don't want to hurt you" and "wrote it all in a letter but I can't just put it in the mail" spilled into my ears like the bucket of hot tar that had spilled onto my feet when I was seven years old. What had happened to my daughter? It felt as though my heart would bang its way right out of my chest and my imagination was running wild. Could she be pregnant? In trouble with the police? Drugs? Everything I knew about Judy reassured me that no, none of these things made sense.

Daughter Judy had made her way into the world on Erev Yom Kippur (the evening before the Day of Atonement). In fact, Ethel distinctly remembers hearing the doctor say, "I hope the baby comes soon because I want to get to Kol Nidre."

I remember what I was like that afternoon, pacing up and back, smoking like crazy. It seemed like "The Baby" would never come. But Judy complied with the doctor's wishes and arrived at about five o'clock in the afternoon, just in the nick of time for him to get to services.

I immediately looked in her mouth and checked her palate. I had taken a course in the anatomy and physiology of the ear and vocal mechanism when I thought I was going to go on for a Ph.D. in speech pathology, and I wanted to check her out. She was perfect. I was tickled that she had been born on Erev Yom Kippur, because Yom Kippur is one of the most important days on the Jewish calendar, whether or not one is religious.

Judy had my undivided attention then and she had it as we spoke on the phone that Sunday night. I set aside my feelings of panic and grabbed a pen and paper so I could jot down whatever details might have to be acted upon. Besides, Ethel was in the shower and I knew she would want as close an account of the conversation as possible. Whatever this was about, I would stand by my daughter. Ethel and I would help.

I listened intently as Judy read her letter. It began by affirming how much she loved us and her sister, Ann...and ended by saying that she believed Jesus is the Messiah.

Of all the crazy thoughts that had run through my mind...of all the things that Judy would find difficult to tell us...it never even occurred to me that this would happen. Judy was absolutely right to fear that it would shock us. She knew we would be hurt. Hurt? Devastated is more like it! So how could she do it?

By the time Judy had reached her punch line, Ethel was finished with her shower. She heard me ask Judy how she could possibly believe in Jesus. And did Judy really believe in Jesus the same way as the Christians do? Ethel paled as she heard my end of the conversation and Judy confirmed my worst fears.

If I could have shouted this crazy idea out of my daughter I would have. A million accusations and arguments came to mind. But this was a crisis, and I knew clear thinking would be the only way out. I forced myself to remain calm. I knew I could help my daughter out of this mess, but I would have to keep my wits about me. I managed to tell Judy not to worry, that we would discuss it in depth later. After all, she would be home for her spring break in a couple of weeks.

Judy was smart, I knew. And I felt that once she saw her mistake, she would give it up. It would be my job to help her see the mistake. I could understand what Judy must have experienced. Questions had come up at college that hadn't come up at home. She'd been given some wrong answers. She needed someone to see to it that she got the right ones. That was my responsibility as her father.

In the meantime it was like an earthquake had shaken our household. The only one who wasn't upset was our housekeeper, a Christian woman named Heidi. She was sympathetic to the pain we felt, and very tactful, but after all, she believed that what our daughter said about Jesus was true.

Ethel, Ann and I felt betrayed. There's no other way to explain it. Ann, especially, felt Judy had turned her back on us. We were a very tightly knit family, but unlike Ethel and me, Ann didn't have that parental protectiveness to balance her feelings of anger and hurt.

Why did we feel Judy had turned away from us? She hadn't rejected us. One couldn't even say she had rejected our religion, since we were not an especially religious family. But we were a Jewish family, and those two words were inseparable—*Jewish family*. So much of being Jewish had to do with family. And so much of being a family had to do with being Jewish.

I would explain to Judy that she hadn't made a decision that affected only her. I would tell her, "Jewish people do not believe in Jesus. Your decision rips you away from being Jewish and consequently rips you away from your mom, your sister and me." I knew she would not want that any more than we did.

I went to the office the next day and called the rabbi. I was able to express to him some of the anger and fear which I hadn't wanted Judy to hear. He was sympathetic and reassured me that what I had hoped was indeed the case: Judy had been carried away at a vulnerable time and had made an emotional decision. Once she was home in a family environment, she would be able to put everything into perspective. She was a bright girl. This wouldn't last. Perhaps it would even blow over before Judy got home for her break.

Two weeks later Ethel and I went to the airport together to pick up our daughter. Her plane was late and the tension was mounting.

When Judy finally arrived, she looked terrific. In fact, I couldn't remember ever having seen her look better.

The underlying tension of our light conversation during the 40-minute drive home meant that Judy had not yet changed her mind about Jesus. She would have blurted out her mistake, maybe even laughed at it. But she didn't even bring up the subject. She was waiting for us to do that.

When we got home we headed for the den. I braced myself and asked Judy if she was ready to tell us what had been happening to her. She knew exactly what I meant and said that yes, she really wanted to talk about it. Ann came out from her bedroom and joined us. The usual excitement she would normally show upon seeing her sister was missing. In fact, as I looked from one daughter to the other it troubled me to see that Judy was the one looking healthy and excited, albeit nervous, while Ann looked pale and withdrawn. If I had been a stranger, and was told to choose which of these two girls had just undergone a crisis, would I have made the correct choice?

Judy told us her story, interrupted occasionally by a question I would ask as a point of clarification. It seemed that she had gotten somewhat introspective living alone in an apartment off campus. Being by herself, she said, gave her cause to think for the first time about who she was and what her life was about. She discovered she was not happy. She felt her life really had no meaning, apart from her close relationships with us, her family. But apart from loving us, she felt her life lacked purpose.

Seeking fulfillment, Judy had taken a job at a crisis intervention center, answering a telephone hotline. I quickly asked her if the center was Christian. Judy answered that it was not, but that one of the people who worked at the hotline, Dick, was a Christian. She had been impressed by his ability to help people, and his spiritual perspective. As they became friends, Dick began telling Judy about Jesus. He gave her a Bible to read. Through a series of events involving one man's attempted suicide, Judy met another Christian who impressed her with the quality of his life. Further, her Bible reading had affected her. All this thinking about life and death...all these Christians...all this Bible reading, that had been the combination. I could see how it had happened.

As Judy realized that she was starting to believe in Jesus, she felt the very things I had felt when I hung up the phone after her big announcement. She found herself upset and frustrated; how could she believe in Jesus—she was Jewish and Jews don't believe in Jesus! As she described the turmoil, the tears over not wanting to embrace something that would upset her family, I realized that Judy's decision to believe in Jesus ran deeper than I had feared. She hadn't jumped into this lightly.

Meanwhile, her Christian friends affirmed Judy's Jewish identity. This did not make sense to me. After all, I reasoned, didn't all Christians want Jews to convert and stop being Jewish? Had they been anti-Semitic, she could have seen that Jesus was not for her. Instead, they told her that believing in him as her Messiah would be a return to the God of Abraham, Isaac and Jacob. Return? How could she return to someone she'd never met? And what gave these Gentiles the right to speak so knowingly about the God of Israel?

Frankly, the questions our daughter had wrestled with were issues which I had shelved long ago. Judy seemed to think that the Bible, including our Bible, pointed to Jesus as the answer to knowing God and the meaning of life. I hadn't looked at the Bible for a long, long time. To help my daughter, I was going to have to look in the same places she had looked, and point out the distortions and the misinterpretations that had led her to Jesus. This, I realized, would take some good, hard study. But I knew if I applied myself to the task, I would be successful in getting Judy out of this.

I listened as Judy finished telling her story. Then I told her, "Judy, you are Jewish. Jews do not believe in Jesus. You can't be Jewish and believe in Jesus. It's not possible."

Judy was not disrespectful, but her answer surprised me. It was not something a child would say to a parent, but something one adult would say to another. "Dad, that's not true. There are lots of Jews who believe in Jesus. I don't expect you to take my word for it. You've got to look into this for yourself and come to your own conclusions. It isn't enough to just say Jews don't believe in Jesus. Please read the New Testament for yourself before you tell me why you don't believe it."

And that's exactly what I promised to do. Relieved, Judy gave me a copy of the New Testament and a couple of Bibles containing both Old and New Testaments. One was the King James Version, the other was a modern translation.

That night, Ethel and I talked privately about Judy. Ethel commented on how well Judy looked—almost radiant. She wondered, could it have anything to do with Judy's new beliefs? I said it was an emotional high that had to do with the new friends Judy had made, and not with any deep convictions she had about Jesus. Judy's behavior for the rest of her break was consistent with what we'd seen that first night. Gone was the heavy makeup and the trendy clothing that she had insisted on wearing (even to synagogue) the last time she came home. But the change was more than clothes and makeup. The defiant attitude that seemed to underlie them had vanished. We had tolerated it because we knew that Judy was a sensible, loving person. Defiance was natural at her age and we knew that she would outgrow it. We just didn't know that it would be so soon, or that it would be replaced with something which we deemed far worse.

When we got back from taking Judy to the airport, I made preparations to keep my promise. I went to the den and pulled out my Soncino edition of the Torah to balance out the pocket-sized New Testament and the larger King James Bible that Judy had left me. I neatly arranged fresh pads of paper and sharpened pencils and told Ethel of my intention to get a fresh start on my project the following day. I knew I could win my daughter back. This was another mountain to climb and the same systematic effort I had employed to climb up the corporate ladder would enable me to come out on top of this challenge. I had the competitive edge.

The following day, Monday, I left work right on time. After dinner I headed straight for the den. I settled in, picked up the pocket New Testament and steeled myself for some unpleasant reading. Whatever was in here was the basis for the Christian religion, and therefore the basis of 2,000 years of persecution.

To my surprise, there was an inscription pasted onto the front page. It was a list of four suggestions for whoever was about to read the book. First, the reader was asked to read at least one chapter of the book a day. That was no problem, since I intended to read the entire book in two or three days. Second, the reader was advised to ask God to show him or her the truth as they read. Well, if God wanted to help me get my daughter back that would be fine but we weren't on speaking terms since I wasn't even convinced that he existed. Third, the reader should look up the references in the Old Testament. I intended to! Fourth, it was suggested that the reader carry this little book in their pocket whenever possible. No need for that!

On the following page there was a prayer: "O God of Abraham, Isaac, and Jacob, show me the truth as I read this book; and help me to follow the light that is given me by Thee. Amen." Beneath, the prayer was translated into Hebrew. What a strange thing to find in a Christian Bible. It was unsettling to find a Jewish prayer in a book which I objected to primarily on the grounds that it was anti-Semitic. Nevertheless, I intended to read the book from start to finish.

The first book in the New Testament is called The Gospel According to Matthew. By the 16th chapter I had switched to the larger King James Bible. The print was easier to read and I didn't want to miss a word. It took me three hours to read through the first book of the New Testament. I was disappointed that I hadn't found any ammunition, yet intrigued; it was all so different from what I'd expected.

Jesus had exhorted the Jews of his day to adhere to the Shema. He could in no way be mistaken for a Gentile. And when Jesus asked his followers, "Who do men say that I am?" one of his disciples, Peter, answered: "You are the Messiah, the son of the living God." I found myself trying to visualize Jesus as he interacted with people, working at understanding what was being said. To my surprise, I'd been reading a book written to Jews, by a Jew who was describing another Jew named Jesus as the Messiah of Israel.

When I finished the first gospel, I made my way to the kitchen and Ethel and I had a cup of tea. I told her how far I'd gotten, told her I hadn't accumulated anything that I could use to bring Judy back, but I was certain I would. She nodded.

The following two nights I plowed through the next two books in the New Testament, and not just the books, but all the references in the margins as well. Many of them were "Old Testament" passages and since I only had the first five books of Moses in what I considered an authentic Jewish version, I went to a Jewish bookstore and purchased a Tenach. I didn't quite trust the "Christian" versions of our Bible, but when I read them comparatively, for the most part they were the same.

My pads of paper were filling up with questions and some of them spilled out of my mouth as well. Poor Heidi! Our housekeeper was facing questions from all sides. None of us had thought much about Heidi's religion before this crisis. Suddenly we regarded her as our resident expert on Christian theology. Our questions were often blunt and not always asked with the same love and respect we normally expressed to her. You see, after nine years together, we had adopted Heidi into our family, and she had adopted us into hers.

Now Heidi was suddenly in the awkward position of dealing with our emotional turmoil over Judy's beliefs. She was so patient with us. I would constantly go downstairs and knock on her door asking, "Heidi, what about this? What about that? What does this mean, what does that mean?" She answered when she could but she continually told me, "Oh Mr. Telchin, don't look to me, I'm just a human being, I'll fail you. Don't look to me, look to God for the answer."

Look to God for the answer? That's what the inscription in the pocket New Testament suggested. Again I was reminded that I had never made a firm commitment as to whether or not I truly believed that God exists.

By Thursday night I was into the fourth and final gospel which would complete the portion of the New Testament describing Jesus' birth, life, death and supposed resurrection. The Gospel According to John was not any longer than the others, but I spent more time contemplating this mini-biography. I wasn't sure why each of these authors had written their own account of Jesus' story, but I definitely found John's the most absorbing.

I didn't read merely left to right. Perhaps my background in drama is what caused me to dig beneath the words, determined to uncover the essence of what was being said. I was envisioning scene after scene. I was especially impressed by the Sermon on the Mount, and impressed by Jesus' desire to see changes in the hearts of the people.

But it was the fifth chapter of the Gospel of John that grabbed me. Jesus told his accusers: "How can you believe when you receive glory from one another, and you do not seek the glory that is from the one and only God? Do not think that I will accuse you before the Father; the one who accuses you is Moses, in whom you have set your hope. For if you believed Moses, you would believe

Me; for he wrote of Me. But if you do not believe his writings, how will you believe My words?"

The words cut through me. The cut wasn't painful; it was more like the shock of sudden exposure. Jesus claimed that those who rejected him were more interested in one another's opinions and interpretations than they were in what Moses had written and what God intended. Did that accusation apply to me? If Jesus was "the god of the Gentiles," as I'd always thought, why was he talking about the "one and only God?" Why did he rebuke his doubters for not believing Moses? How could Jesus say with such confidence that Moses had written of him? It's not as though Moses' writings were not accessible to either disprove or verify that claim. This raised a disturbing point. I had always thought a person could be a Jew and not believe in God, even be an atheist. And yet I was unwilling to concede that someone could be a Jew and believe in Jesus. Here Jesus was indicating the reason his accusers were doubting him was that they didn't believe Moses. And I had rejected Jesus without being sure that I even believed in God!!!

Jesus had thrown up an intriguing challenge and one that I could not ignore. He was saying that I could not come to an honest conclusion about him until I had come to some basic understanding of the God of Israel and the Jewish Bible.

I formulated a logical sequence of rudimentary questions to meet that challenge. Working through the answers would provide the insight I needed to help my daughter and it would satisfy my own curiosity as well. I jotted down my questions:

Do I really believe that God exists?

Do I believe that the Jewish Bible (the Tenach) came to us from God and that he reveals his truth through it?

Does the Tenach prophesy about a Messiah?

Is Jesus the Messiah?

I had calculated it would take me ten to twelve hours to read the New Testament and thus far I was through the first four books. I knew that a few hours after work each night would not be sufficient to answer these questions properly. Where would I find time?

I looked over my questions again. They did not involve easy issues which would be nice to resolve in my spare time. The answers were vital to understanding my own beliefs and disproving

Judy's Jesus. Accordingly, they were my number one priority. Ethel watched with growing interest as I became more and more absorbed in my project. I told her that I had found the Gospel of John the most interesting of the first four books. She concurred; she had also felt it was the best-written and most interesting of the gospels. This came as a shock. I didn't even know Ethel had been reading the New Testament. We decided that to guard against influencing one another's opinions, it would be best to continue our studies independently.

I addressed my first question: Do I believe in God? I had behaved as though there was no God, without being willing to commit myself to that position. When I say I behaved as though there was no God, I don't mean that I pursued a pattern of immorality. I mean that although I could never come right out and say God does not exist, I never wondered what he might expect of me if he did exist.

I remember how confused I'd felt in high school when we were taught the theory of evolution. If God had not created the earth, what did that say about our Scriptures? If Genesis was not true, why should I believe the rest of the books of Moses? To accept evolution, I would have to reject belief in God, who had called Moses to lead the "chosen people," my people, out of Egypt. Passover, Purim, and my entire Jewish heritage would amount to nothing more than an ethnocentric fairy tale. And yet, to accept that God exists, I would have to reconcile the fact that he allowed atrocious things to happen to the people he supposedly had "chosen." It seemed like a no-win situation. Rather than make a choice, I shelved the issue.

Now I was forced to consider what I really believed. I could not deny that deep down inside, I believed that somewhere, there was a God. I could not explain why he permitted all the evil in the world; yet somehow I sensed that I had much for which to thank God, and that disbelief in him was not the solution to the problem of evil in the world.

The next question I had to resolve was whether or not God had inspired the writing of the Jewish Scriptures: should it be counted as his word and his truth? I was already motivated to read the Jewish Scriptures. Jesus' words, "If you had believed Moses and the prophets, you would have believed me" were still ringing in my ears.

As I thought through resources that would help answer my question, I had a "flashback" to Rabbi Adler. Back in the '50s we had joined a reform synagogue. I liked Rabbi Adler's open attitude. He didn't speak in certainties about God and he didn't make us feel guilty. He felt it was important for us to gather as Jews and he expressed the hope that perhaps together, as a congregation, we would find God. This seemed like an honest and forthright approach to me. I signed up for the rabbi's class in comparative religions. I still recall his introductory lecture. "What if all memory of every organized religion was suddenly wiped off the face of the earth? What would happen?"

The dozen or so adults who had come to study with the rabbi began to talk about how chaotic our lives would be with no organized religion. Marriages and other contracts would disintegrate and the fabric of society would unravel. Eventually people would begin asking questions about where they came from, what life is about and whether or not a force existed that was stronger than they were.

The rabbi agreed that indeed, those questions would arise and that when they did, different groups of people around the world would come up with various answers. Organized religions would thus come back into existence. "And," the rabbi concluded, "that's the way it should be! Right? Everyone is entitled to his own opinions! Right?" Underlying his statements was the theme, "We Jews are entitled to our beliefs as much as the Gentiles are entitled to theirs."

Murmurs of approval could be heard throughout the room as people nodded their assent. This seemed a reasonable enough assumption and I accepted it, too. Twenty years later I realized that my assent to the ideas that were expressed that day had been based on an assumption that we had been foolish to accept—and that was the assumption that people were starting from ground zero with regard to belief systems. The rabbi's whole scenario was based on the idea that "all memory of organized religion was obliterated." I know the rabbi meant well, but as I thought about it, I realized the terrible mistake that I had bought into so long ago.

Rabbi Adler had left the Jewish Scriptures out of his scenario.

The Jewish people have been referred to as The People of The Book, but someone had taken The Book away. All I had was the prayer book! Who had ever suggested that I read The Book? I was surprised at the intensity of my feelings as I realized how angry I was at the widespread "open-mindedness" which closed out the possibility that this Book might actually be God's way of teaching us the truth.   Would God leave it to us to make up whatever "truths" might seem appropriate to the time and place?

I tried to recall various things I had learned *about* the Bible, if not *from* the Bible. I remembered how, back in 1973, our tour guide in Israel had been so pleased to describe how the latest archaeological findings supported the authenticity of Scripture. This had given me a certain satisfaction as I sensed that when the authenticity of the Hebrew Scriptures was affirmed, somehow the Jewish people also were affirmed and, in a sense, vindicated. However, I did not make a spiritual connection. This was something good for the Jewish people and that was enough.

I remembered various articles I had read and I also did some additional research in my efforts to reach a conclusion about the Scriptures. I recalled the excitement surrounding the unearthing of the Dead Sea Scrolls and what a major discovery that had been. The scrolls were dated at about 1000 BCE and thus verified the authenticity of later translations.

I concluded that the Hebrew Scriptures were authentic; they had been transmitted by our ancestors through the centuries without contamination. That did not mean they were inspired by God, though the fact that they had been preserved the way they had seemed to point to the supernatural. Still, the bottom line was that I could not determine this issue by comparison or research. Either I believed that the Scriptures came from God or I didn't. It was going to have to be a gut level decision. Over the next couple of days I did a lot of inward looking...and I finally dug out a truth which was small enough to fit in my hand yet enormous enough to change everything.   The truth about God didn't begin in our imagination. It began with what he told us in The Book.

The next question on my list was: does the Bible foretell a Messiah? By now I was talking to all kinds of people: Gentiles I knew from the office who believed in Jesus, as well as Jewish sources, including books and rabbis. The Christians I knew pointed out various Scriptures and it soon was obvious to me that the Jewish Bible does foretell a Messiah. Further, I found myself fascinated by these prophecies.

My daughter Judy was still the motivation behind my study, or so I continued to believe. Part of me still was confident that my studies would reveal whatever I needed to guide her away from her belief in Jesus. But there was another part of me which had been awakened, a part that wanted to know the truth for myself. And that part was not just searching the Scriptures for clues to get Judy back; that part was intrigued with the Bible and eager to learn more. Our Scriptures told where the Messiah would come from, what he would do, how people would respond.

The questions of whether our Bible spoke of a Messiah and whether or not Jesus was the Messiah were often difficult to separate. I found myself constantly reminded of things I had already read in the New Testament as I investigated the prophets. In the ninth chapter of Daniel there was a prophecy which had particularly disturbing implications.

"Seventy weeks are determined upon thy people and upon thy holy city...to make reconciliation for iniquity, and to bring in everlasting righteousness.... Know therefore and understand that from the going forth of the commandment to restore and to build Jerusalem unto the Messiah, the Prince, shall be seven weeks, and threescore and two weeks: the street shall be built again.... And after threescore and two weeks shall Messiah be cut off, but not for himself: and the people of the prince that shall come shall destroy the city and the sanctuary."

I asked one of my contacts, a Christian, how he explained this. It seems that if a week is calculated as a period of seven years, and if one makes allowances for the difference between the lunar and solar calendars, Daniel predicted the correct amount of time between the rebuilding of Jerusalem and the destruction of the second Temple. Further, the Temple would be destroyed after the Messiah was "cut off."

The predicted destruction had taken place after Jesus had been "cut off." I was stunned as I recognized this fulfillment of prophecy. Whether or not Jesus was the Messiah, according to Daniel's prophecy, the Messiah had to come before the destruction of the second Temple!

Seeking balance, I attended a group discussion which was chaired by a rabbi and which addressed the concept of the spirit realm in Jewish literature. As the rabbi took questions from the floor, I asked him to tell us about the Jewish concept of the soul, not necessarily in literature, but in Jewish life today. This apparently caught him off guard, though that certainly hadn't been my intent. He shrugged and said, "What's a soul?" The laughter which ensued gave him a moment to prepare a brief answer to my question: "I don't know." He answered a few other questions and then I asked if he would please tell us about the Messiah. Again, the response, "What's a Messiah?" When the laughter subsided, he did not offer any serious comments. I decided to keep my questions to myself until after the discussion.

When it was over, I approached the rabbi and told him that those questions were important to me, and that I was disappointed that he hadn't given serious answers. He seemed to be studying my face for a few moments, perhaps to ascertain whether I was sincere. Then he asked, "What makes you think I can answer your questions?"

"Because," I said, "you're a rabbi. You've studied these things."

He shook his head and told me he had plenty of questions of his own, perhaps even more than I did. How difficult that must have been for him to admit. I realized that I couldn't assume the rabbis know all the answers.

Despite my disappointment, I continued researching the Jewish perspective of the Messiah. I read such books as *A History of the Jews*; *Jews, God and History* and *My People*. There was nothing there to counter the fulfilled prophecies which had been forecast in the messianic passages of the Tenach. I turned to *The Messianic Idea in Judaism*, and found that the author was not writing from a theistic viewpoint. To him the "Messianic Idea" was just that—merely an idea, not a person.

When I found Joseph Klausner's book, *The Messianic Idea in Israel*, I was excited to see that this book referred to the Messiah as a person. But I was disappointed as I continued reading, for Klausner was merely reporting on centuries of arguments over whether the Messiah would be a person or a "golden age." Klausner himself was noncommittal in comparing these two viewpoints. Rather than venture a specific opinion of his own, Klausner was content to say, "The messianic idea is the most glistening jewel in the glorious crown of Judaism." Pretty words, but unfortunately, pretty meaningless as well.

What a stark contrast the New Testament presented to all of this. When Jesus' cousin, John the Baptist, had a question about Jesus' identity, he sent a messenger to ask, "Are you he that should come? Or look we for another?" John (and whoever "we" were) obviously expected a person, not a philosophy or a golden age. Jesus sent the messenger back to John, telling him to report "what things you have seen and heard: how that the blind see, the lame walk and lepers are cleansed, the deaf hear, the dead are raised, to the poor the gospel is preached." (Matthew 11: 3-5)

John's question and Jesus' reply were having more of an effect on me than I cared to admit. If nothing else, they added to my growing frustration that the leaders, much less the followers of "my own religion" could not agree upon what "the most glistening jewel in the glorious crown of Judaism" was supposed to be.

Meanwhile, I had not given up my reading of the New Testament by any means. I had gone beyond it, so as to see "both sides," but I was still intent on finding that one piece of evidence, that one thread that would unravel the gospel fabric.

After the Gospel of John came the Book of Acts. When I got to the 10th chapter of that book, I was just catapulted. I was transfixed. I read how Jesus was thought to be only for Jews, and not for Gentiles. What a chore it was, getting those early Jewish believers in Jesus to accept that Gentiles could believe in Jesus, without first converting to Judaism.

The switch was mind-boggling. Today, Jesus was only for Gentiles and not for Jews. What happened? How in the world did Christianity change from a religion followed by Jews only to a religion followed predominantly by Gentiles? I say predominantly because by then I knew that Judy was not the only Jewish believer in Jesus. Someone at work had directed me to a local messianic congregation called Beth Messiah where Ethel and I met several Jewish believers in Jesus. Still, there was no denying that today, Christianity is considered antithetical to Judaism. I was bowled over by the question: how could someone who was once considered "for Jews only" now be considered "for Gentiles only"? That launched me into a study of church history which is too involved to mention here.

Sometime in the second week of my search I told my secretary, Jenny, that I had a job to do at home. I wasn't sure when I'd be back. She could reach me at home when necessary. I would come in to sign checks and to see certain clients a couple of times a week.

I thought I would be away from the office for two weeks but the two weeks turned into more like ten.

I became more and more involved—personally, emotionally and spiritually—in needing answers for myself, not just for Judy. I was asking myself questions and flipping back and forth, back and forth, and back and forth between the Old Covenant (Testament) and the New. There seemed to be a genuine connection. In the Tenach I was learning about God's covenant with Israel, beginning with his commitment to Abram. Abram's response: obedience. He became Abraham. He had a direct line to God. I saw that our God is a God of promises and that in the days of old he was anything but distant. He seemed to desire involvement with his people. He was not at all the vague "somewhere out there" deity whose existence had meant so little to me. This was a God who knew his people and wanted to be known by them.

I kept waiting for the New Testament to contradict the "Old." Instead, passages from the Tenach were often quoted in the New Testament. The message seemed to be that mere obedience to the Law of Moses wasn't enough. Jesus and his followers wanted people to understand what was behind the Law so that their obedience would not be to a set of outward regulations but to God.

I was overwhelmed by what I was reading. And I didn't want to believe it…oh, I did not want to believe any of it. It's the last thing in the world I needed. I didn't want my life to be changed. I couldn't imagine what it would do to my family. I wasn't telling Ethel how intrigued I had become with my Bible reading, though she could see it without my telling her. I did not ask how she was doing with her reading, or her extended conversations with Heidi. But it seemed to me that as I grew more and more tense about the issue, Ethel was becoming more relaxed. I often heard laughter when she and Heidi were together. I didn't see how Ethel could have such a sense of humor about all this.

By the time I got to the book of Ephesians, I was ready to turn a corner, but I didn't know it. I spent a lot of time reading and re-reading Ephesians and Philippians and Colossians, which are short books in the New Testament, letters, actually, written by Paul. This man Paul was really sold out to Jesus. He was willing to endure prison and eventually die rather than give up telling people about Jesus. I saw the same kind of thing in his life that I'd seen in movies like "Spartacus" and "The Robe" ...the determination of these characters to live according to their convictions—even if living for their convictions meant dying an ignominious death.

In Paul's writings I saw a certainty of his relationship with God as contrasted with the complete non-existence of my relationship with God. I was jealous. I wanted what he had. Through my Bible reading I was learning about the love of God, the plan of God and God's desire for us to have a new life, just like Abraham got a new life, that would be based on a loving and trusting relationship with the Creator. The way Paul put it was "to become a new creation." And I, who had everything I thought I wanted—everything that was on my list when I went for occupational therapy over 20 years before—I found that I wanted more. I wanted to be a new creation.

Ethel wondered when I planned to return to the office. I assured her that the business was going smoothly, that we wouldn't starve. The insurance business is such that hard work does not pay off immediately. You build and build and build...and eventually the groundwork you lay and the contacts you cultivate come to fruition. I had built up a high enough level of success to know that business would continue to flourish based on work I had already done.

In fact, that was the year that I made "the Top of the Table" and was invited to speak on a panel in San Francisco, at a Million Dollar Round Table convention. I was delighted with the honor. I decided I would take a breather from what had become a spiritual quest, and enjoy some of what the material world had to offer. Ethel would be in Boston visiting Judy while I was gone and Ann would be in Los Angeles visiting a friend.

I had every intention of putting aside all thoughts of Jesus but I couldn't. I enjoyed seeing many old friends at the convention and it was a thrill to speak in front of thousands of successful business people. My contribution to the platform had been very well received and the excitement made me just a little giddy. But as much as I enjoyed the experience, something was different. When it came time to socialize, I found myself cringing at some of the dirty jokes. I was unable to enter into the party atmosphere.

My roommate was an old friend and business associate. I found myself describing to him the major events which had taken place since we'd last talked: namely, what had happened to our daughter, Judy, and how my response had involved me in this spiritual search. My friend had no idea how to relate to what I was saying. He stared at me as though I were a creature from outer space. I was somewhat embarrassed. Still, none of this detracted from the pleasure of the recognition I had received.

After the convention and before I returned home, I made a quick stop in Los Angeles. It was an opportunity to visit with my niece, and while I was there I'd also have a quick visit with Ann and her friend. The four of us got together just before I caught my plane back to Washington. Ann looked terrific. There was no sign of the resentment or depression that had resulted from Judy's news of believing in Jesus. I was glad to see her looking so well. The trip to Los Angeles seemed to have done her some good.

Ethel picked me up at the airport, and naturally I asked her how things had gone with Judy. I was shocked when she told me that they had a wonderful visit. How could it be wonderful when we were caught in this terrible conflict—when our daughter still believed a religion whose followers had persecuted our people mercilessly? You see, while I couldn't find fault with the Bible, I did have proof of the terrible things that were done in the name of Jesus by people who felt they were doing God a favor by persecuting Jews. I had been tempted to use my findings as the ammunition I needed to dissuade Judy from her belief in Jesus. Why hadn't I? The argument had seemed incomplete. I would be telling her what was bad without being able to point her to something good. To do this thing right, it wasn't church history I had to discredit, but Jesus. And I hadn't been able to do this. But that didn't mean I was comfortable with her beliefs. How could Ethel be so calm after a visit with Judy?

Ethel said they had avoided arguing. Then she asked me where I was with regard to my search. She wondered if I'd given up, and if I was going back to work. No, I told her. There were some details I needed to attend to at the office, but after that I planned to get back to my research. She seemed relieved. But I thought I had better check it out. After all, she had pointed out before that I couldn't stay away from the business forever. "Do you think it's time for me to go back to the business?"

116

Ethel paused before saying, "I think you should do whatever you think is right."

It was hard to know what was right. I didn't have the heart to tell Ethel that after all my hard work, Judy's belief in Jesus had begun to make sense to me. There was still the possibility that I would prove Judy wrong, but what if I didn't?

What if I proved her right?

How could I compound the pain that Ethel and Ann had felt when Judy became a believer? How could I do something which I knew would alienate me, not only from family and friends, but from my business clientele, 85% of whom were Jewish?

But that was ridiculous. I simply hadn't found the right combination yet. With persistence, I would certainly find what I needed to win Judy back. I had always stood up for Jewish causes. What Jewish cause could be more important than my daughter, and uniting my family? And yet, and yet, I couldn't escape my own question: "Is Jesus the Messiah?" I had meant it to be a rhetorical question which, by now, I should be able to answer not only with a resounding "no" but with plenty of proof to show why he was not. Instead, the question had become open-ended. And I think I realized, at least subconsciously, that God himself would have to answer it for me.

One day I was playing golf at our club. It was a hot day in June. There were three of us, and I suggested the other two take a cart. I wanted to walk as this would give me some time to be alone. We finished the 13th green and as I walked to the 14th tee, I cried out to God, "If Jesus really is the Messiah, reveal it to me, and if he's not the Messiah, please take these thoughts away from me and don't let me believe that he is." I forgot it soon after; I didn't really expect an answer. I didn't know if I had said the "magic word." Whatever it was that people did to get their prayers answered, I figured I didn't have the knack.

Ethel and I had returned to Beth Messiah, and there I heard about a nationwide conference of "Messianic Jews" who, as I knew by that time, were Jewish believers in Jesus. I was surprised to see that there were enough of these Messianic Jews to have a national conference. And I did a peculiar thing. I decided that as part of my research, I should go.

I asked Ethel if she was interested in coming along. She

declined, but she didn't seem to think I was crazy for wanting to go. In fact, she seemed to think it was a good idea.

I drove to the conference, which was held on the campus of Messiah College in Grantham, PA. I pulled up to the grounds in my BMW, determined that this conference would be no different than any other. I would plan my goals and work toward getting as much as possible in a short amount of time. I would pick the brains of every person who could help me.

But this conference wasn't the same as any other. There was a warmth and a comradery that was different from the customary business conventions I had attended. And there was none of the revelry such as I had felt uncomfortable with at the Round Table convention a few weeks earlier.

I registered and went to the first morning session. We met in a large auditorium and I nearly gasped as I saw that it was filled with over 700 people. While there were some Gentiles present, the audience seemed to be mainly Jewish. How could there be this many Jews who believed in Jesus? I sat and listened to music which had a Jewish sound, but told about Jesus. I watched as a team of dancers combined Jewish folk dances with the music — and I realized these people were all worshipping God. There was the same joy and exuberance that I'd loved in Ha Shomer Ha Tzair but there was something more. They joyously came before the God who'd made a covenant with Abraham.

After the meeting was over I headed back to the dormitory. Latecomers were still arriving and I noticed one older woman who was obviously struggling with her suitcase. I stopped to help her and we struck up a conversation as we walked.

Her name was Lillian. She was Jewish, from Philadelphia, about 60 years old, and one of the most forthright people I have ever met. Rather then talk about the weather or her trip from Philadelphia, Lillian asked me almost immediately how long I had believed in Jesus. I quickly told her that I was not a "believer." I had many questions about Jesus and I was interested in what these people believed, but I was certainly not a believer.

Lillian registered no surprise at my reply. "Let's stop a minute and rest," Lillian suggested, as we approached a concrete bench. After we sat down, she politely asked if I would reach into her briefcase and get her Bible. I pulled out the Bible and before I could hand it to her, she asked me to turn to the 20th chapter of Exodus and read the first few verses to her. I was not accustomed to taking orders but this lady was so sweet that I could not refuse her. I read: "I am the Lord thy God which have brought thee out of the land of Egypt, out of the house of bondage. Thou shalt have no other gods before me."

She interrupted. "Enough. Tell me please, Stan, who is your god?"

That sweet lady just about knocked me over with her question. What a thing to say! Lillian hadn't meant to upset me. I shouldn't be aggravated, she said. I should just think about the question. Whom did I worship? Money? My family? My career? "Or," she asked, looking me straight in the eye, "do you worship the God of Abraham, Isaac and Jacob who delivered our ancestors from the land of Egypt?"

I couldn't answer. Lillian did not try to fill the gap in our conversation which became awkward, at least for me. It wasn't silence that made me uncomfortable. It was the smooth, light-hearted answer I wanted to give but couldn't. My glib reply just couldn't push past the weight of something heavier. I'd been feeling that weight for some time, but I hadn't known what it was until Lillian asked me her pointed question.

I couldn't concentrate on the other speakers for the rest of the day. It was so hot and the air so humid, so heavy. I couldn't remember when I'd been more uncomfortable. As I pondered Lillian's question, I knew without a doubt that I believed in the God who had delivered us from slavery in Egypt, though I wouldn't say I worshipped him. But Lillian's question triggered the whole series of questions I'd jotted down toward the beginning of my search. Yes, I believed in God and that the Bible was inspired by God. I believed it foretold a Messiah. The fourth question had been "Is Jesus the Messiah?" All my efforts, this whole search, had been for the purpose of showing me how to say "No, Jesus is not the Messiah," in a way that would convince Judy.

But sitting there with Lillian, a thought as hard and as heavy as the concrete upon which we sat had intruded. It was the answer to my fourth question which had crowded out the glib remark I'd wanted to make, the answer I couldn't bring myself to say. Jesus is the Messiah. I couldn't say it because there was a fifth and final question that really frightened me. "If Jesus is the Messiah, how does that affect me?"

I could not admit the answer to the fourth question until I was able to accept the consequences. Before I was in turmoil. Now I was in agony. The pressure just kept mounting and mounting and mounting…."I want to believe, I don't want to believe. I want to believe, I don't want to believe." I didn't want to lie, nor did I want to pay the price of admitting the truth to myself or anyone else. I slept very little that night.

I had so many questions, personal questions that no amount of research could answer. How could we have been so wrong? How could I believe something that was so offensive to everyone I loved? Why would God choose a way that was so difficult for us to accept? Why had all those awful things been done in the name of Jesus? I needed to talk with somebody who would be tender and compassionate and not try to make a sale.

There were many young people at the conference, but I found myself gravitating toward people who were my age or older. Shirley Moses Berne was one such person. She and her husband had such patience in answering my questions and gently directing my attention to the main issue: whether or not Jesus was true. This had more of an effect than any of the sessions or teachings at the conference.

Still, I wondered, how could these people stand it? How could they bear having fellow Jews view them as traitors, outcasts? Identifying with the Jewish people and being accepted as one who made important contributions to Jewish concerns had always been a major part of my life. How could I be me if I became an object of contempt to those whom I esteemed and whose esteem mattered so much to me?

No one I spoke to denied the fact that I would be misunderstood just as I had misunderstood Judy. There would be no guarantees as to how those around me would respond. The only guarantees would be the ones the Bible gave. A new life…a new creation…a new freedom to enter a realm I'd never imagined…a relationship with the God of Israel.

When I had stood up on that mountain at Lake Louise, I had a momentary longing for something that was deeper, higher, beyond my grasp. It hadn't occurred to me that my desire was a need which could actually be met.   I only knew the "something" I wanted was like nothing I could know or accomplish for myself. It therefore seemed impossible by virtue of its very nature: unattainability.

I knew now that the "something" I longed for was no longer unattainable. It was a connection with the Creator, and it was worth everything I had achieved in my life and more. I also knew that God was not an acquisition. God would not belong to me, I would belong to him. Everything I had and everything I was would be at his disposal. The freedom to enter into a relationship with God had quite a price tag.

Spartacus had been crucified because he fought for freedom. If I embraced Jesus, I might very well be crucified, both socially and professionally. Freedom could be frightening. One didn't know what to expect. The children of Israel had suggested to Moses more than once that they would have been better off in Egypt than out in the wilderness facing dangers and challenges for which they felt unequipped. But God did not bring them back into Egyptian slavery. Instead he kept them roaming in the desert for 40 years. How long would I roam in a spiritual desert?

On the other hand, maybe I was deluded. Maybe Jesus wasn't the Messiah. Maybe I was agonizing over nothing.

How hot it was in Grantham, Pennsylvania that July! How I perspired from physical and spiritual discomfort! That night the tossing and turning began as it had the night before. I couldn't face another sleepless night. A little before midnight I whispered, "Art, are you awake?" Art was my roommate, one of the people I'd met at Beth Messiah. He was awake, and I asked him something I'd never asked anyone before. I asked him to pray for me. He spoke to God, simply and briefly, asking him to give me rest...both physically and spiritually.

The next thing I knew it was 7 a.m. I felt well-rested and at peace. Art was still sleeping so I dressed quietly and made my way to the cafeteria. I sought out the people I'd been sitting with for most of the meals. I waited for them to say the blessing, as I had grown accustomed to their prayers thanking God for the food. I was startled when someone asked if I would say the blessing this time. I felt a little awkward and inexperienced, but after all, I did believe in God. Why not ask him to bless the food?

"Praised be Thou, O Lord our God, King of the universe. I thank You for the fellowship and friendship at this table. I thank You for what we have learned here. I ask You to bless this food, and I do so in the name of Jesus, the Messiah."

Dear God, what had I said? I hadn't planned it...but I meant it! I had openly confessed to myself, to these people and to God that I believed Jesus is the Messiah. It was like an explosion. There was a burst of light in my soul as the deeper, higher, purer power of God outweighed all my fears.

I hadn't been able to answer the question, "If Jesus is the Messiah, what will that do to me?" Now I knew why. It was a question that God would answer for me moment by moment, for the rest of my life. Whatever hardships might come, God would be with me. None of the repercussions I could imagine would take away the union with God that had been made possible through the Messiah Jesus.

The relief and the joy that I felt did not blind me to other facts of life. The fear I felt as I thought of Ethel and what this might do to our family was very real.

I tried to mentally script out what I would tell Ethel. I imagined her response and how I would deal with it. But the more I tried to plan the scenario, the harder it became to make the phone call. Finally, I just took a deep breath and dialed.

When I heard my wife's voice, all the dialogue I had planned went out the window. I blurted out the news that my search was finally over; that Jesus truly was the Messiah. I braced myself for the reaction, but there was no way I could have been prepared for it. She didn't cry, she didn't contradict...she didn't even ask me why. She breathed a sigh of relief and said, "Thank God. That makes it unanimous."

It was the last day of the conference. There were bittersweet good-byes as I parted from people who had shared in all the joy and tumult of my spiritual awakening. But I was eager to get home and hear how Ethel and Ann had become believers. "Thank God," Ethel had said, and she meant it. She did not want the joy she found in Jesus to rip us apart...and I knew just how she felt!

Ethel, in characteristically good humor, was amused by my amazement over her decision. She had been at least as upset as I was over Judy's decision; perhaps even more so. She had begun reading the Bible with the same goal as I'd had at the outset; find the weakness in Judy's beliefs and disprove the whole thing once and for all. Like me, Ethel had been intrigued by the person of Jesus. The New Testament took her by surprise as it had taken me. This took some of the edge off her anger.

Heidi, too, had been highly instrumental in Ethel's change of heart. It seems our whole family had been a constant subject of her prayers! Heidi's genuine sympathy for Ethel, Ann and me was apparent to each of us. Still, she always gave straightforward answers about her faith and did not compromise her beliefs to appease us. She and Ethel had regular discussions, and between Ethel's growing respect for Jesus as she read, and her respect for our housekeeper, she found it harder and harder to be genuinely upset about Judy's faith.

Even so, Ethel had no intention of embracing that faith for herself. Something happened to her just before I left for San Francisco which she could not explain. It seems my wife went to bed believing that Jesus was merely a good man and woke up believing he was the Messiah!

Puzzled by a belief which seemed to have intruded overnight, Ethel said nothing about it. Perhaps it would pass as mysteriously as it had come. As she prepared to go to Boston for her visit with Judy, Ethel came down with chills, fever, and nausea. She recounted the story, telling me, "I didn't know if I should go to Boston or to bed!" Though she did not feel well enough to travel, she felt compelled to go to Boston.

Ethel arrived at Judy's apartment feeling even worse than before. She was too ill to discuss her belief in Jesus, which had not disappeared in the same way it had come. Judy wanted to call a doctor, but Ethel insisted that a good night's rest was all she needed.

The following day Ethel tried to "perk up" for Judy's sake, but she was feeling just as miserable as before. Judy wanted to invite her friend, Charles, to pray for Ethel. My wife did not want to see anyone, but our daughter was so concerned that Ethel didn't have the heart to turn her down.

Charles arrived and told Ethel the story of how he had come to believe in Jesus. Then he asked if he could pray for her to be healed. My poor wife was too miserable to do much of anything but nod her consent. After he prayed, Charles told Ethel that he was convinced she would be healed. He asked her to call him as soon as she felt better.

After Charles left, Ethel felt overcome by nausea. She headed for the bathroom, but nothing happened. A few minutes later Judy asked if she could come in to keep her company. Ethel told me,

"We sat on the floor talking, and about five minutes later, I realized I wasn't nauseous anymore. In fact, for the first time in three days, I was hungry."

Judy didn't have a whole lot in the house to eat, and it looked like Ethel's main option was fresh liverwurst with mustard on rye. Ordinarily, she probably would have gone out to the store for some chicken broth or crackers. But under the circumstances, Ethel felt that if she really had been "healed" her stomach would tolerate the sandwich.

My wife ate her sandwich with great gusto—enjoyed it to the last bite and felt perfectly fine afterwards. It was then that she told Judy that she had become a believer in Jesus. Judy immediately saw that the concrete experience of answered prayer was just what Ethel needed to confirm that something supernatural really had taken place in her life.

As for Ann, her main objection to Jesus was that he had taken away her sister, her best friend. Judy hadn't cooled toward Ann, but Ann felt, as we all had, that if Judy believed in Jesus, she wasn't Jewish. And if she wasn't Jewish, who was she? Whom did she belong to? Not to Ethel and me, not to Ann.

In addition, Ann was sensitive enough to perceive that her sister's priorities had changed. This didn't mean that Judy treated Ann as though she were unimportant. But their conversations were limited in a way that they never had been before. Judy couldn't really discuss with Ann the things that were now uppermost on her mind. Ann was keenly aware that their talks no longer achieved the same intimacy as they had before. She could not talk about the things that would reach Judy on that deeper level.

Over the next three months, Ann's reaction to Judy's faith softened much as Ethel's had. Though there was no denying that Judy was different, she hadn't deserted her sister.

When Ann arrived in Los Angeles she discovered that the friend she'd come to visit (a childhood friend, and Jewish at that) had become a believer in Jesus! Through the events and discussions of the following week, Ann also took that step of faith.

So the three of us—all in different cities, all within a few weeks of one another, and all nervous about what the others would think—became believers in Jesus.

Believing in Jesus was just the beginning for us. We learned from the Bible that believing Jesus is the Messiah—that he died an atoning death for our sins and rose from the grave—is not enough. God wanted to change our lives, to make us more like Jesus. He wanted us to acknowledge that he is our God and we are his people. He wanted us to live for him through the power of His Spirit.

More than 14 years have passed since the four of us became a "messianic family." The reaction was largely what I feared it would be, though the business continued to thrive. Many former friends wanted nothing to do with us. The fact that we had been pillars of the Jewish community did not help. If anything, it led to more confusion, more feelings of betrayal. There was no one who was going to look at my family and say, "No big deal that they believe in Jesus. They were never that Jewish anyway." We were too well known in our local Jewish community to be ignored or "swept under the carpet."

There were also many steadfast friends who couldn't under-stand what had happened to us, but stood by us anyway. And we gladly told those who wanted to know why we believe in Jesus.

For as long as I could remember, the survival of the Jewish people had been of the utmost importance to me. I had always done my best to donate my time, energy—and as I became older and financially secure, my money—to Jewish concerns. I've been to Israel nine times and have not withdrawn my concern or my support. But what I have done is realize that the survival of the Jewish people is not enough. Just as I had longed for something more than survival for myself, I long for something more than survival for my people. Something deeper, higher, purer...something outside, other, holy...something the Messiah gave his life to achieve for us...the freedom to come into the presence of our God!

The full story of Stan Telchin is available in his book entitled <u>Betrayed</u>, published by Chosen Books of the Zondervan Corporation in Grand Rapids, MI, 49506.

VERA SCHLAMM

I continued going to Friday night services at temple. Even the sermons there seemed to draw me closer to my inevitable conclusion. I remember one taken from a passage in Exodus: "You shall not follow a crowd to do evil" (Exodus 23:2). To me, that meant I should not follow the majority; I should follow God. If I took the verse to its logical conclusion, I would have to obey God even if it set me apart from the people I loved...even if it meant being considered a traitor...even if it meant believing in Jesus.

It was Passover, 1962. I was no longer a little girl, but I wanted to look for the prophet Elijah anyway, for I still believed he would someday herald the coming of the Messiah. My mother was a cautious woman; she did not think it would be such a good idea to throw open the door to look for him. I was living in a nice neighborhood in Southern California, but still, if Elijah wasn't there, who could say what sort of person might be lurking outside my doorway. And so Mama suggested I put the chain on the door before opening it. "But Mama," I protested (though I confess, I thought it amusing), "How do you expect the Messiah to come if we've got the chain on the door?"

My mother felt we needed a chain on the door to protect us. She and I knew that if God should decide to send the Messiah, no silly little chain would stop him. If the Messiah chose to, he could break the chain. Yet tradition tells us to go and look for Elijah at Passover. With the protective chain in place, one cannot go beyond one's door to see if the prophet has come to announce the Messiah. Likewise, with a protective chain on one's heart, one cannot go beyond one's prejudices to see if maybe the Messiah has already come.

Do we have chains on our hearts? If so, what do we fear and from what must we protect ourselves? I've heard some say, "It is a disgrace for a Jew to believe in Jesus after what the Christians did to our people in the Holocaust." I disagree. I have never studied the Holocaust. I don't need to. I lived through that nightmare, I and my family. And I can tell you as one who has suffered through the horror, the Holocaust has nothing to do with whether or not Jesus is the Messiah. We must guard ourselves from doing a disgraceful thing, yes. But we must also guard ourselves from prejudice which can cause us to mistakenly label the truth "a disgrace."

I have experienced all the hatred and prejudice that Hitler managed to dredge up in what was once my country. When I hear my people tell about the Holocaust as though it should justify prejudice against Jesus, it makes me very sad. If we allow the memory of the Nazis to keep us from our own Messiah, we give Hitler the power to reach beyond the grave and destroy us in an awful way that even his evil mind could not imagine.

I didn't grow up asking how I could go about believing in Jesus. It is not something to which most Jewish people aspire. If I had to choose one word to explain how it happened, I suppose the word would be "prayer." One could almost draw a portrait of my life by playing "connect-the-dots"--for my life has been dotted with prayers which shaped both the events and the decisions of my existence.

I trusted God long before I believed in Jesus. I trusted him absolutely, even through desperate times. Many people who saw what I saw turned bitter. They even try to punish God by saying he doesn't exist. It is difficult to say why some turn away from God through hard times while others draw close. I trace my relationship with God back to a time when I was less then 4 years old. I trace it back to prayer.

I was born in Berlin, in 1923. I was a year old when a severe attack of eczema put me in the hospital. It had been serious enough to endanger my life, so when I came home my parents hired a nurse to care for me. She remained with us over the next two years, and taught me a bedtime prayer when I was about 3 years old. It rhymes in German, though not in English: "I'm small, my heart is clean, no one should live in it but God alone." It is a very common German prayer. Actually, the original prayer says "no one should live in it but Jesus alone." She didn't tell me that until years after the war--she had taught me to say "God" instead of "Jesus" because we were Jewish.

My nurse would pray that little prayer each night as she made me ready for bed. I did not say it out loud, but listened carefully and agreed in my heart. It made sense to me and it felt good to tell God: "Yes, I'm small" (I was always very small for my age and still am.), "Yes, my heart is clean," (after all, wasn't I a good girl?), "Yes, I only want God to live in my heart." (I knew God was good and I didn't want anything or anyone bad in my heart.) Many of my childhood memories have been obliterated by the trauma of Bergen-Belsen, but I remember that prayer quite distinctly. I believe God began influencing my young life in answer to that prayer. That was the beginning, the first "dot" in the connect-the-dot picture of how I came to believe in Jesus. From that time on, God was important to me and I wanted to know him better.

As I got older, I would go with my father to synagogue on Friday nights. As we read from the *siddur*, I would concentrate on the translation in German and agree with the prayers in my heart. I learned the *Shema* when I was 10 or 12 years old--Hitler was just coming into power. As times got worse and worse, I began to add my own prayers to the ones learned in synagogue. They were not deep or lengthy prayers--I would ask God to protect my family. I also paid close attention to the Scriptures used in the prayer book, like Psalm 119: "Your word is a lamp to my feet and a light to my path" (verse 105). God was real to me and I often wished our family were more Orthodox, more religious. I felt it was important to obey God, and it seemed to me that being more "Orthodox" was the way to obedience.

Did other people in my family have the same deep interest? No. My father was the most "religious" one in the family. He would see to it that we had *kiddush* on Friday nights; we always did that in Germany. But I remember being concerned that we did not keep kosher or strictly observe the Sabbath.

My parents took my sister Marga and me out of public school in 1935. The rise in anti-Semitism was causing more pressure than any child should have to bear. As the Nazi propaganda began to permeate the educational system, we Jews watched those who had been friendly or at least tolerant toward us turn either ice cold or red hot whenever they saw us. We were excluded from more and more classes and activities which Gentiles were forced to attend. They resented the fact that we had "free time" while they were required to sit and hear classes on the "new socialism" or go on extracurricular field trips. We wouldn't have minded attending the classes at all for it was much harder to bear the resentment of our classmates than it would have been to sit through the lectures. It was a clever ploy on the part of the new government, for the fact that we had "free time" while the others didn't helped foster anti-Jewish feelings almost as much as the propaganda which was taught against us in those classes.

Some of our relatives were beginning to leave Germany and my father seriously considered it. However, well-meaning Gentile friends encouraged him to stay, insisting that the bad times would blow over. Business was still good, so we stayed.

There were isolated instances of Jewish men being taken to concentration camps, but nothing organized. All Jewish businesses were ordered to display a big sign which read "Jewish Store," which everyone knew was an engraved Nazi invitation to vandalize with impunity. It was also to "encourage" our Gentile neighbors not to do business with us, and many who may have wanted to patronize us anyway were afraid. All of this was very bad, but we still hoped it would be temporary. On the 9th of November in 1938, we saw that we'd been wrong, so very wrong, to think that it would pass. And by the 10th, we understood too late that all the harassment had been but a gentle prelude to far more evil intentions which were demonstrated in the "Kristallnacht." That was the night all our synagogues were destroyed. All our stores, so well-marked, were raided. Jewish buildings were burned down; at the very least windows were shattered, and merchandise stolen. Kristallnacht, the "night of the broken glass." Everything Jewish was in ruins by the next morning, including our hopes that better days would come to Germany. Everyone had losses to mourn, and for many, the losses included far more than a business or a building.

Now Jews were being terrorized by arrests for various "offenses." My father was imprisoned for trying to smuggle his own money out of Germany. There was no protection, no one in authority to turn to. Oh, we had some neighbors who did care about us--but though they felt bad about our plight, they did not see what they could do to help. There were laws to protect people--but suddenly, we were no longer considered people. It seemed as though new, unwritten laws were being created to torment us.

My father realized that we had to get out, with or without money. There could be no waiting for this nightmare to blow over. We were a hated people. And there was nothing, absolutely nothing to restrain the people who hated us from violence and even murder. Mother sold everything to get the several thousand dollars needed for illegal passage to Holland--illegal because the visas we had arranged for, visas which could get us safely into Holland, had not come through yet. In addition, my father's passport had been confiscated in prison. Some people were becoming extremely wealthy as a result of the plight of the Jews in Germany. They knew we would pay whatever we had to, whatever we could, to escape. And apparently their love of money outweighed their love of Der Fuehrer. We had found such people to help us, but their help was very slow--and very expensive.

We were given very specific instructions on crossing the German border into the safety of Holland. We would go by train to a tiny station at the border, where we were to meet a man wearing, of all things, a white carnation. So far, so good. He was waiting. He drove us to a soccer field located right on the border of Germany and Holland. The ground was damp and muddy, a foretaste of the swampland we would have to pass through on the other side before reaching "civilization." It was cold and it was very dark. The man with the white carnation said we had only to run across the soccer field and through the goal posts. The score would be Nazis: 0--Schlamms: freedom! Once on the other side we were to wait for a Dutchman who would let us know who he was by making a "tch, tch, tch" sound. It was very important that we wait for him; without his guidance, we were warned, it was very unlikely that we would be able to make our way through the swamp.

We made it across the field and we waited. And waited. And waited. No one said a word, lest we miss the connection with the mysterious Dutchman who would lead us to freedom. We waited for two hours. I prayed the whole time. My prayers that night were the second big "dot" in the dot-to-dot picture of how I came to believe in Jesus. Of course I had no idea that there would ever be such a connection at that time--Jesus was the last thing on my mind! I just wanted God to keep us alive and to keep us together.

As I prayed, I felt assured that he would do so.

After shivering for two hours in the rain and the mud, we realized that no one was going to come for us--at least, no one we'd want to see! The only logical thing seemed to go back through the field to Germany, where, if we were lucky, we'd be told what had gone wrong with the plan and would be able to make another attempt the next day.

We were captured by the Gestapo on the way back. My father was shaking violently; he knew the consequences would be dire if the Nazis discovered he had jumped parole. It was a very scary night. Usually children turn to their parents for comfort in a frightening situation. Marga and I did not have that luxury, for the danger was even more frightening to our parents, who understood more about these things than we did. I only knew that we were in great danger. Yet I was able to whisper to my father, "Don't worry, God will get us out of this." Normally, those who were arrested and questioned by the Gestapo knew they were in a hopeless situation. I had more than hope. Somehow I knew God would answer my prayers.

The Gestapo was willing to release Marga, Mother and myself, but they wanted to hold my father for suspicion of attempting to cross the border illegally, because he had no passport. Yet he also had no suitcase while the rest of us did, which may have been what caused the Nazis to believe our story. We told the Nazis that father was merely accompanying us to the border with no intention of crossing himself. My sister became the spokesperson for the family. Why couldn't they just send one of their men to take us to the train station and make certain that we were headed back to Berlin? She was so convincing that the Gestapo decided to take her suggestion--after making a quick call to Berlin to verify our story.

Thank God, the lines were jammed and after half an hour they lost patience and decided it wasn't necessary to verify our story after all. They selected a man to drive us to the station--and it turned out to be none other than the man with the white carnation who'd instructed us to wait on the soccer field! He thanked us profusely for not saying anything which might have incriminated him before his superiors. He said he would take us over the border himself--in the trunk of his car. We didn't know if we should trust him and so we declined the offer. Instead, he drove us back to the station where he had originally met us.

The next morning, my father went with some "shady-looking" mercenaries, and he managed to make it over the border, promising his "helpers" payment on the other side. The rest of us still had no visas. We had to wait a day while my father procured money from his business in Holland for all four of our visas. Sure enough, after he paid, our visas arrived. To our dismay, we saw that the pictures on those visas did not even remotely resemble us. Surely we would be caught! We came to the border at night and as the guard shone his flashlight at each of us, I thought the frantic pounding of my heart would give us away. To this day I don't know if someone bribed the guard on our behalf or if God simply blinded him, but he let us pass. We were reunited with Father--God had come through!

Marga and I joined a Zionist youth group shortly after we arrived in Amsterdam. There I, the shortest one in the group, became fast friends with the tallest girl in the group, Lore. Lore and I maintained contact over the years and, in fact, she was one of the few in whom I later confided when I was beginning to consider whether Jesus might be our Messiah. More about that later. The other thing which occupied my time in Holland was business school, where I learned how to do bookkeeping, which came in handy in my father's wholesale business.

I went into the hospital in October of 1939 and stayed until March of 1940, being tested to see if there was any way to prompt my growth. As a teenager, I was still conspicuously smaller than my peers. I really missed being able to participate in the Zionist group while in the hospital, but Marga and Lore would visit and tell me about their meetings and activities; that helped ease my frustration over being cooped up. I left the hospital with no more hope of adding inches than I'd had when I came in.

In May of 1940, the Germans attacked and the trouble began all over again. For five days, we were constantly racing between our apartment and the bomb shelter. When those five days were over, so was our freedom. Holland was defeated. Dutch Jews began leaving for England. Everyone had to register with the Nazis for identification, and we were once more at the mercy of a government bent on our destruction. The Dutch were friendly to us, and did what they could to show kindness and let us know they would not join in the Nazi anti-Semitism. Often they would offer one of us a seat on a crowded bus--a small gesture, perhaps, but we were grateful to know that we could still expect to be treated like human beings by some non-Jews. Nevertheless, they could not prevent the inevitable. In 1942, the Third Reich began taking over our businesses and all Jews were forced to wear the yellow star.

1942 was also the year that Marga and her fiance, Eric, were married. Two months later, Eric received a summons to report for transport to a concentration camp. Shortly after, Marga and I received a similar summons. The day before we were slated to leave, I was given a reprieve for medical reasons. My small size had come in handy for a change! Marga and Eric were slated for Auschwitz. Thank God, they were never taken. Between delays and bribery, we managed to avoid being transported despite three separate summonses. In June of '43, the fourth summons came and this time there was no more stalling. We were all shipped to Westerbork.

Westerbork was not so bad. There were no gas chambers and there was not really forced labor--just daily chores. The worst part was that for most, Westerbork was merely a waiting place. Each Tuesday, at three o'clock in the morning the names of 1,000 Jews were read over the loudspeaker. Those whose names were called were sent to Auschwitz. The suspense was the worst part. It was just a matter of time before the Jews at Westerbork would be sent to a "real" concentration camp.

Within two weeks, my parents and I were released. Marga and Eric stayed at Westerbork for another month and then they were transferred to Vught. This was far worse than Westerbork--more in line with the camps you've heard about. We'd heard about people losing their sanity there. We'd also heard that as soon as prisoners at Vught were no longer capable of labor, they were sent off to Auschwitz and certain death. A month later my parents and I were picked up once more and taken back to Westerbork. And then it happened: my parents were taken to Vught as well. I was left alone.

I prayed and prayed for my family to be returned to me. On Yom Kippur, the Day of Atonement, I formulated the idea that God would bring them back to Westerbork by Hanukkah. There was no reason to think this would happen. Yet, I told my friends with great certainty that God would answer my prayer. Meanwhile, I had learned that lists were everything to the Nazis. Everyone was on this list or that, and when numbers of people were to be transported, exterminated, or whatever, your entire life often depended on which list your name appeared on. Through Eric's relatives in Sweden, we were able to obtain Ecuadorian passports. I don't know how they did it, but I thank God they did, for these passports later saved our lives. The day we left Westerbork, the Nazis happened to be sending Jews with papers for Palestine to Auschwitz, which we now knew to be a death camp. Those with papers to South America went to Bergen-Belsen. You could die of starvation, beating or lack of medical treatment in Bergen-Belsen--but at least there were no gas chambers.

It was rumored that a German woman was coming to Westerbork to straighten out some of the lists and take care of relegating the whereabouts of Jews who had passports. I managed to see her and blurted out my story, telling her that I had papers for South America and my family were all on the same passport and shouldn't we really all be kept together? This woman was not cruel; she simply had a job to do. My request seemed to fall within the boundaries of her job, and she told me there was a good chance my family would be transported back to Westerbork. However, there were many other details and duties which would take priority over reuniting a Jewish family--even if it was for the sake of maintaining the proper lists.

As Hanukkah approached, I began to hoard whatever food I could so that we could celebrate our reunion as well as the holiday. My greatest treasure was a store of eggs I'd been able to save up--hard-boiled eggs which I'd been given only because I was sick. The eggs would not last past the expected arrival of my family at Hanukkah. I knew they would be considered a gourmet feast after the food at Vught. Being sick did not get you hard-boiled eggs at Vught. It got you a transport to Auschwitz.

Not only did my family return in time for Hanukkah, but the four of them were the only ones aboard the transport! As far as I know, sending a transport to carry only four people is a unique event in the history of Nazi concentration camps. I saw that as a clear answer to prayer. This prayer, and the many others I offered up for the survival of my family during our time in the camps, comprised the third major "dot" which helped to shape my faith.

In February of 1944, the five of us were shipped off to Bergen-Belsen. The fact that we all managed to survive there until we were freed in January of 1945 can only be attributed to answered prayer. I shall only describe a few of the gruesome details of life in a Nazi concentration camp, for books and museums have been devoted to the subject and you can easily research some of the things which took place there. But you must understand that whatever you read or hear from camp survivors, it is impossible to exaggerate the nightmarish suffering. It is simply impossible. Nothing you read or hear can convey the horror of it.

Once a month we were required to take showers which were more humiliating than hygienic. Each shower outlet was shared by four people who could barely wet their wasted, diseased bodies with the trickle of water which came out. The guards watched, often laughing at the sight. Lice were a constant source of torment. We stood for hours in the freezing cold to be counted. And we watched one another starve to death.

Families would fight over an inch-and-a-half square of bread. Mothers would trade a cup of milk intended for their children for a tiny triangle of moldy cheese which they would eat themselves. Thankfully, our family did not quarrel like many of the others. We shared and made sacrifices for one another. Many just could not maintain the sanity to treat one another as family should be treated. Everyone was obsessed with food. Every day, there would be the all-important question regarding the soup: "Thick or thin?" "Thick" meant there was maybe a piece of turnip floating in it, or on very rare occasions, a piece of horse-meat. "Thin" could mean just the regular watery soup--or it could mean just plain water, with a few flakes of dried parsley sprinkled on top. You were always hungry--until just before you died. Then you didn't care anymore--about food, or anything else. To give you an idea of how hungry we were--my father weighed in at 180 pounds when we came to Bergen-Belsen. When we left, in January of 1945, he weighed 70 pounds.

Did my thoughts and feelings about who God is and what he means change during the time I was in camp? No. Did I discuss God or religion with anyone there? No. You discuss very little in camp. In fact, I don't remember any real conversations there at all, other than answering when I was spoken to--except to say a few words to my sister before we went to sleep--we slept in one bed. Even when we stood to be counted we were not allowed to talk. I knew a friend of mine from school in Berlin had also ended up in Bergen-Belsen but I never saw or spoke to her. People were just too busy trying to survive to think about doing anything else. One exception that I recall was due to my continued concern that my family wasn't Orthodox enough. Once I stood by my father's bed and asked, "If we get out of camp, couldn't we be more Orthodox? Couldn't we keep kosher and keep the Sabbath?" And he said, yes, we could, but I don't think he paid any great attention and I doubt if he even remembered I had asked him that question--but I never forgot because I meant business.

Anyway, I was never angry with God. I never stopped believing. I never gave up thinking that God is a good, loving God, although we cannot understand many things about him and about the world in which we live. Sometimes he protects people, sometimes he doesn't and we don't understand why. I do know one thing: when people say, "Where was God when 6 million Jews were killed?" I always say where he always was, in heaven, grieving over what was happening to his people. The Bible says the Jewish people are the apple of God's eye and he is concerned about what happens to us, and I believe it.

I'm thankful that I never blamed God for what was happening. I heard one person in camp say something about God and it bothered me. I felt he was blaspheming. I was praying all the way through camp. I hoped from one week to the next that we would get out and God answered my prayers. It never occurred to me to blame him. I have seen over and over how the bitterness toward God which seems intended to punish him ends up harming the bearer of bitterness instead.

Each member of our family, except for my brother-in-law Eric, experienced illness at one point or another which could have brought an end to it all. As it was, after a year in Bergen-Belsen, our phony South American papers finally resulted in our freedom, as a large group of us were released. Even the release was an ordeal with questions to answer and the emotional trauma of wondering whether it was really possible that we would be freed, or was it all a ruse to send us quietly to the gas chambers.

But it was true...we were free at last! In November of 1947, just a few months short of our two-year anniversary of being set free, we finally arrived in America. We'd been shuffled from place to place and treated like dirt by people who had no idea of the conditions in camp and just assumed that we Jews naturally wore tattered clothing and carried an entourage of lice.

The relief of being in America! We headed for the Detroit area, where Eric had family. It was time to build a new life.

I felt a sense of destiny in having been spared from death in the camps--I believed God must have something special for me to do. I was determined to finish my education and learn a meaningful vocation. I only hoped that somehow I could make something out of my life. I had no idea what that should be, except that I liked children. I thought that being a practical nurse might be something I could do, so I went to an orphanage where training was offered for that position. While there, I observed the kindergarten teachers and that vocation appealed to me even more.

I went down to Wayne University, now Wayne State University, at the suggestion of Eric's family in Detroit. The school administrators told me what I would have to do to become a kindergarten teacher. Had I not received the encouragement to speak to people at the college, it would not have occurred to me that it was even an option. My parents had taken me out of school at 15. If anything, I expected to finish high school in America.

The admissions officer at Wayne University didn't say, "Well, go and get a high school diploma and come back." He said, "I'd like you to take our entrance examination for guidance only, just so I can advise you." After I'd taken the test, he came and said, "We'll take you on a trial basis." I think they called it "special student" status, and I had to make a "B-plus" average in order to receive credit for my classes.

I did well in my studies and intended to pursue a career as a kindergarten teacher, when I heard a rumor that there was a height requirement for that position. To this day I don't know if there really was a height requirement or not. But I questioned one of the faculty about it, and his response was very discouraging. If I had to ask about it, he said dryly, perhaps I should look into another field. I'd shown more aptitude and interest in science than anything else, so I chose medical technology. My parents had moved down to San Antonio, Texas, and my father wrote and suggested I join them there. Reuniting with my family sounded good, and I was ripe for change, so in 1951, I transferred to Trinity University.

I liked Trinity. It was not exactly a "Christian school" but it was connected with the Presbyterian church, and they did require each student to take two religion classes. I selected "Old Testament" and "Comparative Religion," feeling that these would be the two least offensive courses to my Jewish faith. Both classes were taught by the school's chaplain.

One day a student was giving the chaplain a hard time

because he believed in the Genesis account of creation. The chaplain was not at all ruffled. He responded by saying, "You can't go wrong by looking for the truth," and he added, "There's only one truth." He opened his classes with prayer, which fascinated me. Prayer, after all, was a very important thing in my life.

As for our family's religious pursuits, we were attending a Reform synagogue. We liked the rabbi, and we didn't mind that they read the prayers in English instead of Hebrew. In fact, I felt they displayed more reverence than in Orthodox shul--perhaps because they understood what they were saying. However, it did make us uncomfortable that the men did not bother to wear yarmulkas.

Many of the courses I was taking at Trinity were the same ones required for all the pre-med students, but it never occurred to me that becoming a physician would be an option for me--so much schooling--so expensive! But a girlfriend whom I studied with began to encourage me. She kept saying, "I wish you could go to medical school with me so we could keep on studying together."

Finally I blurted out, "Please, don't keep saying that because there's no way I can afford it." She invited me to her home for dinner, and her husband, a dentist, explained about scholarships and school loans. My friend and I spoke to our biology professor about it the next day, and he was very enthusiastic. That was the last nudge I needed to make my decision.

I had been praying about what I should do since I arrived in America, because I was grateful that God had saved me and I wanted to obey him by doing whatever it was that he had saved me for! The odds seemed stacked against my getting into medical school, but I remember saying to my sister, who was not particularly "religious," "Well, if God wants me to go to medical school I'll be accepted, and if not, well, that's fine too." I thought that as a doctor, I could be of help to people and maybe that was what God had in mind for me. It was. I was accepted into medical school.

I had only been in this country a little over four years when I began to study medicine. The language used in those classrooms is very sophisticated, and the professors went so fast in their lectures that I really had a hard time trying to take in what they were saying and take notes at the same time. Remember, English was not my first, nor even my second language. I had a choice--I could give my attention to understanding the lecture, and try to write it down later or I could try to take notes without really understanding what I was writing. Somehow I managed to grasp enough to do well--but oh, what I would have given for a tape recorder!

1953 was a landmark year for me--I became a citizen of the United States.

During the summers of my second and third year of medical school I worked as an "extern" at a private San Antonio hospital. I was put in charge of the Emergency Room during the day and during some evenings. On weekends I was responsible for intravenous feedings and other such procedures. It was very good experience. A woman obstetrician was very kind and allowed me to assist with quite a few deliveries.

I applied for internship during my last year and was accepted at U.C.L.A. for pediatrics. I would be able to work with children after all! I graduated from medical school in 1956, packed my belongings and moved to Los Angeles.

Two months after I came to L.A., my parents joined me there. (My mother's brother also lived in the area.) A year later I finished my internship and began residency at Children's Hospital. I moved into the housing there and to my surprise, ended up with an old friend from Trinity as my roommate!

Residency was a time when I began to seriously investigate my faith. I'd come through medical school, survived my internship--the dust was settling, the end was in sight! I now had more mental energy to devote to this issue--I could foresee having my own life, my own schedule, my own decisions. And I knew that an important part of that life, that schedule and those decisions should be God. I thought about how to be a good Jew and I prayed a great deal about it. This time of prayer and reflection is the fourth "dot" in my connect-the-dots portrait of how I came to believe in Jesus.

My roommate, Le Claire, was a faithful Catholic. She asked me many questions about Judaism and I didn't always know the answers. As we compared our religions, I explained to her that I didn't need to confess my sins to a priest as she did. I did that once a year on Yom Kippur, by reading a list of sins and asking God's forgiveness. I "felt" forgiven. After I had explained it to her, I began to question it myself. How could I feel forgiven when I knew I would be committing the same sins, many of which had to do with being observant? The two issues that troubled me the most were the dietary laws and the Sabbath. These two things had always bothered me, even at Bergen-Belsen.

A friend named Werner was my connection with Orthodox Judaism. His parents and my parents had become friends in Holland because we had both fled there from Germany and went through similar experiences. We also went to the concentration camp together and when I was alone in Westerbork, they became my substitute family, so to speak. We met again later at the repatriation center in France, and so the friendship continued. Werner and his mother ended up in San Francisco, so when I was in Los Angeles, it was very natural for me to fly up there occasionally to visit. We were not dating, just friends. I especially liked to go up for weekends, as we would have a good, Orthodox Shabbat celebration.

I felt that Le Claire was doing what she thought was right to serve God and so was I--each according to our own upbringing. Eventually she seemed to accept this and I was proud of myself for having brought her to my way of thinking. Meanwhile, I made plans for what I would do to be "more religious" once my residency was over.

My idea was to find out more about God through reading the Bible. No one told me to do this--I was more interested in reading what I considered the Word of God than hearing what other people had to say about being Jewish.

Much as I appreciated Werner's sincerity and diligence in doing what he felt was right, I began to see things which made me feel uncomfortable. It dawned on me that the Judaism of my friend Werner and the Catholicism of my friend Le Claire had more in common than perhaps either may have liked to admit. Each seemed to have traditions which he or she regarded as important parts of the religion-- traditions which were not commanded in the Bible, yet to violate them would be considered sin. This was not troublesome to me in the case of Le Claire's beliefs, for I felt that what she believed and did was fine for her. There was no need for me to judge or criticize since I had no intention of adhering to the religion myself.

But it was different with Orthodox Judaism. Judaism, after all, was my religion, and something to which I did intend to adhere. I was exploring Orthodox Judaism with the intent of becoming "more religious." Therefore, when I saw things which seemed inconsistent, it did trouble me.

For example, I remember asking my friend about driving the car to synagogue on the Sabbath. It seemed to me as though it was no more work to drive than to walk to the synagogue. Werner explained to me that this was not a matter of "working," but it was to prevent us from violating the injunction against building a fire on the Sabbath. Starting a car involved igniting a spark, and was therefore considered a violation. This did not make sense to me. Further, my parents would not be able to attend synagogue if I didn't drive, for it was too far for them to walk. To my dismay, I learned that our Orthodox rabbis taught it was better that one should stay home than to drive a car on the Sabbath. I did not know as much as the rabbis about the Talmud, and about a great many other things, I'm sure. But I knew enough about God to believe that he would rather have my parents come to worship him in synagogue than to stay home in order to keep from breaking a man-made tradition.

I remembered back to my youth in Holland, when an Orthodox friend of mine who had asthma refused to take the elevator on the Sabbath. She would climb up five flights of stairs each Sabbath to avoid offending God, and she could barely breathe by the time she reached the top. I did not think God required that of her. But I had no proof of that. Little things like that troubled me; still I admired the Orthodox and wanted to emulate them.

The trouble spots of man-made traditions did not turn me against Orthodox Judaism, they simply made me cautious. I saw much beauty in the religious lifestyle, but I also concluded that I would restrict my obedience to what I knew was communicated by God, through the Bible. At the same time, I was troubled over the fact that one could not possibly be obedient to God by keeping the entire Law. Parts of it were antiquated--impossible for practical reasons. What should one do to please God?

The more I considered these things and wrestled with the issues of obedience to God, the more I began to formulate a plan to go somewhere that would help me fit the pieces together. Surely, I would be inspired and would find answers in Israel. I had some dear friends as well as family in the land and so I arranged for a long-awaited visit to take place within weeks of finishing my residency.

As I boarded the plane for Haifa, I remembered the days of the Zionist youth organization, and how Marga and I had helped to collect money so that trees could be planted in the land. Once I arrived, it was thrilling to see the "bloom in the desert." The transformation we'd dreamed of had come to pass and in our small way, we'd helped.

As we went from place to place in Israel, I was deeply moved to know that I was in the land where all I had read about in the Bible had actually happened thousands of years ago. This new dimension of reality added to my hunger to know about God. I'd always had a sense of the Bible as God's Word to us, and now I was even more eager to read it. From that perspective, being in Israel was a step forward in my search for God.

At the same time, I was disillusioned by the secularism, and even, it seemed to me, the irreverence of many Israelis. It seemed as though people were either extremely Orthodox or not religious at all. The Orthodox were a definite minority. I stayed in Israel for seven weeks, feeling glad for the experience and especially for the opportunity to see old friends, particularly Lore, my friend from the Zionist youth group in Holland. She was, and is still, a very dear friend.

I returned to Southern California and began working with a group of doctors who had set up a private practice in Glendale. I began working with them twice a week, then four times a week, then much to my delight, in January of 1960 they asked me to join them on a permanent full-time basis.

The great desire I'd had to do something meaningful with my life was met beautifully in my pediatrics career. I had the opportunity to care for children that had drawn me to teaching, but I was able to do so in a way that was much more suited to my abilities and temperament. I was truly thankful to God. The sense of destiny I'd felt since I was spared from death at the hands of the Nazis was fulfilled. What satisfaction!

My schedule was still hectic, for one never knows when a child will become ill or have some sort of accident, but to a large extent, I was now "my own boss" and able to devote more thought to pursuits which I'd limited myself in during my internship and residency.

Now was the time to resolve questions about my religion and to decide what kind of a Jew God wanted me to be. My birthday (February 28) was approaching and my sister wanted to know what I would like for a gift. I asked her for a Bible--a "whole" Bible with what I then considered the "Jewish" and "Christian" parts. She and Eric had one and it hadn't made heretics of them, so I decided I would have one, too. After all, I was constantly in contact with people who I assumed were Christians (mainly because I knew they weren't Jews). I wanted to understand something about what they believed, just so I wouldn't be ignorant.

I began in the book of Genesis and soaked up page after page of the Bible--occasionally glancing at portions of "the other" Bible, the Christian one. I felt a twinge of uneasiness at first, but I remembered what the chaplain of Trinity had said: "You can't go wrong if you're searching for the truth," and that gave me courage. God knew I only wanted to know more about him, wanted to learn what he required of me. He knew I wanted to be a good Jew, and that I didn't have any conditions or agendas attached to these desires. I would obey God on his terms if he would just show me how. After everything he'd brought me through, I didn't believe he would allow me to be tricked into believing something I shouldn't. I wasn't taking these occasional looks at the New Testament because I had intentions of becoming a Christian. My friendship with Le Claire and the many discussions we'd had made me curious to understand what she believed. In addition to reading my Bible, I attended Temple Emanuel every Friday night.

I read Isaiah 53, and though it seemed to be obviously pointing to Jesus, that didn't trouble me. My first thought was, "Oh well, I'm reading the King James Version. It's obviously slanted to sound that way." So far there had been nothing else to make me wonder if there was something wrong with the translation. But of course, anything which seemed to be pointing to Jesus was obviously an error.

The very next Friday night when I was in temple, I took the Scriptures from the pew and opened to the fifty-third chapter of Isaiah. I was surprised to find that though the wording was a little different, the general meaning was the same. If somebody had said to me, "You have to study with a rabbi to understand this," I suppose I would have been open to it. The interesting thing is that with all my regular attendance, spiritual matters were not really a topic of conversation and it did not occur to me to seek the rabbi's advice.

I finally decided it was a bit far to schlepp from Glendale to temple in Westwood each week, so I decided to become more established in my own neighborhood. I began going to the temple in Glendale which was smaller, and of course more convenient. I recall the rabbi saying, "Well, we'll have to have you over some time." And I said, "That would be very nice." I thought to myself, "Well, I can ask him some of the questions that I have on my mind." He never repeated the invitation. I got to be good friends with a family called the Palmers, whom I met through my profession, and eventually asked them my questions instead.

My profession, meanwhile, was providing a great deal of satisfaction. There's really no such thing as a "typical day" in any doctor's life and certainly not in the life of a pediatrician. You get night calls, you get weekend calls. You often work closely with the parents, to comfort them, to give them guidance on how to care for their child. To me, being in private practice was like seeing friends all the time. After meeting with the parents two or three times, a bond develops. However, it is a limited friendship, for one cannot be personally committed to spending time with every person with whom one comes in contact professionally. So, while I enjoyed these limited friendships, I made it a personal policy not to socialize with them outside of the professional relationship. I made an exception in the case of the Palmers.

On May 17, 1960, Tommy Palmer was born. His adoptive mother, Lisa, called to ask if I would be his pediatrician. I agreed to meet with her, and thought as I hung up, what a pleasant voice and manner she had. I soon discovered that Milton Palmer, Tommy's proud papa, was a minister at a local Baptist church. As I came to know the Palmers through our regular visits, I was impressed that their faith was a part of their daily living. They spoke of God as though he had an important part in their life. They talked about answered prayer. They seemed to have a confidence in knowing and relating to God. I'd never seen that kind of faith in any of the so-called Christian friends I had made. I admired this and it made me a little jealous.

Another thing which attracted me to the Palmers was their genuine love for me. They accepted me as a person; it didn't seem to make any difference if I was Jewish or not. It never seemed to enter into their thinking, except on those occasions when I mentioned it as a roadblock to believing in Jesus. Then they were interested and answered me gently, without making me feel our friendship depended on whether or not I agreed.

Eighteen months after Tommy was born, and we had come to a mutual respect and fondness for one another, the Palmers invited me to spend a weekend with them up at Milton's brother's home in Lake Arrowhead. Lake Arrowhead is a resort area about two hours away from Los Angeles. This was really the first time they had extended a social invitation, and because I felt a special fondness and respect for them, I accepted. They did not preach to me or even mention God during the weekend, except at brief prayers before meals. They listened as I told about the camps. I let them know of my Bible reading, because I wanted them to understand that I, too, was religious--in my own way.

After that weekend, I continued to spend time with the Palmers. I would invite them to my home for dinner, and accept invitations to go to theirs. The first time I came to their home, I asked Milton, "How can anyone know what is the right religion? You're born into a religion and you do the best with it that you can." I'd made that statement to some of my other "Christian" friends (I'd assumed they were Christian since they weren't Jewish) and I'd never gotten an answer. I suppose I didn't expect one from him, either. But he responded without hesitation, "I knew when I accepted the Messiah as my personal Savior."

That opened up two new ideas to me--first, he used the word "Messiah." I knew Christians believed in Jesus, but I hadn't really thought about the fact that they believe in him as the Jewish Messiah. If you had pinned me down, maybe I would've known that "Christ" and "Messiah" were synonymous. It wasn't really part of my working knowledge though. He brought that into focus for me.

The second idea which interested me was the fact that he said, "When I accepted Jesus as my Messiah." Hadn't he been born a Christian? Apparently not. I was surprised to hear how, as an adult, this man had become a Christian. Further, at one time he had been a very heavy drinker. Jesus had changed him, he said. I could not imagine Milton Palmer drunk! He was a godly man, not because he used a lot of religious words when he talked, and not because he talked about how sinful everyone else was. God just mattered very much to him and was a real presence in his life.

Well, Milton had answered my question and now he felt free to ask one of his own. "What happened to the sacrifices in the Jewish religion?" I didn't know. I offered to look into it.

I asked my friend Werner about the sacrifices and he explained that since the destruction of the Temple sacrifices could no longer be made. We now had prayer and good deeds instead. I felt that God could make a place for sacrifices if he wanted them. Why didn't he want them any longer? This puzzled me. I continued to pray, read the Bible and wonder.

One Sunday afternoon I was visiting the Palmers and they asked if I would like to come with them to church that evening. Milton was going to give a sermon on the first Psalm. The Book of Psalms, that was in the Jewish Bible. It should be safe enough, yes, why not? Still, as I walked into church with them, I recited the Shema. Like many Jewish people, I thought Christians worshipped three gods and I wanted God to know that I believed in him alone. I thought he'd be jealous if I believed in Jesus.

Milton's sermon was impressive. He expounded on the ungodly and the righteous from the Jewish Bible. I saw that he was teaching from the text and everything he said was true, according to God's Word. Then he quoted something Jesus said from the Gospel of John: "I am the way, the truth, and the life. No one comes to the Father except through Me." It dawned on me that he was saying one could not be truly godly without Jesus. I was very angry. But angry as I was, those words seemed to haunt me. True, I'd been praying and trusting and wanting to obey God all these years with never a thought about Jesus. The thought occurred to me that if God was shedding more light on what it means to obey him, I was now responsible to act accordingly. I didn't want to believe in Jesus. But I didn't want to reject him if he really was God's way for me to be obedient. And there was the matter of Isaiah 53. It had sounded like Jesus without anyone there to pressure me. Could it possibly be that we didn't make sacrifice for sin anymore because Jesus took care of the sacrifice once and for all? I began asking God to show me if it were true. And that was the fifth big "dot" in my faith picture.

Nobody else knew how seriously I was searching, except my girlfriend, Lore, in Israel. I wrote to her and told

her some of my thoughts, and even so, I didn't
much. Mostly, I talked to God about it.

I didn't even let the Palmers know how muc[h]
thinking about all this and how the things they wer[e]
impressed me. At one time Milton suggested, "You
read the Book of Luke and the Book of Romans. Lu[ke]
written by a doctor just like you who wrote an accu[rate]
count, just as you write up a chart in your office. [A]
reasoning in the book of Romans might appeal to y[ou]
never let them know that I actually read those books. I was
very careful because I did not want to be pushed in any way,
shape or form. I wanted it to be between me and God.

And you know, the closer I got, the more I tried to
cling to traditional Judaism. I felt, how can I go into enemy
territory? After all, the people who persecuted me were
Christians as far as I was concerned. I certainly didn't want
to be a Christian. I just wanted to be right with God.

I brought out my old Orthodox siddur and started
reading. I began to read the morning prayers and I would
recite the Thirteen Articles of Faith. I knew that every Jew
ought to firmly believe these and rehearse them daily, so I
did. And I read, "I believe with a perfect faith that all the
words of the prophets are true." I zeroed in on that--I had
read Isaiah by that time, and Pastor Palmer had pointed out
some prophecies which I was very much aware had been
fulfilled. And of course, the Articles of Faith affirmed the
fact that the Messiah was an important aspect of Judaism as
well. They even mentioned belief in a resurrection. Resurrection, in Judaism? Wasn't that something that the Christians believed? Apparently, it was a Jewish concept and I'd
never realized it before. God used the siddur to help me
along the way to Jesus.

I continued going to Friday night services at Temple.
Even the sermons there seemed to be drawing me closer to
Jesus. I remember one taken from a passage in Exodus:
"You shall not follow a crowd to do evil" (Exodus 23:2). To
me, that verse meant you should not follow what the majority of people are doing, you should follow God. If I took
the verse to its logical conclusion, it would mean that I also

had to do what was right, even if that meant being considered a traitor.

On June 30, 1962, I went to spend another weekend with the Palmers in Lake Arrowhead. We talked openly about Jesus. I asked question after question, among them was the question of whether or not a Jew who believed in Jesus would be expected to give up his or her Jewishness. Milton said no, because Jesus came as a Jew to Jewish people in fulfillment of Jewish prophecies. Believing in him would certainly put me at odds with what the rabbis taught, but then it was God, and not any person, who'd made me Jewish to begin with. It all made sense, but I did not want to make a rash decision. When Milton asked if I wanted to accept Jesus as my Messiah that night, I said no. I prayed once again before I went to bed that God would show me if it was true. I slept soundly through the night.

At six o' clock the next morning I awoke to hear God speaking to my heart. I say he was speaking to my heart because it was not something audible that I heard in my ear. But I was not a stranger to talking to him and I recognized his answer. Jesus was the Messiah. I was responsible to believe and obey. My search was over.

At that point, I had no clear concept that accepting Jesus as Messiah was what being a Christian was all about. When I accepted him, it was strictly because God showed me, yes, Jesus is the expected Messiah, and that was reason enough to believe in him. When I told the Palmers of my decision, Milton prayed with me, and the last dot in my connect-the-dots picture was in place.

It was really after I came to believe in Jesus that I began to understand what it means to be a Christian, and that I had, in fact, become one. I learned that Jesus had ushered in a New Covenant prophesied by Jeremiah. The realization that I had become a Christian never made me doubt for a moment that I was still Jewish.

So now you see the connecting dots that make the picture of how this Jewish woman came to believe in Jesus. Some might object that the first four don't "connect" with believing in Jesus. My prayer as a 4-year-old for God to live in my heart, my prayers during the night we were captured by the Gestapo, my prayers throughout the duration of our time in the camps, and my prayers of searching during my residency--what did these have to do with Jesus? I'll tell you the connection. All these prayers (and, of course, the answers to them) gave me a sense of God's reality. This resulted in my trusting God and wanting to obey him. Because of that, I cared more about knowing him than I cared what any person or people might think of me. A person, especially a Jewish person, is unable to believe in Jesus until he or she reaches that point, for believing in him will not win them any popularity contests. Then, of course, the last two major prayers related directly to Jesus and my eventual faith in him. I was born Jewish and I will die Jewish. My belief in the Messiah is the natural result of my search for God and fulfillment of my Jewishness.

As it was, I was able to make peace with each member of my immediate family, though I will not pretend that my faith did not put a strain on our relationships. Not only was I able to make peace with them, but they were able to make their peace with Y'shua. My sister died in 1970, after accepting Jesus as her Messiah.

In the days before my father's death, I requested that he ask the Almighty if the only way to God is through Y'shua. He agreed to pray and ask God to show him if that were true, and said he was willing to believe it if God showed him. I don't know whether it was that prayer that finally led him to believe, but I know that he did believe in Jesus as his Messiah before he died. He gave definite evidence of his belief.

My mother lived with me for the last six years of her life after he was gone. I'd prayed for 19 years that she would have faith in Jesus. She was always very adamant and gave me a hard time the last six years that she lived with me. She would keep on bringing up the subject, and when I would start answering her she would say, "Oh, how did we come to talk about religion again? Let's not talk about it." I'd drop it until the next time she opened the subject, and we went on and on like that. Though I couldn't see it, God was answering my prayers on behalf of my mother. Eventually she believed and I had the privilege to personally pray with her when she accepted Jesus as her Messiah. Anyone who knew my mother knows that if she could believe in Jesus, anyone can! Anyone who is willing to sincerely ask God to show him or her the truth, that is.

Do we need to protect ourselves against the "disgrace" of becoming Jews who believe in Jesus? Should we keep a chain on the door of our hearts so we don't have to see if he is out there, if he is real? No, for if Jesus is the Messiah, it is no disgrace for a Jew to believe. True, the anti-Semites accuse us of killing "their Lord." But the Bible says the Messiah gave himself willingly as an atonement for sin. True Christians recognize that everyone (Jews and Gentiles) needs the atonement that Jesus' death and resurrection provided. Thus, the Christian understanding is that everyone for whom Jesus died (again, Jews and Gentiles), shares the responsibility for his crucifixion.

We must not be swayed by the irrational accusations and behavior of ignorant people who don't understand what Christianity is about. If we respond to them by letting so much fear and malice into our hearts that we have no room left to thoughtfully consider who Jesus is, then their madness has triumphed. Do we need a chain to protect us? Let the protection be from our own fears and malice.

Let us remove the chains that keep us closed, that we might open the door of our hearts and go beyond our prejudices to look for the Messiah.

For more about Vera Schlamm, a longer biography entitled Pursued *is available through Regal Books, a division of Gospel Light Publishers in Ventura, California.*

JAY SEKULOW

I left the courtroom feeling like the Beatles must have felt as they were leaving Shea Stadium. If you don't know the Beatles, I felt like "Rocky" after the fight. If you've never heard of Rocky, how about a prima ballerina after her first performance? Okay, so a ballerina I'm not, but I felt great! I knew God had brought me through that trial--and he'd brought me through it much better than I'd even dared to hope.

I came to the courtroom early, before the proceedings began. The podium was adjustable, right? I lowered it. I'm five feet seven and a half inches tall and the last thing I needed was to be standing up on the tips of my toes to reach the podium! When I came back later, for the proceedings, I looked in the back row and there, sitting all together, were my good friends, Moishe Rosen (executive director of Jews for Jesus), Tuvya Zaretsky, Susan Perlman and Russ Reed (three of Jews for Jesus' board members), plus my wife, my parents, and a lady from the Los Angeles Board of Airport Commissioners who accidentally sat in the wrong row! The thing that struck me was, when I looked back at the "Christian row," my parents were right in there. Whatever their feelings may be about my beliefs, they were there to support me. And I felt God's presence in that courtroom.

I wasn't too nervous until a couple of weeks before the trial, at which time I became pretty tense. I mean, for a while there, I was physically sick. I knew I was not the best. I don't generally lack confidence, but this was definitely the "big leagues." Despite all the commercial success I'd achieved as a lawyer, I knew that in the Supreme Court of the United States, I was basically just a kid. At age 30, I had to get special permission to defend the case. Yet, by the time I walked into the courtroom I felt great. I should have been a nervous wreck but I wasn't. People were praying for me and God came through.

The stairs I had to climb to get into that courtroom seemed like they were made for giants. And it felt like 14 flights, though I'm sure that's an exaggeration. I signed in with the clerk of the court, who, if I were Catholic, I would say ought to be canonized. His job, in addition to the paperwork, is to create an air of friendliness which helps soothe last-minute jitters. He tells you how it's going to be fun, you're going to enjoy it; everybody looks great--he helps everyone relax.

Next, I met the Marshal, who was decked out in a full-length tuxedo. Once the clerk helps the participants to relax, the Marshal underscores the formality of the whole procedure. He is the one who says "Oyez, oyez, oyez. The Supreme Court of the United States is now in session. All these gathered, draw nigh and speak your piece."

The room itself is awe inspiring. The ceilings in the Supreme Court of the United States are about 30 feet high, or at least they seem like it! They are painted very elaborately--lots of gold, with "Equal justice under the law" in big, fancy letters--and the most ostentatious Greco-Roman architecture imaginable. The justices come walking out in their big dark robes and slam down the gavel. I'm telling you my heart skipped a beat--it was very impressive. I was sitting about eight feet away from the justices, maybe ten. My opponent was just across a little podium from me; we were practically staring into each other's faces.

I knew God was present. It was clear. Even my parents, who don't believe like I do, said "the calmness was eerie." My wife (who does believe like I do) put it a little differently. She said she sensed the presence of the Spirit of God. My parents weren't sure what they sensed, but they knew it was something very much out of the ordinary.

The actual proceedings began with announcements of verdicts from previous cases. Then they started the day's docket. Our case was the first to be heard that day. I could hardly believe it when I heard them say, "Now we'll hear case #86-104: Board of Airport Commissioners et al. versus Jews for Jesus." While the justices were busy raking the opposing counsel over the coals, I was sitting with Barry Fisher (the civil rights attorney who assisted me) changing the strategy of our case. We saw where the judges were headed and we knew we'd have to reply to what was being said.

Half an hour later, I heard a voice call out, "Mr. Sekulow?" And I went up there. Me, a short Jewish guy from Brooklyn, New York, went before the justices of the Supreme Court of the United States to defend the constitutional right to stand in an airport and hand out tracts about Jesus!

I'd prepared my first sentence carefully, because I knew it might be my only opportunity to make a statement. I said: "Mr. Chief Justice, may it please the court, local governments have important interests to protect concerning the efficient operation of the airports under their

156

jurisdiction; however, the facts in this case do not justify the repression of cherished first amendment freedoms based on a broad ban prohibiting all first amendment activities to take place." That's all I got to say. That was it. Because for the next half hour, they grilled me.

Justice Scalia and I got into a dialogue that reminded me of the teacher-student interactions from my days back in law school. He'd say "What if this and this?" and I'd have to answer him. There were times when I had to say, "Your honor, that's exactly what I did not say. You left out such and such." And so it went for the next thirty minutes of what was probably the most intense experience of my life.

I left the courtroom feeling like the Beatles must have felt leaving Shea Stadium. Or for those who might not know the Beatles, I felt like "Rocky" after the fight. If you don't know about Rocky, how about a prima ballerina after her first performance? Okay, so a ballerina I'm not, but I felt great! I knew God had brought me through that trial-- and he'd brought me through much better than I'd dared to hope.

I had walked into the courtroom thinking about Jesus and how he overturned the moneychangers' tables at the Temple. Jesus was an activist; he stood up for what he knew was right. I drew strength from his example.

This case had already been decided in our favor by two lower circuit courts. The judges had ruled that people cannot be excluded from exercising first amendment rights in the airport.

I know it's a sidetrack, but the lawyer in me can't resist cautioning the reader against sympathizing too quickly with the airport commission, which is trying to restrict the distribution of religious literature. Whether or not one appreciates seeing individuals clad in "Jews for Jesus" T-shirts handing out literature at the airport is immaterial. If their rights of free speech are denied in the airport, who knows when and where you may eventually be denied your freedom of speech?

So now you know about my big day in the Supreme Court. And you've probably surmised that my interest in the case was from more than a purely legal perspective. So how did a Jewish kid from New York get involved with Jesus? It happened like this....

I was born on June 10, 1956, in Brooklyn, but we moved to Long Island just after I was born and lived there until I was into my teens. My family attended a Reform synagogue in Long Island; it was not a fancy building, but I remember it had thick, plush drapes. It's funny, the things one remembers. I was very impressed with those drapes; I don't know, maybe because my friend's dad donated them. I liked Friday night services, which we attended about once a month, but Hebrew school, well, unfortunately, none of the kids in our class liked Hebrew school. We were not very well behaved. Sometimes I had the feeling the only reason the cantor didn't kick my friend and me out of the class (which he threatened to do) was because that was the friend whose dad donated the drapes!

"Religion" was not a big topic of discussion in our home. Sometimes my father referred to "The Supreme Being," but he usually reserved such references for the holidays. I didn't think much about God either. I do remember that when I was 13 years old, I'd exchange friendly insults with a Gentile friend of mine, a Catholic. We'd tease each other about our different backgrounds. We were never really serious about it, but I do remember wondering for a brief moment whether Shaun could possibly be right about Jesus. It seemed strange that such a thought would even enter my mind, but it left about as abruptly as it had come. I was pretty secure in my Jewish identity, which, as far as I knew, included not believing in Jesus. Although we weren't "religious," we did many things to reinforce our culture and our heritage. I especially enjoyed the many Jewish celebrations: my bar mitzvah, for example.

That was a red-letter day. Instead of my usual blue yarmulka with the white lining, I wore a white satin yarmulka with gold embroidery, and a tallis to match. Maybe my performance was leaning toward mediocre, but still, to be bar mitzvah signalled the end of Hebrew school and the thrill of "growing up."

Two years later, my family left New York and moved to Atlanta, Georgia. We joined a synagogue which I would describe as "very Reform." In contrast to our little Long Island synagogue, this one was quite elaborate. An ornate chandelier hung from the center of the beautiful domed ceiling; the ark was made of marble and gold, and we had gold velvet cushions on the seats to match.

As with the synagogue, our new home was also fancier than what we had in Long Island. It was a traditional two-story colonial brick house. Even with all the extra space, we still ended up congregating in the kitchen. It wasn't just for meals, although you'd better believe, my mother makes a great meat loaf. The kitchen was also the place for my parents, my two brothers, my sister and me to *shmues* and enjoy each other's company.

My high school grades were pretty much like my bar mitzvah Torah reading—mediocre. It wasn't dull wits or laziness, just a short supply of motivation. I actually enjoyed hard work. In fact, I went out and got a job just as soon as I could. By the time I was 17 years old, I was a night manager at a large department store called "Richway." I had my own set of keys and adult responsibilities. I always loved to work; it's just that I waited until college to start working at my grades.

My original plan was to attend a two-year college for some business education courses, and go straight back to work. After a short stint at the local junior college, I developed an appetite for learning and decided to enroll in a four-year school.

My desire to stay in Atlanta was probably the main reason I looked into Atlanta Baptist College (later known as Mercer University). I visited the school and found the friendly, small campus atmosphere appealing. To add to the appeal, the campus was only a five-minute drive from our house! "Dad," I asked, "Will it bother you if I go to a school that calls itself a Baptist college?" But my Dad is a pragmatic man.

"Baptist-shmaptist," he told me. "I'm glad you decided on a four-year college. Go ahead, get yourself a good education."

I enrolled in Atlanta Baptist College with a competitive determination to outstudy and outsmart "all the Christians." I did well in my pre-law studies, and attacked the mandatory Bible classes with a cynical confidence, certain that it would not be difficult to disprove "their" idea that Jesus was the Messiah.

I met a guy named Glenn Borders, whom I immediately labelled a "Jesus freak." Glenn took his religion seriously. There could be no doubt of that; he wore a big wooden cross around his neck! I knew of Jewish people who wore a rather large "chai" but I'd never seen anything the size of Glenn's cross. Despite his outward appearance, Glenn turned out to be a "regular guy." When we talked, I forgot about the big wood cross--maybe because Glenn wasn't trying to shove it down my throat. It turned out that Glenn played college sports, was active in the student government association, and he even managed to find time to be a good student. Glenn was the kind of person who was there to help if you needed him. He was a good friend. It was partly due to our friendship that my competitive attitude toward the Bible courses I was taking changed to an attitude of genuine curiosity.

Glenn suggested I read Isaiah 53. My mind was boggled by the description of the "suffering servant" who sounded so much like Jesus. I had to be misreading the text. I realized with relief that I was reading from a "King James" Bible, and after all, that's a "Christian" translation. So the first thing I said to Glenn after I read it was "Okay, now give me a real Bible." I grabbed the Jewish text, but the description seemed just as clear. Even though this caught my attention, I wasn't too worried. It still sounded like Jesus in the "Jewish Bible," but there had to be a logical explanation.

I began to research the passage and I started to look for rabbinic interpretations. That's when I began to worry. If I read the passage once, I'm sure I read it 500 times. I looked for as many traditional Jewish interpretations as I could find. A number of them, especially the earlier ones, described the text as a messianic prophecy. Other interpretations claimed the suffering servant was Isaiah himself, or even the nation of Israel, but those explanations were an embarrassment to me. The details in the text obviously don't add up to the prophet Isaiah or the nation of Israel. Did I ask the rabbis? No, I didn't ask the rabbis. I read what the rabbis had written over the years, beginning with ancient times, but frankly, I hadn't been too impressed with anyone I'd met lately. My last impression of what to expect from the Jewish religious establishment had been in a service where, when somebody sneezed the rabbi said, "God bless you." Then he said, "What am I saying? I don't believe in God."

I kept looking for a traditional Jewish explanation that would satisfy, but found none. The only plausible explanation seemed to be Jesus. My Christian friends were suggesting other passages for me to read, such as Daniel 9. As I read, my suspicion that Jesus might really be the Messiah was confirmed. That decision, however, was strictly intellectual. I'd been struggling to resolve this question for about a year, and I was glad to have finally arrived at a decision.

How did I feel about believing that Jesus was the Messiah? Actually, I was half relieved. Once I'd gotten past the point of not wanting to know, once I took out my paper and pencil and began my lists of why Jesus was the Messiah on one side and why he wasn't on the other--I realized something. I had never felt the need for a Messiah before, but now that I was studying the prophecies and reading about what the Messiah was supposed to do, it sounded pretty good. I'd always thought my cultural Judaism was sufficient, but in the course of studying about the Messiah who would die as a sin bearer, I realized that I needed a Messiah to do that for me. When I concluded that Jesus was that Messiah, I was grateful. It didn't occur to me that I needed to do anything about it.

A few days later, one of my Christian friends invited me to hear Jews for Jesus' singing group, The Liberated Wailing Wall. You have no idea what a relief it was to see other Jews who believed that Jesus is the Messiah. Their presentation of "Jewish gospel music" and some of the things they said helped me realize that if I really believed in Jesus, I needed to make a commitment to him. At the end of the program, they sang a song called "I Am Not

Ashamed of the Gospel" and they invited people who wanted to commit their life to Jesus to come up the aisle to meet with them at the front of the church. I responded to that invitation. It was February, 1976.

I wasn't concerned about how my parents would respond. It didn't enter my mind that they might be upset. After all, Jesus was a Jew. I knew that much. I didn't see what the big deal would be about my believing he was the Jewish Messiah. He was Jewish, I was Jewish, I didn't see that there was any reason for us not to believe in him.

As I walked up the aisle in response to the invitation, I got my first hint that Jews who believe in Jesus are sometimes ostracized by family and friends. A lady I'd never met said, "If you get kicked out of your home tonight, you can stay with us." I had a very good relationship with my parents. I didn't smoke, drink, use dope--I didn't give them grief and we were always very close. Did this lady know something that I didn't?

As it turned out, my parents did not react the way I know that some families of Jewish believers have. But after what this woman had said, frankly, I was a little scared. I wasn't prepared for that kind of a reaction, so I decided I wouldn't say anything at first; I'd wait a while. But my relationship with my parents was such that I just couldn't do that. I could not keep such a major decision from them. I tried, but I really couldn't. I got home at about 11 p.m. and went to sleep. I woke up at about two o'clock in the morning. I couldn't go back to sleep, so what did I do? I went and woke my father. I told him I'd decided Jesus was our Messiah. His response was, "*You* decided?" And of course, he was implying, "Who are you to decide?" but he didn't elaborate. He just shook his head sleepily and said, "We'll talk about it in the morning."

Well, morning came, and he didn't say a word about it. Neither did I. My parents knew I believed in Jesus; they knew I was getting literature from Jews for Jesus because I was living at home and they saw it. In fact, I know they read some of it out of curiosity. Sometimes I'd find it in the "reading room" (the bathroom)--not in the trash--just out where it was obvious that my dad had been looking over it.

Since I was living under their roof, I felt if they didn't want to discuss it, I should leave well enough alone. Our relationship didn't change and I have always been grateful that whatever my parents might think of my beliefs, they love and respect me enough to prevent any disagreement from tearing us apart.

It wasn't until three years later that my parents and I actually discussed the subject of Jesus. I was in law school at Mercer at the time. Jews for Jesus ran a gospel statement in the Macon paper, "The Messiah has come and his name is Y'shua." My parents either came across the ad, or I showed it to them; I don't remember which. We discussed it; they didn't agree, but they were never hostile. They knew I was still Jewish; they knew I hadn't undergone any drastic personality changes--I wasn't involved with some strange cult.

I got married in 1978 on my birthday, June 10. I had just completed my first year of law school. I went on to graduate from law school in the top 5% of my class. I began my career at law as a tax prosecutor for the IRS. It was the best experience I could have had. In one sense it's a miserable job; prosecuting people for fraud and tax evasion never won anybody a popularity contest. I even had a few death threats from time to time. What made it worthwhile was the fact that I was trying as many as twelve cases per week. It was phenomenal. That kind of experience can really launch a person into a terrific career--if the person wins his cases, which I did. I stayed with the IRS for about eighteen months, then my name came up for a transfer which I didn't want to take.

At that point, I figured, "If I'm going to set up private practice, now is the time to do it." So I rented space with a friend from law school. Our monthly overhead was about $1600. I thought that was a fortune! I didn't have a client, not one, but I did have some good contacts. In less than eight months, my firm was up to nine lawyers, two full-time CPAs and three para-legals. We were the fastest growing firm in Atlanta. How did we do it? We took on some pretty controversial cases and won. We were known as very tough litigators and we developed a rapport and a good client base. When people were in trouble, they went to Sekulow and Roth.

Stuart Roth and I could hardly believe that our clients were paying us these $25,000 and $35,000 retainers, and here we were just 26 years old. But despite the fact that we were very young, when clients walked out of our office, they knew we were taking care of them.

Both my family and business life were flourishing. My wife and I had a son. In addition to the law practice, I began a real estate development firm which grossed over $20 million after the first year.

I kept in touch with Jews for Jesus and became a member of their board of directors. Business continued to flourish and Pam and I had another son. Yet there was some - thing else I wanted to do. I thought more and more about using my legal skills to serve God. In 1986 I became the Jews for Jesus General Legal Counsel. That is how I happened to be defending a case before the Supreme Court of the United States, as described at the beginning of my story.

Incidentally, the verdict on that case was unanimous. The decisions of the lower circuit courts were upheld, and the Supreme Court declared the airport's resolution to curtail first amendment rights unconstitutional. Since the trial is over, however, I can devote myself to C.A.S.E: Christian Advocates Serving Evangelism. That is what we've named the new organization which will be defending the legal rights of individuals and organizations who are telling the gospel--specifically in issues relating to access, as in parks, college campuses, street corners, and of course, airports. We will work with other groups to ensure that the access to first amendment rights remains protected. It's pretty scary to think that the day could come when people might be prohibited from expressing their beliefs in a public forum. The public, of course, has the right to refuse the literature. If people are annoyed that there are Jews (and others) who believe in Jesus, then so be it. But there are people who are looking for God, for answers to the question of how to know him. They need to hear the good news about the Messiah, and we must protect our right to tell them.

JOSEPH CAPLAN

Joseph Caplan was on his way to becoming a "lord," a nobleman of British society. His father's business was the rag trade, so one might consider this a "rags-to-riches" story... except the story doesn't end there. Caplan's empire crumbled; his wealth, his status and even his health were reversed in a terrible twist of events.  But the story doesn't end there either, for Joseph Caplan went from rags, to riches...to righteousness.

I was determined to joust with the British upper class on their own playing field, and I was absolutely set upon winning whatever they possessed. Jews in Britain are not likely to receive much acclaim or recognition unless they're very wealthy and/or have ties with people "in high places." I wanted the elevating elements of education, profession and personal fortune. And I got them. I got them all. What I didn't get were the words of wisdom and warning from Moses for persons such as myself. These words are set in black and white in the Torah, yet I'd never read them:

> ...then you say in your heart, "My power and the might of my hand have gained me this wealth." And you shall remember the LORD your God, for it is He who give you power to get wealth, that He may establish His covenant which He swore to your fathers, as it is this day. Then it shall be, if you by any means forget the LORD your God, and follow other gods, and serve them and worship them, I testify against you this day that you shall surely perish.

Had I read, understood and accepted those words as a youth, surely my life would have been drastically different. Now I clearly see that the material and social status which I had gone after, were indeed, "other gods."

It is not as though I was a complete stranger to Scripture. My father taught me to read the Torah long before I was 13 years old. Unlike the education many Jewish boys received, the lessons were not merely for the sake of my bar mitzvah; it was very important to my father that I pronounce the Hebrew well as I read from the Torah. Yet, I never learned what the words meant in English. I learned to lay *tefillin*, which I did faithfully each day. My father taught me the appropriate Hebrew prayers for daily Jewish ritual. We celebrated all the Jewish holidays and we spent a great deal of time in the synagogue. But my main impression was that people went there to see and be seen. They dressed up to meet their friends. Our synagogue was not, for most who attended, a place of worship. It was a formality, a tradition, a part of family social life. I also attended cheder three times a week until I was 16 years old. And so I received my religious training. Then I went out into the world to be educated.

Mine was the first generation of Jewish people to be schooled in London. Our grandparents had fled the terrible persecutions of Russia and Poland; our parents, then children, were far too busy learning to survive in new surroundings to bother with schools. Their classrooms were city streets and they learned their lessons quickly, for such teachers as one finds on the streets are not known for their gentility.

My father worked with all his might to support Mother and me. He left our home before the sun rose and did not return until well after it had set. Father ran a small factory in what our people commonly refer to as the *shmatte* business, or the rag trade. He bought rags from "totters." Totters were people who'd roam about the city in little vans--some even used a horse and cart--collecting rags and scraps of metal. On bad days when they couldn't find much, they would steal from here and there, usually bits of lead off churches.

My father employed 20 to 30 people as sorters. After he'd bought the scraps, he'd have them sorted out and then resell them in volume. I spent some time sorting as a boy, but I didn't know much else about the rag trade and I wasn't keen on learning more. It was a gruelling business and I could see that my father only did it because it was the way to put bread and butter on our table. He spent nearly every waking hour at work and thus managed to save enough money to enable me to attend one of the finest British schools.

Most Jews could not attend the top schools in Britain back in the 1940s because they were "church foundation" schools, and routinely barred Jewish pupils and various other "non-Christians" from admission. I was fortunate enough to win the "Junior County Scholarship," which meant I'd graduated with the top few hundred teenagers in the whole of London. The colleges were compelled to give a few places to minority students whose scholastic record placed them "at the top of the heap." I learned at an early age that when one is Jewish, it isn't enough to be merely "very good." One must be the best in order to gain even the smallest bit of recognition or acceptance...at least, this was so where I grew up.

Off I went to college in Dulwich, where I studied for about seven years. I obtained an "Oxford and Cambridge Certificate," which is the equivalent of an American Bachelor of Arts in languages. I proceeded on to the Honorable Society of Lincoln's Inn and earned my law degree, which is called "the Utter Degree of Barrister of Law." I'm not certain, but I believe it would be considered a Doctor of Jurisprudence by American standards.

How I became so keen to study law is still a mystery to me, for I certainly never received encouragement to do so from my family. They are hardworking folk who could not understand why I would spend years studying books instead of earning money, which we all needed. But study I did, and eventually became a criminal lawyer in London and the surrounding towns.

In addition to my formal schooling, I was trained at the Bar with some of the most erudite, famous people in English legal history. My particular mentor was a man by the name of Sir Christmas Humphreys, who was Senior Crown Counsel for the British government. As his pupil, I was present at literally hundreds of murder trials. This was the finest preparation I could possibly have had.

Much of my early experience as a defense lawyer was in the British Armed Forces. Military service was compulsory in Britain--you could do it before or after concluding your studies. I chose to graduate and pass the Bar before enlisting, so I was already a qualified lawyer when I became an officer in the British Army.

I was sent to Northern Ireland where I discovered court-martials taking place daily with absolutely no one there who was professionally qualified to defend the accused. I became something of a public defender once my qualifications were known, since soldiers in the British Army may select any willing officer to defend them. The General in charge was annoyed at having his men defended by a qualified lawyer, but I continued despite his obvious displeasure. It was a very exciting time for me because I had cases to defend every single day.

There was a lot of anti-Semitism in my day in Britain--and I imagine there probably still is--but particularly in the army. I was the only Jew in the officers' club, and was given a rather cold shoulder by my peers. Despite my Orthodox upbringing, I was not religious. My Jewish identity lay more in somehow beating the system--gaining the acceptance and respect of those around me without compromising my Jewish identity. I was a bit like a character in a movie which was popular some years ago--"Chariots of Fire." The film was about champion runners, and their range of motivation and personal standards in competition. One of the characters, Harold Abrahams, was Jewish; he was an excellent runner, very fast. He ran races almost with a vengeance. He ran to prove a point, so that people would know he was a winner and a Jew. Like him, I wanted the respect so often withheld from my people, but I wanted it on my own terms: as a winner and a Jew.

At one point, several officers were arrested for unauthorized driving of an army vehicle with a civilian passenger. It might seem like a small infraction, but the forces take these prohibitions and regulations very seriously and punishment could have been quite severe. The men asked me to defend them and though things looked pretty bleak, I was able to defend them successfully. I was quite popular after that. Between the easing of social tensions and the opportunities to practice my new profession, I rather enjoyed the rest of my time in the service.

The day I was discharged from the British army my father met me at the train station, and I recall thinking he looked terribly ill. He didn't complain of any sickness so I thought perhaps his age was just beginning to show. He continued on with his business and I began practicing law in London.

I loved being an attorney. Britain has a "two-tier" legal system: there are "solicitors" and there are "barristers." Solicitors deal with legal matters but are not members of the Bar and may not plead cases in superior courts. A barrister is a court attorney, and that was my profession.

Criminal lawyers deal with very ordinary people, at least beginners do. I defended crooks and homosexuals, prostitutes and people who simply "stole a loaf of bread." Britain has a means by which legal counsel is made available to everyone--it's known as the "Legal Aid System." The courts have a "dock brief," where all the barristers who are looking for a case line up opposite a row of people who are about to be tried. One man points a finger and says, "I'll 'ave 'im," and the next nods his head at another lawyer and says, "I'll 'ave 'im." Young barristers get experience by becoming the "him" someone fancies will do a good job of pleading his case.

I'll always remember one man in particular; after he'd received a two-year sentence for stealing, he put his arm around me and said, "I know, guv, you worked very 'ard, you got nothin' for it, but never mind. I got a smashing job to do when I get out, and I'll see you all right." Well, I would've liked to have "seen him all right" but I never heard from the man again. I was young, just starting really, and his promise had made a strong impression on me. He taught me an important lesson--that people break their promises. In fact, as I later learned, very few people keep them.

I was finishing my second year as a barrister when my father was suddenly taken to the hospital with a massive heart attack. I had no brothers or sisters who could take over my father's affairs. Consequently, I had to leave my profession overnight to handle my father's business--the condition of which was nearly as grave as my father's health. There was simply no other choice. It was like being shot from a double barrel; the grief and fear of knowing my father's life was in mortal danger was compounded with the grief and frustration of losing my career in law.

The business was in a district called Camberwell, in London. It was, and I imagine probably still is, one of the worst parts of London. It was a very rough neighborhood. People who drifted in and out of prison would congregate there and perhaps they still do. It was completely bewildering to dive head first into a place like Camberwell after spending nearly two heady years as a barrister.

I'd gone from the utter dignity of the English Bar, where lawyers still wear wigs and gowns in court, to the profane language of a profession which horrified me. I'd never heard my father use a swear word in my whole life, not ever. He must have warned his men to guard their tongues when I was around as a boy. Now he was in the hospital and in his absence, everyone with whom I came in contact felt quite free to swear and cuss.

I, too, learned to speak a language of filth as I adapted to the conditions of my environment. That, of course, was wrong. One needn't go up or down to anybody else's level in order to be successful with them. But of course when you're young and battered, you don't know that.

Suddenly I discovered myself facing large debts from a business about which I knew nothing. My father, out of concern for old friends, had been reluctant to sack workers he could not afford to pay. I had no partners, no money, and no credit, whatsoever. I had to pay cash on delivery on any goods--on absolutely everything from the moment my father was in the hospital. An array of small creditors climbed onto my back and became my constant but unwelcome companions.

The creditors demeaned my dignity and utterly humiliated me. It was a hellish ordeal. I became very bitter and very angry. People ask what motivated me to create the financial empire I eventually built, and I think it was largely to do with pride. My pride had been violently attacked and terribly wounded, but not destroyed.

I'd spent years studying for a profession, and I'd had to fight for every inch of progress. Now, just as I was getting on my feet, my career was obliterated by circumstances completely beyond my control. I was angry with my father for I felt he'd let me down; I was angry with the world, I was absolutely penniless...and I was determined to show everyone that I would come out on top, even though they were, so to speak, spitting on me down the phone every single day of my life. Fueled by anger and bitterness, I was very motivated indeed to succeed.

I had to dismiss nearly all the staff. I didn't want to let them go; I simply had no money to pay them. Twenty-eight people lost their jobs within 14 days. This in itself was a tragedy because Father had employed many of those people for 10 to 20 years, some even longer. The pain and humiliation was compounded. I had to bear the stress alone--my father was incapable of speaking to me at that time--he was far too ill. And so I went round from house to house, collecting rags myself with only two or three people to help.

I immediately formed a new little partnership with an uncle, in which we shared 50/50. I formed another small partnership with a cousin, also 50/50. Next, I rented out part of our premises to bring in a little income. With whatever was left, however meager, we kept things going. In addition to my anger and bitterness, I was very confused. I was a young man. I didn't understand why all this was happening to me. I certainly couldn't see how I was going to get out of it.

I did deals, I did whatever I thought I had to do to survive. People fight harder when they've seen better times and they have something to aim for. I'd never been wealthy, but I knew what it meant to live normally, as opposed to sweating out each day in a pit of despair such as Camberwell.

I never planned to return to the Bar as a practicing attorney. But I did plan to reestablish what I felt was all-important--my dignity. No one lifted a finger to help. It was quite the reverse. I was subjected to constant insults and abuse. Perhaps my pride invited some of the ill-mannered behavior. It's part of the British way for people to relish puncturing what they regard as self-inflated ego.

My father made a very slow recovery. He was in the hospital for months, I've forgotten how long now. I do remember that religion was absolutely no comfort to me during that time. I didn't feel there was anyone to whom I could turn. It never occurred to me that I should speak to God. I was still able to recite the prayers I'd learned in perfect Hebrew, but it never occurred to me to do so. No messages or words of comfort came to me from the Bible. No ritual offered the strength and consolation I needed. Thus, when the worst was over, I felt I had no one to thank but myself for the grip I'd been able to keep on my father's business and the grip I'd been able to keep on my sanity. I managed, by myself, thank you very much, to get his business back on an even keel.

Eventually, my father was able to return to the rag trade. It was about that time that Valerie and I got married. She is better than I at telling the story so I'll ask her to carry on.

Valerie: It was 1959 when Joseph and I met at a Jewish hotel. There are a few such places in Britain, strictly kosher. They were quite the social nests, where Jewish people could come to meet each other. Joseph's grandparents, the Hersches (formerly Hershkovitz) spent a great deal of time at this particular hotel. I happened to be there with my mother, who knew the hotel owner.

One day, the owner told me that the most fabulous boy had arrived, Mrs. Hersch's grandson. She then went into a long description of this "fabulous boy," and I thought, well, that sounds nice. It was "off season" and there were no other teenagers around.

The owner of this hotel sat by the entrance to the dining room and she more or less controlled everything. She'd keep an eye on who came in and who went out, and she had a word for just about everybody. One evening my mother and I were on our way out, and since she'd known my mother for many years, she stopped us to have a little chat. Once again, she mentioned this "fabulous boy." Then she caught sight of him and called him over to introduce us. Joseph was very polite; he said "How do you do?" and then he walked away! I thought to myself, "She can't mean him. That can't be the wonderful boy she's been talking about." But it was.

We were one or two generations younger than everybody else at the hotel, so we were sort of thrown together; we had no one else to talk to. And that's how we got to know each other. Joseph turned out to be much nicer than my first impression had led me to believe. He was very intelligent and showed tremendous depth of feeling. I found I enjoyed his company immensely. And I came to the conclusion that he was a fabulous boy after all. Convincing my parents of that, however, took some time.

My family lived in an upwardly mobile Jewish suburb of London. Like Joseph, I was an only child. My father was moderately successful, and we led a comfortable middle class Jewish life. My parents were not quite as observant as Joseph's, but being Jewish was definitely central to our family identity.

I was perhaps a bit more conscious of the "religious" aspect of being Jewish than my parents. When I was 16, I was quite ill and it was thought that I had polio. During that illness, I made a commitment to God that I would be the best Jew I could be. I recovered, and began a "search" for God. My concept of God, however, was vague--I just knew he was there and I always believed that if I prayed hard enough, he would hear and eventually answer. It troubled me that I didn't know what to do or how to keep the promise I'd made. I felt a sense of responsibility, but I didn't know how I could meet my obligation.

I did begin by aggressively searching for ways of getting closer to God via Orthodox Judaism. I spoke to rabbis and others whom I regarded as Orthodox whenever I had the opportunity. I asked a lot of questions, but seemed to reach a lot of dead ends. Nothing anyone told me made me feel any closer to God or any closer to being a "good Jew."

I'd like to jump forward in time for just a moment regarding this same issue. Years after Joseph and I were married, I was still trying to figure out how to keep the promise I'd made to God. One night, I was flying from Kennedy International Airport in New York City to Monte Carlo (where we were living at the time) and my flight was delayed for three hours. As I sat in the airport, I found a pamphlet on the seat beside me. It said something about Jews and Jesus on the cover. I looked at the pamphlet for several moments, trying to decide whether it was all right for me to read it. I had nothing else to read, I had plenty of time, and I was curious. So I read it. It was a Jews for Jesus tract telling about Jesus being the Jewish Messiah. As I read, everything seemed to come together at that moment and make complete sense. It was as though a light bulb went on

174

in my head. When I got back to Monte Carlo I asked some people whom I considered knowledgeable whether or not Jesus could be the Jewish Messiah. They told me no, he definitely could not. They had heard about Jews who believed in Jesus, but those Jews were crazy, and there was nothing to their ideas. That was all I needed to hear. I dismissed, for the moment, the idea of Jesus. But I never forgot it.

Coming back to Joseph and the situation when we got together--he didn't seem particularly interested in religion at all. His Orthodox background hadn't given him the experience with God that I was seeking. When we began courting, I became less aggressive in my search for God, although it was a constant thought in the back of my mind.

We'd met just about the time Joseph failed his first bar exam. He was still a long way from being a practicing barrister; once he finished his studies and passed the exam, he'd still have two years of service in the army. My father didn't understand why I'd "waste my time" with him.

You see, my parents had always assumed that I would marry some wealthy young lord, Jewish of course. I don't know where they thought I was going to find this wealthy young Jewish lord, but Joseph didn't fit the picture. He came from a poor family and that wasn't what my parents had in mind for their daughter. I remember the evening that Joseph showed up at our door to escort me to dinner-- without a car. My father was very upset. Joseph had to borrow my father's car because he wasn't about to allow me out of the house with a man who expected me to take public transportation.

At any rate, Joseph went through a great deal before we finally married in 1959. Though he was far from being a wealthy young lord, I'm sure Joseph earned my parents' respect and admiration for the way he was able to keep the business afloat during his father's illness. And then, later, he did go on to distinguish himself and was, in fact, able to provide all the things my parents had hoped I would someday have.

When we returned from our honeymoon, I told Joseph, "Whatever else you choose to do in life, you must not go back to the rag trade--it's just not you. You can go back to the Bar, or you can go into something else, but please don't go back to a job that will only make you miserable." Joseph agreed.

Joseph: When we came back from our honeymoon I told my father, much to his anger, that I was not going to stay in the rag trade. He was quite scornful about it; he couldn't imagine what else I could do.

In the 13 years that followed, I worked all the hours a human being can work without collapsing. And what did I have to show for it? I was chairman and chief executive of what became a $350,000,000 business. I had 26 banking branches throughout Britain as well as businesses throughout other countries. We owned the second largest pharmacy group in the United Kingdom with 256 pharmacies. We were very powerful and had enormous drawing facilities. Our turnover in dollars must have been $5 million a week at least, perhaps more. Including the money market turnover, I suppose it was $10 to $20 million a week. People described it as a financial empire, with assets in several countries and between ten to fifteen thousand employees. One might wonder how we got from the rag trade to the situation I've just described.

Valerie and I began our life together in a modest apartment in an area called St. John's Wood in the northwest of London. We lived right opposite the Underground station--I couldn't even afford a car, although my wife did have one.

But I remember taking the Underground. I particularly remember a day when other people stayed home and played bridge because we'd had an unusually huge snowfall, and the trains weren't running. Everyone else seemed delighted to get off work. I wasn't delighted--I walked all the way from Highgate (where we were then living) into the city of London because I couldn't bear to go one day without working. That was the Jewish way.

When I left the "rag trade," I began working with a little business my father had. It was called a loan club. People saved up money each week, and at Christmas they would get their money back with a small interest. I took over and began dealing with the seven or eight customers involved. I expanded the business by going from door to door, encouraging others to join this club. I obviously couldn't go to the elite professionals from the Bar to collect five, ten, twenty dollars a week...so I stayed in Camberwell.

One day I noticed a tailor shop on Camberwell High Street (the main street in town). They advertised extended credit for customers; if a person wanted a suit, they could buy it over a period of 20 weeks. I did a quick calculation of how much more people paid using this installment plan, and the rate of interest worked out between 30% and 40% true annual return.

That was my first lesson in moneylending. I then looked up a man whom I'd met through my father, a man by the name of Sidney Keston. He was also in the shmatte business, and he also had about 20 of these customers in a loan club of his own. By then I had 10 or 15 customers, and we merged our two "businesses."

Sidney and I went from door to door, day after day and night after night. We drank whiskey with people and we talked to them about handling their savings. We were a very good team. I was young, energetic and educated, while Sid was an old man and not educated, but an earthy and practical person who knew everyone in the East End of London.

Soon we had dozens of customers saving a fraction of their weekly earnings. We printed up little savings cards. Then we began lending the money out on a 20-week basis. Before too long, maybe a year or 18 months, I'd taken a two-room office on the third floor of a building in a part of town which was about to be demolished. I still remember the rent: it was ten pounds per week, which was then about $30. That little office served us well for a couple of years.

I began to outgrow the loan club. I searched for ways to expand, and discovered a hundred-year-old defunct company which had been in the discount business. Its value was approximately $50,000. I borrowed about $20,000 from one bank and my wife borrowed $20,000 from another. I think it was a cousin of mine who borrowed the rest. And we bought this business.

Once I had a "real" business, my whole perspective widened considerably and I began to look at things from a legal standpoint. I needed a moneylender's license, which I promptly acquired. However, it's very tough being a licensed moneylender in Britain. Under the 1923 Moneylending Act, there were piles of paperwork you had to provide each customer, with a lengthy document for him or her to sign. If any mistakes were made or documents left unsigned, all the money you lent that person was forfeit-- the customer could simply refuse payment. It was a very complicated business!

It was much more desirable to be a bank than a moneylending institution, because banks do not operate under a moneylending license. Growing from a moneylending business to a recognized bank in Britain was a process which literally took years. One of the first things one had to do in order to become a bank was issue checks. I printed up checks, but it wasn't easy to persuade our customers to bring them to their banks!

A person can write out a check on an egg, and that would be considered legally binding. It's what the check represents that counts, not what the check looks like. Nevertheless, people balk when they see something different, and although my checks were meant to have dignity, I'm afraid they didn't quite appear that way to most people. The name of the company I'd purchased was a long-winded, non-banking, non-professional name, and of course, it was one nobody had ever heard of--"London and County Advance and Discount Company." It sounded nothing like "Lloyds Bank" or "Barclays Bank." And so people were bound to look askance when they saw the name on our checks.

There I was on the third floor, way in the back of an office building in the Strand area of London. The clearing banks, such as Lloyds, Barclays, Midland, and National Westminster were obliged to come to our little premises and collect payment on the checks our customers had brought them.

Well, the big banks refused to accept our checks as payment; they wanted cash. When one is just starting out, keeping enough cash on the premises to meet the checks one's customers have written is a ludicrously impossible task. It was hysterical; it was absolutely amazing. The bank couriers knew we didn't have that much cash on hand. We had to keep them waiting while we ran downstairs to the "real bank." We'd pick up the cash needed to cover the checks, run back upstairs, and give these couriers the money. They really didn't like it any better than we did, and after a while they complained to the big banks that they didn't want to carry around all this cash anymore.

Finally, after many months, instead of insisting on cash, they began to take our checks. At first, they wouldn't take an ordinary check; they wanted what is known in the States as a cashier's check. I couldn't issue my own cashier's check so I still had to keep the messengers waiting while I went downstairs to get a cashier's check. But it was a step in the right direction. And over a period of time, the banks finally recognized the fact that we were able to back our checks, and they began accepting them.

Recognition comes slowly in Britain, and it's next to impossible unless you have someone with you who "knows the ropes." I was fortunate enough to employ a man who'd worked most of his life as a manager in one of the major banks in London. He was in his sixties and was virtually retired, otherwise he wouldn't have come to work for me. Nevertheless I was very happy to have him; he showed me all the steps one needs to take in order to become a bank. We began getting various minor licenses and recognitions and then, as we began to grow, we acquired the more important licenses until eventually, we became one of the recognized banks in London, England. What finally shifted the scales in our favor was the volume of business we were doing.

How did we grow? We purchased mailing lists and used them to advertise nationwide. We sent out about 5,000,000 brochures which described our little company and invited people to deposit with us at a rate of interest which was probably a point or two higher than the national rate. I could barely afford the mailing and I had no way of paying for the return postage on our "postage-paid" business reply envelopes. We relied completely upon money coming in as a result of these advertisements to pay the bills, and that's exactly what happened. By 1973, we had over $300 million on deposit.

The years went by and as we grew, we began to take over other companies. My strong point was the merger of corporations; I dealt well with people on the negotiating level. I was known as a person who would keep his word. I stood behind my promises and agreements, even when it turned out that the deal wasn't so good for me and I knew I could get away with backing out. As a result, people grew to trust me and they began to bring me deals...and deals...and deals. We thus arrived at the point of success which I described earlier.

Our days of apartment dwelling and taking the Underground were over. This was the sweet victory I'd dreamed of when I was sweating it out with the small creditors in the rag trade. This had been my goal: to be in a position where no one would ever be able to humiliate me again--to be in a position which would be the envy of those who had thought I would never make it.

By the time we had achieved what I considered success, Valerie and I owned four homes. In Totteridge (an elegant outer suburb), we owned "Dell House," a mansion overlooking 100 acres, all laid out by a famous Victorian architect. The views were breathtaking. Then there was "The Tower House" in Regents Park (central London). That home had been built for Queen Victoria's physician by the Prince Regent. It was designed by Nash. House number three was a villa in Malta, where I had frequent business dealings. The fourth home was for holidays; it was in the South of France, overlooking the Mediterranean. And that is how we lived.

I was very conceited, very headstrong, very sure of myself. My wife's social diary was booked up one year in advance, from December to December. I felt I was entirely responsible for my own success. It was very important to me that I was finally "vindicated" for the insults and abuse I'd borne years ago as a young man, bewildered and broken-hearted over my father's sudden illness, the loss of my career, and the burden of taking over a business about which I knew nothing. Having survived all that, I finally had what I wanted--wealth, power and recognition.

I was not the least bit interested in spiritual things, although Valerie felt some discontent in that area.

Valerie: I can recall this as if it were yesterday, though it was actually many years ago. Joseph and I owned a yacht and on that yacht there was a large sunbathing deck. We were out at sea and I was stretched out on this sunbathing deck holding a rather large glass of champagne. I looked around and I saw the gorgeous view; the sun was delightful, as was the champagne and I thought, "This is really wonderful...why aren't I happier? What's missing? And what about everybody else? They must be absolutely miserable--after all, I've got all this and I'm not overjoyed. Why am I not overjoyed, and how can people who have less stand the unhappiness?" I realized that I lacked the satisfaction I had assumed this lifestyle would bring, and I couldn't think what else I could add to my life that would give me more joy.

Joseph: Well, those were Valerie's feelings about our success and our lifestyle. I was feeling highly ambitious and still eager to see what more could be gotten, what more could be done, how much higher I could climb.

What happened was this: The bank was very successful. It hadn't reached its peak, but it was successful enough that some rather important people were beginning to take notice. And I was suddenly approached by a very close personal friend of the Right Honorable Jeremy Thorpe, who was then a Member of Parliament and a Privy Counselor. This man, Robin Sallenger, suggested I put his famed friend on my board of directors. After paying Sallenger a fee of approximately $30,000 to meet the man, that's precisely what I did.

Thorpe was the leader of the Liberal Party in Britain at that time. He was a very charismatic person, and he commanded the balance of power between the Conservatives and the Labor Party. There were many who thought he was likely to be the next Prime Minister of Britain. His party was growing and I felt this would be a very advantageous connection. I was about to open up several banking branches, and had visions of the publicity he would bring and the confidence he would inspire in potential depositors. The possibilities were intriguing.

So I made the Privy Counselor a director on my board. This gave me prestige, which was very important to me at the time.

I discovered that his reason for joining the board was financial. He needed the income we paid and he also hoped I would make substantial contributions to the Liberal Party, which I never did because I was basically Conservative. Yet I did not let my politics interfere with the obvious business advantage of having such a well-known public figure on my board.

As I opened new branches throughout the United Kingdom, my celebrated board member was always there to officially open the bank. We always got the best publicity...the Liberal Party's public relations people saw to that.

I never intended to become actively involved in politics. I expected that in return for what I'd done for Thorpe, (the publicity and the salary which his position on my board afforded him) I would receive a title. I could see myself being knighted...and for a Jew to be knighted in Britain was a rare achievement. One would not only have to be very wealthy, but very well-connected. And you see, this man had very close ties with royalty in Britain. His wife, Marion, former Countess of Harewood, had been previously married to the Queen's cousin. He left her for another woman, but the Countess of Harewood remained in the Queen's favor and maintained her ties with the royal family after she remarried.

These are the sorts of connections one pays attention to if one has aspirations of joining that most elite layer of the "upper crust." And having acquired most of the material things I desired, the status of being knighted seemed the next logical thing for me to pursue. Jeremy Thorpe had the power to confer knighthood upon two people per year. I might well have attained my goal had it not been for the cataclysmic events which followed. I was completely unaware of the scandal which was brewing up around him.

Nevertheless, the attack which was finally launched against him was of incredible proportions. As was mentioned, this man was becoming a major political force in the United Kingdom and had the potential of becoming Prime Minister if his support continued to grow. So, of course, there were those who were intent on bringing him down. They began a campaign against him with accusations involving my bank, and the attack escalated when it became known that Thorpe was apparently being blackmailed by his homosexual lover. It is now a matter of public record that in the year of 1978, he was accused of attempting to murder his blackmailer. His private life became very public--a national disgrace. For all the appearance of propriety which he presented, apparently there seemed to be a great deal of impropriety which the press had a field day exposing--and, of course, that didn't do me a bit of good.

Much of the problem I faced in 1973 was due to the scathing publicity I received because this man was on my board of directors. Many hundreds of thousands of dollars of deposits were withdrawn from my bank because every time he was attacked, I was the *coconut shy*. At one time, I was warned that if I didn't get him off my board, I would be in great trouble. I spoke to him about resigning a number of times, but each time I did so, he would call me "Sir" or "my lord" and assure me that my forthcoming title would more than compensate my company for whatever damage the adverse publicity might do. By the time I realized that would not be the case, it was too late.

At first, the publicity had to do with interest rates. One of our banking divisions conducted what is known as "second mortgages," or the lending of money against second mortgages. The rates of interest on such loans were very high, not only at our bank, but throughout Britain. Suddenly, I found our bank plastered on the front page of most London newspapers. Imagine my surprise when I read about the sky-high interest rates at "Thorpe's bank." The attacks on this man and "his bank" (which, of course, was actually my bank, although my name was never mentioned in conjunction with it) continued relentlessly. At no time was the press willing to see or talk to me regarding these allegations.

That was the beginning of the end for me...in January of 1973. I had another warning from one of my best friends in the press. His name was John Davis; he was the financial editor of *The Observer.* He was told that there would be trouble with Thorpe; in fact, someone bet him a case of champagne that my company wouldn't survive it. Mr Davis lost his case of champagne. Lest you think he was being hard-hearted, he told my wife with tears in his eyes that he was sorry things had turned out so badly for us.

The collapse of the bank came about during a horrendous time in British economy. Oil costs were quadrupling and interest rates went up to 22-25%. Money became very scarce. All the "secondary banks" (those such as mine which were not one of the "big five") had difficulty maintaining credit lines.

When signs of trouble appeared, we began to have meetings with the Bank of England, and what was called a "consortium" was put together. A consortium is a group of banks and institutions which are brought together for a financial purpose. In our case, the purpose was to provide temporary financing, perhaps a $100 million or some such figure which would enable our bank to get through our temporary liquidity problems.

The consortium consisted of Keyser Ullman, a major bank (one of the largest in Britain, which also "went to the wall"), Eagle Star Insurance Company, the Bank of England itself, and several other interested institutions. The consortium was not antagonistic to our interests; their object was to support us and help us through the rough waters.

Together, we designed a program which would have easily enabled my bank to continue until the bad publicity died down. But the whole country was shivering from high interest rates--major groups were producing balance sheets showing lost capital due to the stock market collapse which took place at that time. And we were double-crossed by the Bank of England; they changed their mind about helping us.

It turned out that my own attorney, Leonard Sainer, was also a director of First National Finance, a company which was trying to take me over. Eventually, the Bank of England allowed them to do so. (Incidentally, a year later, they went bankrupt.) It was Jeremy Thorpe who actually signed the takeover of the bank to First National.

It was three o'clock in the morning at a meeting of the consortium; I was exhausted and Sainer said I might as well go home because there was nothing more I could do that night. During my absence, and with no other board members present, Jeremy Thorpe signed a document which was accepted by the Bank of England as legal. Of course I started major lawsuits against him immediately, but Britain is quite different from America. Many attorneys were just unwilling and unable to take action against such a powerful figure. Everyone was warned off the case. And that was that.

The whole of the financial field in Britain was in a terrible mess from September of '73 to about the same time in '74. About 28 banks collapsed after mine and I was accused of causing it all. The devastating loss of my own empire was bad enough--but to be held responsible for losses all across the nation was unbearable. The anger, the intense frustration I thought I'd left behind me with the rag trade came rushing back with even greater force.

My business was dissipated by liquidators and many assets were sold for a fraction of their true value. I was blamed for all the losses. This led to a "Board of Trade Inquiry." When a major company collapses, it is normal to have a Board of Trade Inquiry--it's something like the Better Business Bureau, only it's at a higher level. It's a government-sponsored body, and it's out to look for trouble. The Board of Trade Inquiry was a very prolonged, humiliating experience.

I came to every meeting of that Inquiry that I was asked to attend. I was accompanied by Sir David Napley, who, at the time, was my attorney. Later on he became Jeremy Thorpe's attorney.

There was a stream of events which I went through very much in a daze. I was taking a great deal of valium and drinking a great deal of whiskey. When one has worked for 13 years to build an empire and suddenly it seems the fruit of all one's labor hangs upon what somebody else happens to decide on a given day, it does something to one's mind. It makes it extremely difficult to function normally.

Valerie and I didn't realize that I was in what is known as a deep clinical depression. I was suffering from shock after the collapse of the bank. I would say to Valerie, "Is it Monday or Tuesday?" and she would answer "It's Wednesday." Five minutes later I'd say, "Did you say it's Monday?" And we'd go over it time and time again. That's what happens when people are in shock. Obviously, the combination of whiskey and valium didn't do much to clear my mind. Valerie just thought, "Well, he'll be alright next week, he'll get over it soon...," and it went on for about three years.

If you've ever gone skiing, you know that it takes a long time getting up the hill, but you go down very quickly and it's all over.

On the way up, many people were in constant touch with me, wanting to know what great deals I was making, what shares they should buy and so on. In the first year that I went public, Sir Isaac Wolfson, later Lord Wolfson, telephoned me. I'll always remember what he said: "Mr Caplan, you've had a great success in the market. Will you come and have a cup of tea with me?" And surely I went to have more than one cup of tea with him. I visited him many times. He owned the Anglo-Israel bank. He wanted to combine his bank with mine. But that was the first year of my career, and I was much too headstrong and full of my own success to submit to Sir Isaac Wolfson, though he was a great financial figure.

On the way down, there were no phone calls or words of encouragement from those who had taken an interest in my success. I was alone.

We lost just about everything. We had to sell the lease on The Tower House. Our beautiful home in

Totteridge went to pay off my debts. I owed a great deal of money--millions and millions of dollars--to just a few people. We brought all these people together and offered our house with all its wonderful antiques--we put the whole thing together and I said, "Look, this is what we've got. You can make me bankrupt, or whatever all this is worth, you can take it." And take it they did. When I left Britain, I was free of debt, because it had all been settled by my attorneys with various banks and individuals.

We emigrated from Britain in November of 1974. Valerie and I, with our daughter (who was only 2 years old at the time), moved to Monte Carlo--we had kept the "holiday home" which became our residence until 1977. Our son stayed at Mill Hill School in London...at least for a while.

My wife's parents and mine both lived close to Mill Hill, so our son boarded there. We wanted very much for him to finish his schooling there. But kids can be very cruel to each other, and all the bad publicity about me prompted much slander.

My son was constantly getting into fights. His teachers were not sympathetic; no one helped him. I could do nothing for him. My phone calls and letters served no purpose at all, because he was trying to live a teenage life in a hostile environment. Finally, it became utterly impossible for him to stay in Mill Hill. We sent him to school in Switzerland.

I spent most of my time in Monte Carlo feeling sorry for myself--"licking my wounds," as they say. The one constructive thing I accomplished in France was to stop drinking like a fish. I occupied myself by practicing judo quite regularly. But I continued taking the valium.

Every now and then we would take what remained of our furniture--which was all antique--and we'd sell it for money to live on. My wife was incredible. Valerie's the classic wife: the wife who doesn't leave the husband when there's trouble, the wife who knows when not to nag him about going back to work, the wife who carefully watches diminished family finances and doesn't put pressure on at the wrong time. She was just wonderful and I thank God every day of my life for blessing me with such a family.

At one point, I did try to do business in France. I formed a consultancy called "European Business Consultants." I lasted with that for about a year, until a sudden upsurge of more publicity was precipitated by the publication of the Board of Trade Inquiry report.

I'd been in northern France on business and when I flew back to Monte Carlo, my three partners, an attorney, an accountant and the businessman who'd financed our venture were all awaiting me with glum faces. I was thrown out of the company within ten seconds of my arrival. There was no point in resisting resignation, because there'd been such bad publicity following the publication of the report.

The British approach to failure is quite different from the American approach. Americans tend to sympathize with the "underdog." In Britain, we don't really have underdogs--we have scapegoats, of which I became the classic example. Once the press condemned me, there was little I could do to reverse my situation.

There was a time period when I had hundreds of interviews with newspaper reporters. Nothing I said to clear the issue was ever published for two reasons. First, I was the guy they were driving to the wall, so they didn't want to publish any good news about me. Second, in Britain there is a much higher danger of libel and slander suits than there is in America. It's astonishing, the accusations the press can make here in the U.S. without fear of lawsuits. In Britain, newspapers are incredibly vulnerable to lawsuits for libel and slander. And there I was, accusing some rather important people of doing the things for which I had been blamed.

Instead of meaningful press coverage, they wanted photographs of me, my wife, the baby, the car--the kinds of things that the public likes to read about. All sorts of articles appeared in the newspapers, none of which were even remotely accurate. There comes a point where one simply will not deal with the press any longer, and at that point they seem to enjoy what is perceived as the intrigue of one's refusal to grant an interview.

And so the press hounded us frequently. One night we came home to find Scruffy, our Welsh Collie, unconscious. At first we thought he was dead--then we realized they'd drugged the dog in order to get into the house. They'd tried to open the garage to see what kind of cars we had. This is typical press "follow-up," not at all unusual. The "what are they doing now?" stories are very popular.

One incident which summed up the press's attitude happened before I had to leave the business consultancy. I was in a restaurant with a businessman from America and one of my partners. We were discussing a potential transaction, when into the restaurant walked a man who later proved to be a reporter. I didn't know who he was; I'd never seen him before. He had a large camera, and he knelt to take my photograph. I reached in before he could do so, removed his camera, lifted him to his feet and walked him to the door. There, a restaurant employee ordered him off the premises. I had not said one word to him other than, "I do not want you to take my photograph with my friends." That's all I said to him. There was no interview, no discussion.

About three days later, an article appeared in a newspaper to inform the public of how I played regular tennis with my good friend Prince Rainier, and that I was seen sipping champagne with various important people in a restaurant overlooking the palace. I've never played tennis in my life, nor have I ever met Prince Rainier. I was abstaining from alcohol; my drink at the time was tomato juice. There may have been a very distant view of the palace, but the restaurant was hardly overlooking it.

It became obvious that living in France held no solution to our problems, so we finally decided to come to America in 1977. At first, I refused to see the press here as well. Later, I did everything I could to meet with reporters because I hoped I'd have an opportunity to tell my side of the story.

I formed a small company with an American partner. We brought people together as a syndicate to purchase land. It is a common practice here for finders to collect 20% commission on a purchase by locating the land, bringing the

189

buyers together, managing the transaction, making the profit and then keeping 20%. With no capital of my own, that was all I could do. But it was something; it kept me occupied and, of course, we needed the income.

In the midst of this, I was totally unaware that the British government was planning to bring me back to England to stand trial. There was a vital connection between the Thorpe trial which was about to take place there and the desire of the British government to bring me back at the same time. The people on my case, Chief Inspector Challis and Inspector Constable (his surname really is "Constable"), were the same two people who were on Thorpe's case. The authorities believed I was involved in his "attempted murder" scandal. They wanted to get at my bank statements to try to prove that I'd been involved in hiring the killer. Why they thought a man in my position would involve himself in hiring a "hit man" is beyond me. Nevertheless, the only way to get at someone's bank statements in Britain is to accuse them of some violation. And you can look into the books of virtually any major company and find all kinds of technicalities to throw at someone if need be.

We now have reason to believe that it was Thorpe the authorities wanted more than me. I would have been a strong asset to them had I stood trial in Britain, no matter what the charges, because of the publicity. Thorpe was involved in one of the most sensational trials Britain has ever seen. If they could have brought in a former colleague to stand trial as well, any adverse publicity I might receive would help to drive a few more nails into Thorpe's coffin. Accusations against me would reflect on him, since he'd been a major presence in my bank. In addition, they knew he had dealt dishonestly with me, so they assumed I would not go out of my way to protect him.

Shortly after I learned that the British government was planning to extradite me, the most dramatic and frightening experience of my life occurred--a crisis from which I believe God himself delivered me.

It began with a very routine procedure. I needed company medical insurance, so I went for an examination. As far as I was concerned, I was very fit. There was no place for me to practice judo, but I was practicing karate regularly instead. I felt great physically; I was working very hard, trying to build up a business again. The doctors put me on a treadmill--I'd never been on one before--and they hooked me up with all the wires and gadgets.

I was going along on this treadmill and they kept saying to me, "Are you out of breath?" I said "No." "Do you have any pain?" I said "No." "How do you feel? Do you want to stop?" I said "No." I plodded on for about 12 minutes and they told me they wanted me to come back the following day. I returned the following day and did the same thing again. They then took my wife into another room and told her that I should have surgery the following morning at 8 o'clock. Otherwise, they said, and I quote, they would "not be responsible for him [me] reaching home alive."

Of course I didn't believe them. First, I felt fine. Second, I hadn't lived there long and I was very wary. I assumed these doctors were looking for a $50,000 fee, or whatever the fee for such a procedure was. We went to another hospital in Santa Monica and saw a different cardiologist, who ordered an angiogram for me. The results of the angiogram showed that I had three major heart blockages. Two of my valves were completely blocked, and a third was about 90% blocked.

And then it was a reality. Three or four days later, I began to feel chest pains. The physical pain did not compare with the emotional anguish it caused me to realize how very helpless I'd become--seemingly, once more--overnight. I'd been very fit, or so I thought, very active--and now I was experiencing pains which the doctors told me were an indication that very soon, I must have surgery. If I didn't have the surgery I would die. If I had the surgery, there was still a good chance that I would die. And the situation was totally out of my hands. I hadn't been so helpless since my father had gone to the hospital with a heart attack all those years before.

The feeling of helplessness was absolutely devastating. It completely stripped me of my ego. I knew nothing of

God and therefore my strength was based on my ego, my successes, my ability to survive financially. The prospect of being physically unable to work was shattering. I was told to avoid stress at all costs--my heart could not survive an attack of any magnitude, no matter how slight. Had there been a heart attack, I would have died instantly. Somehow, I never had one. When I had the surgery in Cedars-Sinai, the doctors were of the opinion that the judo and karate had saved my life because the exercise had kept the blood flowing through my arteries.

Prior to the surgery, I was suddenly accused by the British government of stealing what amounted to about $12 million from my company. They asked the American government to extradite me from Los Angeles to Britain. They even sent about eight men over from Britain to fetch me. I shall never forget the smug expression on Constable's face as he brought me, handcuffed, into the courtroom. And I shall never, ever forget the look on my son's face as he saw his father in handcuffs, flanked by armed guards. (The British government had told the American government that I was dangerous.) The doctors had told me that stress at that point in my life could literally kill me. Why I didn't have a heart attack and drop dead then and there, I don't know.

The end result of the legal battle was that after three years of lawsuits (with major surgery taking place in the middle of it all), it was shown that no money had been taken. I was vindicated, but there was more to it than that. In the attempt to extradite me, I had been accused of 66 different charges. That is important when you consider that they did not have to prove the case against me in order for me to be dragged back to Britain. All they had to prove was what is called "probable cause" for any one of those 66 charges. They simply had to show that there was a possibility that I might be guilty, and that would have been enough to extradite me. I mention that with great emphasis because to have had all 66 charges thrown out was, and I use the expression without any difficulty at all, a miracle.

There's no question in my mind that it was a miracle. Why did I deserve this miracle? I didn't. I can't think why God was so good to me, of all people, when I had ignored him all my life. Perhaps it was because I'd had the good fortune to marry a wonderful woman who'd made a commitment to seek the Lord when she was 16 years old.

But the whole thing was an incredibly frightening experience. I was so very ill; I was waiting for open heart surgery, and suddenly faced with these horrendous charges. was running both the extradition lawsuit and a civil lawsuit, stemming from the liquidation of the assets of my company back in Britain. I was being sued for about $12 million dollars and I'd filed a counter suit for about $18 million. And, of course, the legal fees were eating us out of house and home. We couldn't pay our house mortgage so our attorneys took a third mortgage on the house for their legal fees...after I'd been told to avoid stress on pain of death, it was simply amazing that my heart kept on beating.

One might say I was lucky; one might say that right prevailed over might, or one might say that the Lord intervened, which is how my wife and I interpret the amazing outcome of that most terrible time in our lives. However, we had no idea how it would all turn out as we were facing open heart surgery, possible extradition, and a third mortgage on our home. We were in despair financially, physically, legally and emotionally.

Valerie: Joseph was in the hospital, and the doctors had told me the chances of him coming through the surgery were very slim, 20% I believe. The medical report said that he'd reached the lowest possible ebb a human being can sink to without losing all hope of recovery. He was very sick. And the most peculiar thing happened. A newspaper reporter called me on the telephone--I think it may have even been the night before surgery. I'd had enough experience with newspaper reporters to realize that you don't trust them; you don't talk to the press. But I let down my guard with this reporter for some reason. He was very kind; he told me all about what was going on with Thorpe back in Britain, and he provided me with a lot of information. I, in turn, told him how I was feeling. I really poured my heart out to him. After we'd finished our conversation, I put down the phone, went on my knees and prayed. I said, "Dear God, if you see Joseph through this surgery and bring us through all this...I know I've made this commitment before and I didn't keep it, but I will give the rest of my life to you--only this time, you'll have to show me how to do it." I found out later that the reporter I'd been speaking to was a Jewish believer in Jesus. As soon as we got off the phone, he prayed for me. He wrote me a note to that effect. As I was praying for Joseph, this reporter was praying for me!

Joseph: As for me, after all those years of Orthodox Jewish upbringing, all those years in synagogue, all I could summon up on the night before my surgery was a prayer that may have lasted about twenty seconds. All I could think of saying to God was. "I've worked so hard and I've done so well, why are you letting this happen to me?" And with that, in June of '78, I had major open heart surgery.

There were three surgeons present and six bypasses were performed. I believe that was the largest number of bypasses which had been successfully performed on anyone on the West Coast at the time. Someone on the East Coast had seven bypasses, and he's number one. He's welcome to it; it's the only time in my life I didn't want to be number one!

Valerie was convinced that it was the hand of God which had brought me through the surgery against such incredibly low odds. As for me and my prayer, if God had chosen to answer my complaint then and there, he might have said, "Well, it took you 40 years to come around to talking to me. Now you have to get in line." And that's the reality. People turn to God when they're desperate, and often, after a lifetime of ignoring him, they feel he owes them some sort of explanation or solution to their problems. The amazing thing is that God chooses to answer us at all. In my case, I believe it was Valerie's prayers on my behalf which he chose to answer.

He granted Valerie's request, obviously, that I live through the surgery. The doctors were surprised at how well I came through it. I began to get up and about, although I still felt weakened compared to my former vigor. The effect of realizing one's mortality is staggering. It did not make me think about God. It did not make me think about what, if anything, I should be doing differently. It simply made me realize that I was not in control of my life. I had survived many crises because of my wits and my determination. I had survived this crisis because (I thought) I'd gotten lucky for a change. There hadn't been a blessed thing I could do for myself when I was stretched out on that operating table. It was not a spiritual awakening, but rather an ego-shattering experience.

Later, of course, I learned that God was indeed concerned and that I had been restored due to his grace in answering Valerie's prayers. Not that she'd been able to "bribe" God with her promise of commitment. She actually wanted to devote herself to him, but she didn't know how. God answered that part of the prayer, too, and he did it in rather an unusual way.

We met an older couple, Fillmore and Marion Cohon, in a stockbroker's office in Beverly Hills one day. The lady--a total stranger--came up to me, grabbed my sleeve and said, "God has sent me to you." I believe she told me she needed help understanding a financial matter...I don't recall her particular request. I do know I was never the sort to bring home a total stranger, much less would I invite this lady and her husband to our home based on the fact that she seemed to feel God had sent her to me. God meant nothing to me. In addition, I was not the most trusting soul in the world. To this day, if you ask me why I responded to this woman, I cannot tell--other than the fact that God had obviously chosen her as his instrument in my life.

Despite the fact that neither Valerie nor I were in the habit of bringing strangers into our home, before I knew it, the four of us were standing on our front doorstep. The Cohons saw the *mezuzah* and one of them said, "You're Jewish, aren't you?"

It might be of interest to know that the chief *Lubavitch* rabbi (Vogel) in Britain had given us the mezuzah. We'd had many Lubavitch meetings at our home in London. My mother was Orthodox, more so than my father, and it was through her that we knew Rabbi Vogel.

195

At any rate, they noticed the mezuzah right away, and, of course, I replied, "Yes, we are Jewish." We walked into the house and Marion asked, "Do you believe in God?"

"Yes," I replied once more. I didn't elaborate on what I believed about him because I'd never thought about it. But I was Jewish, and I therefore felt obligated to answer in the affirmative. This couple was also Jewish, so I was surprised when Mrs. Cohn said, "We can see you're an educated man. What do you know about Jesus?"

I didn't know a thing about Jesus other than the fact that he had posed some sort of political problem in ancient history. I knew Christians worshipped him, but I didn't know they thought he was the Messiah--in fact, I didn't even know what "the Messiah" was supposed to be. I grew up as one of the most active boys in synagogue because my father was so Orthodox. Yet, with all the classes I attended in London, I don't remember ever being told about the Messiah. This still amazes me. The whole of the Old Testament, starting with Genesis, is filled with messianic prophecies. And I knew nothing.

Now this woman was asking me about Jesus, who I realized was a significant figure in history, if nothing else. I felt stupid--stupid and very ashamed that I could say nothing to answer her question. Then she began speaking about "end times," and the biblical predictions regarding the future world, including economy. She had no way of knowing the financial trauma I'd experienced, but after my bank collapsed (and not just my bank, but many banks in Britain), I was convinced that the end of the world financial system as we know it was near. So when Marion Cohn began talking about the future of the world situation from a biblical, prophetic perspective, I was intrigued.

It had never occurred to me that the Bible had anything to say about "here and now," much less about the future. So when this couple invited Valerie and me to a Bible study, I saw it as a challenge. Here was something about which I knew nothing, and I was curious. I wanted to know more. At that point, my life was spiritually empty. You've no idea how oppressive "nothing" can be until you realize that you need "something" to replace it. I wanted a few drops of something to put in the cup and this couple said I would find it at a Bible study. Maybe I would and maybe I wouldn't, but I was determined to see for myself. Even if I didn't agree with their beliefs, I would remedy my ignorance. The next time someone asked me what I knew about Jesus, I'd have an answer.

Valerie was curious, too, so on August 29, 1979, we both went to see for ourselves what this Bible study was all about. It was nothing elaborate, just a group of mostly Jewish people who believed in Jesus. They met weekly in the home of a man named Paul Herne, now deceased, who was also a Jewish believer in Jesus.

I was skeptical. I had no idea what I was about to see or hear, I only knew it would be something new. And though I was skeptical, I was looking for something new. The "old" had left me in despair--physically, spiritually, legally and financially. I was ready to explore. I didn't have my guard up, but I didn't have it down either. Valerie didn't know what to expect any more than I did. My wife and I never quite agreed about things like this, about considering new things, that is. We always had a completely different approach, and we're both rather opinionated. So it seemed logical that we not sit together during this Bible study; that would make it easier for us to make observations and draw conclusions on our own. The house lent itself to that plan beautifully, because the meeting was set in a living room/dining room area. The front of the meeting area, where the speaker stood, was open to both rooms, but the rest of the area was divided by a wall separating the two. I sat on one side of the wall, and Valerie on the other. We did not see one another during the course of the entire meeting.

It began with a time of singing. I watched everybody very carefully, as is my custom; I'm always interested in watching people. I didn't know the words, of course, and I didn't know what they were singing except that it was scripturally based. What I did notice, and this made quite an impression on me, was the fact that there was some sort of commonality there. I did not know what drew this assortment of people together. Some appeared well-dressed, others looked rather *schlocky*, yet there was a cohesiveness. I couldn't understand this "togetherness," but it was very obvious to me, especially during the singing. I'd come from a background where there was no togetherness. In our synagogue, this one would pray loudly, that one would quietly mumble. This one *shockled* a lot, that one shockled a little. People either said their prayers or they didn't say them; the only thing they did together was socialize, and then everyone went home. This Bible study was different. These people were worshipping God together, and I'd never seen that before. It made me even more curious.

After the singing, the people prayed. They didn't read from a book or repeat a liturgy they'd memorized. They discussed various situations and problems and then prayed about the things they had discussed. My emotions began to deepen. They were talking to God and I was extremely jealous. I had never in my life spoken to God, other than my quick complaint to him just before open heart surgery. What I felt at that moment was completely unexpected and new. I wanted so much to participate in their kind of praying. I longed to understand what qualifications I needed, what knowledge I had to lay hold of to stand there with other people and talk to God. I was an outsider looking in on all of this. I had to learn what it was they had that I hadn't.

These people not only felt the freedom to come before God, but they cared so much for one another that their prayers were not even focused on themselves. They were either expressing appreciation to God for who he was and what he'd done for them, or they were asking him to help someone else. I had never in my life heard anybody pray for another person!

Next on the agenda was the Bible lesson. This was still more amazing. I didn't know whether to be fascinated or irritated. There was I, an "Orthodox Jew" who'd gone to cheder at least three times a week for years and years, and who knew how to read the Torah in Hebrew. And here was this man, a very calm, middle-aged, pleasant Jewish man telling me what was in the Old Testament. What was worse, he was telling me things I didn't know. Naturally, he was speaking to the whole group, but I took this very personally. What right had he to tell me such a simple story from the Old Testament? I don't even remember the content of the lesson. I just remember suddenly realizing there was more to the Bible than being able to rattle it off in Hebrew without understanding what it meant in English.

That realization was like turning a corner. I suddenly had a whole new perspective. What a shock it was to realize that, with all my Jewishness, I had no idea what the Bible said. If it was the Bible which taught the things I'd seen reflected in the conduct and behavior of those people, then I needed to know more about the Bible. I was convinced in that moment that there would be no higher priority in my life until I got this issue clarified. I would have to read the Bible for myself to see if what this man said was truly in the Scriptures or if he was just presenting his own ideas based on some loose interpretation.

Further, there had been talk of sin and forgiveness during the prayer time as well as in the Bible lesson. Up until that night, it had never entered my mind that I needed to be forgiven. If anything, I would have thought the world should ask my pardon for having treated me so insufferably. They, not I, needed to be forgiven, for I'd worked hard and been cheated out of what I deserved. But as I sat in that living room, watching and listening, my life came into focus and I saw things very differently. I realized I was a sinner. I knew I needed to be forgiven, not only for things I'd done, but for ignoring my Creator all those years, for not thinking of him or caring what he thought of me.

In retrospect, what happened in my heart spiritually was very close to what had happened to me physically. When I'd gone to the doctor for a routine checkup, I discovered my heart was terribly blocked. I had been mortally ill without knowing it; I was completely oblivious to the problem which was endangering my very life. But the pains came soon after, to reinforce what the doctors had told me. Those pains let me know for certain that something was wrong. From the moment I knew, I wanted one thing. I wanted my heart to function properly. I wanted the doctors to cure me. I wanted to live.

Now I was hearing about another heart condition. Sin. And though nobody pointed a finger at me, the diagnosis rang true. I experienced, for the first time, the pain of not knowing God, the anguish of being separated from him. And I wanted one thing. I wanted to be forgiven. wanted my heart to be right. No doctor could cure me. wanted God.

Well, the Bible study ended and there was a time for socializing afterward. People were milling about and they were all pleasant, but there was one lady in particular who approached me very purposefully. She was an elderly woman, in her eighties, I believe. Her name was Miriam Marks, and she was a tiny little thing but very sharp and very bold. After she'd introduced herself to me, she offered a simple description of who Jesus is, what he had done and why. Her speech lasted less than two minutes, and she ended it by asking me, "Would you like to be forgiven for your sins?"

That was the turning point of my whole life. I didn't hesitate. I knew that God was speaking to me. When heard Miriam say the name "Jesus," it was as though I was filled with a sort of light--a cleanliness that I had never known in the whole of my life. I didn't understand it. knew it was real, I knew it was right. It was a warmth and a sudden understanding that there was a whole world in front of me that I'd never experienced. I'd been brought up to believe in God, but though I'm ashamed to admit it, think that night was probably the first time I realized that God matters. I'd had no time for God. I'd known he existed, but had never reached out to him. With all the problems I'd suffered through, I had never reached out to God. I'd reached out to my brains, my ability to conduct legal arguments and to fight my own battles. But that evening, I'd witnessed people who knew God. I wanted to know him too, and throughout the meeting, I'd been wondering how could. When Miriam Marks invited me to step into this new world, this personal relationship with God, there was only one thing to do...and that was seize the opportunity.

I accepted what she said and immediately prayed to acknowledge Jesus as my Messiah. I asked God to forgive me of my sins. I did not, at that time, have any Bible knowledge. I just believed.

The swiftness with which I made my decision was not out of character for me. My normal process was to decide things quickly. I'd had a great deal of experience with business decisions and found I usually did well to rely upon my instincts. Yet there was one aspect in which this decision differed from any commercial decision I had ever made. I decided this from the heart and I knew it was from the heart, whereas my other decisions came from the head; they were based on a quick assessment of the facts. Here, I didn't know enough to assess the facts. But something was stirring so deep inside me as Miriam spoke, that even if I couldn't explain how I knew she was telling the truth, I couldn't deny that truth without denying the very depths of my soul.

After I prayed, I wanted to get on my knees and cry. For the first time, I felt humble and totally undeserving of the wonderful thing that had just happened to me. All the other "wonderful things" I'd experienced in life: wealth, power, recognition, I had received with the feeling that I very much deserved them because of all my hard work. But here was something worth infinitely more and there was no reason why I should receive it other than the goodness and the grace of Almighty God. Nearly a decade has passed and I am still overcome with wonder and joy when I think of God's goodness to me.

Nevertheless, I was in somebody else's home and there were people about, and obviously I did not want to display my emotions.

I didn't know what would happen next. I don't think I had any expectations at that point. I didn't feel that I was entitled to any promises or any "deals." I felt what I had done was genuine and real. I felt that something in my life had changed radically, and that I was obligated to find out what it all meant. And clearly, that obligation could only be measured by knowing what the Bible said.

Everything happened very quickly. Before I could even think how to explain all this to my wife, Miriam Marks was telling me that Valerie had already prayed with

201

her, just as I had. Well, not quite just as I had. Valerie will tell you what happened....

Valerie: If I had known what the evening would consist of, I probably wouldn't have gone. I didn't know these people were going to be believers in Jesus. I would have dismissed it as "un-Jewish" and therefore, not for me. After all, I had committed myself to God and told him that I would be the best Jew I could be. In my mind, this would not have included going to a meeting of Jewish believers in Jesus!

But like Joseph, I sensed God was present in that room, and that these people knew him. How were they able to confide in him and trust in him so intimately? I wanted to know if whatever allowed them to do so would be available to me. It seemed too good to be true. As I listened and realized they were talking about Jesus, I remembered the leaflet I'd read in the airport three years earlier. Hadn't it talked about Jews believing in Jesus? Hadn't it seemed to make a great deal of sense at the time? Hadn't I thought that it might even be true? But that pamphlet had been written by strangers. I'd needed to ask someone I could trust. And when I did, I was told that only crazy, unbalanced Jews would believe in Jesus. I accepted that as true because I felt the people who told me were more qualified to know about such things than I was.

Now I realized they were wrong. Perhaps I was not learned enough to make a scholarly decision, but it didn't take a scholar to see that these Jewish believers in Jesus were not crazy, and further, I could see that I wanted what they had.

I will admit, I was taken aback when I heard the Scripture where Jesus says, "I am the way, the truth, and the life. No one comes to the Father except through Me." I always assumed that God would be there for me. It didn't seem fair that there was some sort of qualifier on having a relationship with him. But when Joseph was in the hospital, I had prayed and asked God to show me the way to keep my promise to him. And I believed wholeheartedly that I had found the answer in Jesus, though I wouldn't have looked to him on my own. I had seen in these people a deep, strong joy. It was the joy which I had been so aware was missing that day, years ago, when I lay sunbathing on our yacht. I saw the fulfillment that comes regardless of one's financial status--the fulfillment that comes only through the Messiah.

So when Miriam spoke to me after the Bible study, I was ready and I wanted to pray with her. God had finally shown me how to keep the promise I'd made to him as a 16-year-old.

Still there was one problem. No matter how much I believed Jesus was the answer and wanted him in my life, I had been raised to consider his name as a swear word only. Joseph always viewed the anti-Semitism we'd experienced as ethnic or social injustice. I, on the other hand, had grown up believing that it all had to do with Jesus. I told Miriam, "I do believe it's true and I would like to pray, but I don't think I can say that word."

Miriam understood. She said, "Y'shua is the Jewish pronunciation for Jesus, you can say that instead." With a sigh of relief, I thanked God for Y'shua, my Jewish Messiah, and committed my life to him.

Then Miriam asked if I thought it would be alright for her to go and talk to Joseph. I couldn't imagine what he would think of all this. As was mentioned, we did not see one another's reactions to what was going on that evening. I told Miriam I supposed she could go ahead and try. I was very happy and relieved when I saw Joseph and he told me what had happened. It would have been difficult to explain my decision to him, but he obviously understood.

We stayed at the Hernes' late that night, talking to Paul and his wife Leonore long after everybody else had gone. When we did leave, the Hernes gave both Joseph and me a Bible. We walked out of the house, got into the car, looked at each other and said, "What on earth have we done?"

Joseph: It was like stepping outside of a movie house. While you're watching the movie, you're immersed in a different world, but then suddenly you go outside and you're back in the "real world." It was late and we were tired. But whatever changes had been wrought by our prayers of commitment--they were still in effect when we awoke the next morning. We both had a tremendous hunger to learn more, and especially to read the Bible.

Our desire to know what the Jewish Bible said became our entire life. At first we read it to make certain that the things we'd been told and believed that night really had a basis in Scripture. Once we were satisfied on that account, we discovered that the more we read about God in the Bible, the deeper our relationship with him grew. Through reading God's Word, we developed standards and a value system quite different from those we previously held.

Nothing had changed so far as the outside world was concerned. We still faced tremendous burdens and difficulties that had to be worked through. What had changed was inside. God was enabling us to deal graciously with our circumstances. And I suddenly had an incredibly deep desire to understand what God says in his Word, to find out every way that God communicates to man. Once I got hold of that Bible, I read voraciously. I had a job to do. I had to find out everything I could about God and what he might want of me.

I became so keen on studying the Bible that I enrolled at Talbot Theological Seminary (the graduate school of Biola University) from which I graduated with a Master of Divinity degree. I received my ordination from a council of 18 pastors and seminary professors in the early part of 1985.

Perhaps that sounds fanatical. But you must understand, I had asked the Lord, "What do you want me to do?" And the answer which immediately came to mind was that I should serve God with the same energy and the same intensity with which I had once tried to serve myself. The fervor which had driven me to build a financial empire was redirected. I would do whatever needed to be done to increase my potential to know and serve God. This remains my concern. Education and formal training are not the only ways to prepare oneself for this; however, this was what I felt I should do.

As to how our families reacted to all this, it varied. My parents went straight to the rabbi. Whenever I spoke or wrote to my father, I would suggest questions which he might ask the rabbi regarding various portions of Scripture, messianic prophecies in particular.

It had never entered my father's mind to question the rabbi as to the meaning of Scripture passages, but when I put it to him, he decided to do so. Because you see, even though he was utterly convinced it was wrong of me to believe in Jesus, there was (and I think this is true of many of our Jewish people) a small area of uncertainty. Instead of dealing with that uncertainty by searching through the Scriptures, most deal with it by saying to the believer in Jesus, "Why do you think you know more than all the rabbis?" I challenged my father to see for himself how the rabbi would explain Scripture.

He was very surprised when the rabbi didn't give answers. He was so certain that the rabbi would explain everything that it rather stunned him when the answers were not forthcoming. Instead, he was told things like, "We'll talk about it another time." I don't think that satisfied my father. He always attends services on Saturday morning and very often on Friday night. He is very keen to be involved in anything Jewish. And I hope someday he and my mother will see that believing in the Messiah is the most Jewish thing they could do.

Valerie's mother reacted with complete horror. She suggested that Valerie divorce me and go back to England to live with her because I had clearly gone mad. At a later date, she visited and saw what a wonderful difference faith in Jesus had made in our lives. Though she admitted seeing a positive change, she still lamented; how could we do this to her--it was such a disgrace.

Valerie's father's reaction was very interesting. He called her up and said, "I'm an atheist; you can believe what you like, but you'd better keep quiet about this Jesus because it's driving your mother crazy, and she, in turn, is driving me crazy. So please stop."

Our daughter was only 7 years old when we came to faith, and she accepted that he is her Messiah at an early age. Valerie and I pray that as Julia grows older, the commitment she made as a child will become more and more significant in the context of her own life experience.

Justin, on the other hand, was 19 years old when Valerie and I committed our lives to God, and he didn't have any time for religion whatsoever. We had many Bible studies in our home and even had baptisms in our swimming pool, and Justin would just disappear to his room upstairs and we wouldn't see or hear from him until morning. Or if he did come 'round, he hadn't anything positive to say.

One time a pastor and his wife were in our home and they said, "Justin, can we pray for you?" He replied, "I'd rather you didn't." And he went upstairs.

Then a rabbi, Rabbi Kravitz, called my son, who was attending the University of Southern California at the time. And the rabbi asked to meet him. Justin had never been approached by a stranger in this fashion and so he said, "If my father gives permission, I'll meet you." I gave my permission and Justin went to see Kravitz, who showed him two film strips. One depicted a young Jew who had supposedly become a Christian and then "saw the light" and "returned to Judaism." The other was a film which showed how Orthodox Jewish people celebrate the holidays and perform various other rituals as an affirmation of Jewish identity. Justin came home and said, "You're not a Jew anymore, Daddy." And that was that.

I'd learned there is only one thing to do in such a situation--talk to the Lord about it. That's exactly what Valerie and I did; we prayed for our son every single day. And one day, Justin came and he said to me, "I'd like to borrow a Bible." He wasn't pleasant; he was quite abrupt. And I said, "Alright," and gave him a Bible. We had refused to discuss anything with Justin up till that point because he hadn't read the Bible.

His only reason for deciding to read it was in order to argue and prove us wrong. He made that quite clear. He said, "Well, I don't want to read any of that New Testament stuff, I want to read the Old Testament." Justin hadn't believed in anything at all and he certainly hadn't been interested in the Bible until his meeting with Rabbi Kravitz. We did not discover this until later, but after the films, the two of them discussed the Bible. Justin asked the rabbi questions concerning some of the passages we had pointed out to him. He particularly wanted to know what Kravitz thought about Isaiah 53. And he found Kravitz's answer inadequate. The rabbi told him that the passage was referring to Israel.

Justin later said, "I didn't know much about the Bible, but even then I could see that it is a logical book. I felt like the text was talking about apples and Kravitz was trying to convince me that it was really oranges. I left dissatisfied, and I knew I had a decision to make. The decision was not whether or not to believe in Jesus, but whether or not to believe the Bible. I remember praying; in fact, I think it was the first time I ever prayed, sincerely, that is. I asked God to show me what was true. And that night, my heart began to turn toward the Bible."

We owe Rabbi Kravitz a debt of gratitude for although he apparently intended to discourage our son from believing in Jesus, he ended up having quite the reverse effect.

Justin read that Bible and over the next six months, he began to change. He started to spend a lot of time at home with us, and saw the enormous change in our lives. Justin, of course, was well acquainted with the dilemmas we faced legally, financially and health-wise. He wouldn't admit it until later, but he couldn't help noticing how prayer and our new relationship with God was bringing us through. He was amazed at our calm in the midst of the storm. He'd say, "It's so nice to be with you. I think you're crazy, but I like being with you." Of course we were delighted because we knew he was aware that the difference in our life and in our values was a direct result of our faith in Jesus.

We told him, "We're very happy to have you around the house, but you'll have to accept that we're having these people over and the meetings here are going to continue." He said, "Oh no, I like these people." It was a complete turn-around! We hadn't argued or tried to coax him--we just left him alone with the Bible.

Six months after we'd given Justin the Bible (and unbeknown to us, he'd read the "Old" and the "New" Testaments), the same pastor and his wife who had once offered to pray for him came to our home for dinner. I was in the kitchen washing up and I heard Justin say to the pastor, "I want to believe in Jesus; please, how do I become a Christian?"

I cried at the sink. I cried and I cried. The tap was pouring and my eyes were pouring and the two were quite equal for some time. Justin became a believer at about 10 past midnight one winter night in 1981.

It is a great joy for us to have Jesus in common. Justin and I don't work in the same firm, but sometimes we still discuss business problems. He'll say to me, "Well, we have to talk to the Lord about it and see what he wants us to do." I'll be wrapped up in thinking of the business end and my son jogs my memory and reminds me of our priorities!

I am the senior partner of a real estate investment company. That is how I now make my living. I also work as a consultant for various Christian organizations, offering financial counsel to those who are having difficulty in that area. That work, however, is gratis. For the time being, it is my way of investing the talents God has given me to serve him.

I no longer seek the personal fortune I strove to achieve as a younger man; yet God has been restoring our finances and for this we give him thanks. I want to say that I do not think one must take a vow of poverty to believe in Jesus. However, God's blessings should be shared with others and seen as evidence of his goodness and grace rather than evidence of our own self-sufficiency. I now see that I must not allow myself to care more for money and material things than for the Lord.

Since coming to know Jesus, I not only view my finances differently, but my Jewish identity also has new meaning. I am no longer like Harold Abrahams in "Chariots of Fire." I no longer run the race in bitterness, striving to prove myself a successful Jew in a Gentile world. I no longer suffer the confusion of seeing my Jewishness both as a burden as well as a badge of honor. For as I study the Bible, there is great joy in knowing that I am part of the people of Israel, included in God's plans and his promises. And the wonderful privilege of being included in this people far outweighs the problems caused by prejudice against us.

Yet with privilege comes responsibility. To know God means we must make him known. I believe we are a people of destiny, and without a knowledge of God and his Messiah, that destiny cannot be fulfilled. I see how God has had his hand on me and I realize that he has kept his hand upon us as a people in much the same way. We have been stubborn and stiff-necked, as the prophets of Israel said, often not recognizing the Lord as our Creator and Benefactor. We have suffered much. We have attributed our survival, and often our successes, to our own wits and abilities. We have been proud of our achievements. But without obedience to God, all we can hope to gain are things which we build with our own hands--things which eventually will crumble.

Only the hand of God can create that which is of everlasting value. To fulfill our destiny, to be a "light to the nations," we must put our hand in the hand of God, and build with him, according to his plans. The Messiah came so we could do just that.

> **For**
> as the heavens
> are high above the earth,
> So great is his mercy
> toward those who
> fear Him;
> As far as the east is from
> the west,
> So far has He removed our
> transgressions
> from us.
>
> PSALM 103: 11,12

SUSAN PERLMAN

It had never occurred to me that I had "spiritual needs" because I didn't know what that meant. If I would have heard the phrase, I might have thought it meant a lack of meaningful activity, a lack of meaningful relationships, a lack of self-esteem, or some other social or psychological deficiency. I was not lacking in those areas. Yet, I was faced with the fact that a holy and just God created me and had certain expectations of me. I realized that I barely knew him and I felt inadequate to draw closer to him. He was worthy of my devotion, yet I was not capable of winning his approval. All this added up to spiritual need.

We piled onto the bus, a group of friends and strangers united in our purpose. It was a special bus destined for a big march in Washington, D.C. The Pentagon, the military-industrial complex, was our target. While this was serious business, the mood was light and festive. People chatted and joked. Now and then someone would burst into a song and others would join in.

When we reached the halfway point between New York City and Washington, D.C., the bus pulled into a highway rest stop/restaurant. Everyone made a beeline for the restrooms, and as is often the case, the line for the ladies' room was much longer than the line for the men's room. Suddenly, I had a brainstorm: "Why not liberate the men's room?" I told my idea to the women waiting next to me. Their enthusiasm helped me muster up the courage to lead the onslaught on the men's room. We "stormed" the door and successfully "liberated" the men's room, making it coed--much to the astonishment of the proprietors of the restaurant, not to mention the bewildered men who were inside!

My confidence was really bolstered as I stepped back on the bus. People continued to chat, sing and laugh, right up until the time we were close enough to see the familiar monuments of our nation's capital. Then the tension, the uneasiness began to set in. There was always the possibility of violence on such demonstrations and I, for one, did not want to be maced or get my head bashed in.

Ironically, like the police we expected to face, we had our own uniform of sorts: faded denim jeans, T-shirts and sandals. Those who were more experienced wore closed shoes. I began to cringe as I saw some of my fellow marchers putting on homemade riot regalia that seemed to almost invite attack: motorcycle helmets, construction hardhats; the assorted gear looked more appropriate for a professional football game than a march for peace! Did they know something that I didn't?

Our little contingent converged with thousands of others to an open area where a platform had been erected. There was a long program of speakers and folk singers, but what I remember most is the march that followed. We began with the chant, "All we are saying, is give peace a chance," which we repeated over and over. Then the slogans became more strident, more clipped, "Ho, Ho, Ho Chi Minh, N.L.F. is gonna win!!" I remember when we crossed over the area marked "No trespassing." We could see, in the distance, the symbol of our nation's military might: the Pentagon. We could hear the tactical police with their bullhorns, warning marchers in front of us that they would be arrested if they continued in that direction.

I wished at that moment that I was not on the line of march. I had no chance to retreat as the crowd pushed forward. I felt the burning sensation of tear gas in my eyes. I saw the police attacking marchers and I saw marchers attacking the police. It was ugly. Then everyone started running. There was no longer a line of march, just hundreds, no, thousands of people scattering in all directions. "Off the pigs! Off the pigs!!" I was running too, only I wasn't exactly sure where. I didn't know which way would take me away from the shoving and hitting and pummeling.

It wasn't until later that I had time to reflect on the day's events. We'd gone to Washington for a noble and just cause. We supposed ourselves to be the voice of sanity in an insane world as we protested the war in Vietnam. I knew that it was beyond my ability to even imagine the human carnage going on over there. The death toll I heard every night on the news was obscene to me. I remember thinking how sick the world must be if words like "a just and honorable peace" were considered more important than life itself. Was it "honorable" for people to be napalmed to death? I felt I had to raise my voice to protest this evil. So there I was, part of a peace demonstration that had turned into a hostile, bloody mess.

I survived the march on the Pentagon, but I was never the same. I rode back on the bus feeling helpless, unable (at least for the moment) to do anything that would really make a difference. All too often "might" triumphed over "right," and a few people in high places made decisions which affected the rest of us--decisions in which we had no voice or choice. This was particularly frustrating because I have always been a person who values the ability to choose.

This is a fact, family and friends tell me, I made apparent at a very early age.

In fact, if I could have chosen where to be born, I would have! Though I was in no position to do so, I feel that my mother made the right choice for me--Brooklyn. I was born at Beth El Hospital on December 29, 1950. It was later renamed "Brookdale"--probably for someone who donated a large sum of money--but I still like to think of it as Beth El, which means "House of God."

I was quite secure in being Jewish. As far as I knew, everyone in our neighborhood was Jewish. Our schools were closed on the Jewish holidays. All our teachers had names like Mrs. Katz and Mrs. Epstein. Our merchants were also Jewish, like Mr. Warren, the pharmacist and Mr. Pincus, the grocer. We didn't know from O'Rourke or Rodriguez. We never saw Christmas decorations or other "Christian" symbols unless we wandered to faraway places like Fort Hamilton.

I was particularly proud of my heritage when, at age 8, I was chosen to play the part of Queen Esther in the Purim pageant put on by the Young Women's Hebrew Association. My flowing white robe with specks of glued-on glitter and my crown, though only of cardboard and dimestore gems, truly made me feel like a queen. I didn't always know the difference between a genuine Bible story and a "rabbi story," but I knew Queen Esther was a real heroine. As I recited my lines from the stage of the YM-YWHA, I was Queen Esther, the fairest maiden in all of Shushan. My family and friends smiled proudly from the very front row. The play became a wonderful, magical experience and a trace of that glow still warms me whenever I recall it.

I was aware that non-Jews existed. I even had a Gentile friend, who didn't live in the neighborhood, but attended my school. Her name was Priscilla. One day, she came to talk to me on the playground. She was very upset because her Sunday school teacher had said that "I" killed Jesus! I protested, but after all, her teacher was an adult and I was just a kid. People our age just naturally trusted adults to be smarter and wiser--especially those in authority, such as religious instructors. I could do nothing to convince

Priscilla of my innocence. From then on, we'd acknowledge one another with a glance now and then, but we never played together again. That made me sad but I also remember thinking what a crazy religion Christianity must be, if Christians taught lies about little Jewish girls killing "their God."

I didn't think much about God, other than the fact that he was there. Then when I was 12, my father died. It was very sudden and unexpected and our family was in shock. Most 12-year-olds don't have to come to grips with the weighty issues of life and death, but I did. As we sat *shiva* (seven days of mourning), friends and relatives tried to console us by assurances that our memories of my father would live on. The rabbi spoke of my father's virtues at the funeral service, but his words seemed empty to me. He hadn't really known my father. Part of that time is blurred in my memory, but I do remember asking if my father was in heaven. The question only seemed to cause embarrassment and I didn't really get an answer.

I was bewildered. How could a great, all-powerful God allow this to happen? Didn't he know that my father was a good man? He was only 34 years old...couldn't God see that my mother, my two sisters and I needed Daddy? I was angry with God, but more than that, I questioned whether or not he was even real. Maybe he only existed in my imagination and in the traditions of our religion.

Regardless of whether or not God existed, my positive feelings about my Jewishness remained strong. I considered Judaism superior to other belief systems. I reasoned that if I was going to believe in God at all or be a religious person, I would certainly not be anything other than Jewish. In comparison to my image of Christianity, I felt ours was the more practical, responsible religion. I viewed Christianity according to what I had seen in movies: a killer walks into a confession booth to confess all his crimes and tell the priest how he wants to make a new start. The priest says, "My son, you are forgiven," and that's that. How convenient! It just didn't seem right to me.

On the other hand, I felt Judaism taught people to take responsibility for their own actions. There was no need for me to cry to God when I did something wrong, nor to give him credit when I did something right. I felt good about that and really worked hard at doing things "right."

I was an above-average student and rapidly advanced through junior and senior high. During that time I was in a sorority, on the cheering squad, helped coach the swim team, wrote for the yearbook and was captain of the student patrol. I graduated from high school in a January term and had a one-week break before entering college at age 16.

I had enrolled at Hunter College in Manhattan for a four-year nursing program. Unlike the liberal arts students, I was able to live in a dormitory. It concerned my mother to have me leave home at such a young age, for even though Manhattan was not distance-wise far away from Brooklyn, it was really a whole new world. I saw it as a great opportunity, a real adventure.

It turned out that I was one of two Jews in the entire nursing program; everyone else seemed to be Irish Catholic. It was a strange sensation to be in the minority. I'll never forget Christmas at the nursing dorm of Hunter College. The lobby was almost all glass windows and the students traditionally decorated them with holiday scenes. Most everyone was busy designing their holly wreaths, jingle bells and jolly old Santas. I was given a window all my own and felt a responsibility to Jewish people everywhere as I defiantly drew a Hanukkah menorah with a Star of David on it. I created a "Jewish corner" lest anyone think there were only Irish Catholics in our dorm!

I didn't last too long in the nursing program, but it didn't have anything to do with being Jewish. I quickly discovered that I had more aptitude and interest in my liberal arts classes than in the science courses nursing required. When I left the nursing program, I also had to leave the dorm. I had enjoyed the taste of independence and could not see myself moving back to my mother's apartment in Brooklyn.

It didn't take long to find some roommates, and together we rented an apartment above "Poor Philip's Head Shop" on St. Mark's Place in Greenwich Village. The location wasn't ideal and after a few weeks, I started looking as weird as everyone I passed on the street. This frightened me. I moved out of Greenwich Village and into an apartment with three other girls on the corner of West 103rd Street and West End Avenue. We actually lived on the 13th floor of a very nice high-rise...but as is the custom in many such buildings, they had labelled it the14th floor. It was an unusually large four-bedroom apartment--unusually large for Manhattan, that is. We bought a huge, carved oak table for our dining room; the living room had beautiful high ceilings and a lovely fireplace. It was a perfect place for lots of entertaining, and we made full use of it.

I continued with my studies, shifting my major to communications. I liked my life as a cause-motivated, action-oriented independent woman. I continued to participate in marches like the one described at the beginning of my story. Though I was eventually disillusioned with this, I never gave up my efforts to "make a difference." I was an active member of our block association and worked toward building a sense of community in our neighborhood. I helped raise funds for a dog run along Riverside Park, and took part in a neighborhood recycling center for glass and aluminum. I even helped with the hiring of a security guard to keep junkies and dope dealers off our street.

I also became active in guerrilla theater (street drama) as a creative means of making social statements. I played the part of "Mother Nature" being choked to death by toxic waste! I was a box of cereal going stale on the shelf at a local supermarket known for charging unreasonably high prices. I was a "city official" determined to evict squatters in an abandoned building near Columbia University.

These roles were a far cry from Queen Esther, but in my way, I tried to protect and defend what I felt was basic to human survival. I kept up much of this activity after college, and got a good job writing advertising copy for J.C. Penney as well. I was productive and pleased that my life had purpose and great potential. I was not looking for God.

One day, I was walking in mid-town Manhattan on my lunch hour, I couldn't help noticing a young man who was conspicuous because of his extremely blond hair. He was wearing a campaign button on his shirt. Being a naturally inquisitive person, and also finding this young man somewhat attractive, I wanted to know what his button said. My curiosity was mixed with caution so I didn't want to ask about the button directly. If he were some sort of fanatic, I did not want to waste my time entangled in a discussion that was not of my choosing.

I decided the best solution would be to find a pretense for getting close enough to read the button myself. All this happened within seconds, you understand, so I stopped him with the first thing that came to mind: "Excuse me, I was wondering, would you mind telling me...is your hair really that color, or do you dye it?" Larry smiled, and assured me that his hair was not dyed. Meanwhile, I was able to read the button: "Smile. God loves you."

Such a statement would not have caught my interest, except I had recently read a cover article in Time magazine about the "Jesus People." When I read his button, I recognized it as one I'd seen a number of people wearing that week. This guy certainly didn't look like a New Yorker; with his extremely blond hair and what I considered sort of a "Beach Boys" look, he seemed to fit in with the people whose photos I'd seen in the Time article. Who knew, maybe the Jesus People were having a convention in New York that week. Maybe they were all staying at one of the big hotels. I could picture the sign: "Welcome, Jesus People." At any rate, I was curious to know if I was talking to "one of them." So I mentioned the article and asked if he was a "Jesus Person."

Larry told me he wasn't exactly one of the "Jesus People" I'd read about, but that like them, he did believe in Jesus. It wasn't until much later that I discovered this young man, Larry Norman, was a fairly well-known Christian folk-rock singer. He did tell me that he was going to be playing guitar and singing at a church that night, and invited me to come along. I was semi-interested in his offer, but ended up accepting a date with a lawyer that night instead.

Larry and I became friends and I grew to respect his convictions, though I assumed their validity was confined to Gentile boundaries. Still, he was an activist in his own way, and I respected that. Because of Jesus, Larry had certain standards of morality that one didn't often come across in the big city.

My friendship with Larry, my curiosity and my avid interest in reading combined were enough to convince me to look into the Bible. That was a life-changing experience. Now to me, "the Bible" meant "the Jewish Bible." I began in Genesis. It didn't take very long before I discovered the fact that God is holy. That might sound obvious, but I had never contemplated God's holiness. I also realized that the Bible was not an ordinary book and the God of Abraham was no ordinary "god." I had not been interested in God before because, quite simply, I did not know who he was. The Bible revealed so much about him and it made me want to know more. The revelation of God's holiness led me to another discovery--I was unholy. My own spiritual need had not been evident to me before that time.

It had never occurred to me that I had "spiritual needs" because I didn't know what that meant. If I would have heard the phrase, I might have thought it meant a lack of meaningful activity, a lack of meaningful relationships, a lack of self-esteem, or some other social or psychological deficiency. I was not lacking in those areas. Yet, I was faced with the fact that a holy and just God created me and had certain expectations of how I should behave and relate to him. I realized that I barely knew him and I felt inadequate to initiate any move to draw closer to him. He was worthy of my devotion, yet I was not capable of winning his approval. All this added up to spiritual need.

I continued to read the Bible and to discuss these things with the new acquaintances I'd met through Larry. My awareness of this spiritual need caused me to view the things they said in a different light. Only days later, I went to a "concert" at a church in New Jersey. I should have been very happy that night. I had just been promoted from junior copywriter to full copywriter at J.C. Penney. I had the love of my family and friends--a nice place to live, a promising future. But as I sat in the church, all I could think of was the fact that I was in the midst of holy things, and I felt unholy. I knew I didn't belong--not because I was Jewish or because anyone had passed judgment on me. I knew I didn't belong because these people had a relationship with God, and I didn't.

I left the church building and sat out on the front lawn. It was a summer night and the air was warm. I sat cross-legged as I looked up at the stars (something you can't do in the city!). There's something about looking at a slice of creation like that which makes conversation with the Creator very appropriate and natural. I told God that I, too, wanted to have a relationship with him. I found myself tearfully confessing to God on the front lawn of that church that I believed Jesus was the Messiah. I accepted the fact that he had taken the punishment for my sin, just as the prophet Isaiah had written. I told God that I wanted the forgiveness he offered through Jesus, and that I wanted to live for him.

As far as I knew, I was the only Jewish believer in Jesus on the face of the earth. Now I was faced with finding a place where I could worship with other people who believed that Jesus was the Messiah. I dismissed what I saw as "establishment churchianity." Instead, I gravitated toward a black church. While it wasn't culturally Jewish, at least it was culturally ethnic, and that made me feel more comfortable. In the beginning, I attributed a number of things to Christianity which were simply a part of the culture of that particular church. All the women wore hats, so I assumed that just as Jewish men wear yarmulkas in synagogue, Christian women wear hats in church!

I didn't expect my family to be overjoyed with my decision, but the priority of God in my life overshadowed whatever fears of rejection I may have had. Still, I wasn't quite prepared for my mother's reaction. "Susan," she said, "it would have been better if you had come to tell me you were pregnant." I was also completely taken aback by the way my Gentile roommates responded. None of them had ever used the name of Jesus as anything other than a swear word until I decided to believe in him. Then they tried to "shake me loose" of what they saw as "archaic superstition." Church and Christianity had been present to some extent in all their upbringings, though mostly as a cultural experience.

Each felt shocked and disappointed that I, as a Jew, would "regress" to a religion they felt they had outgrown.

Meanwhile, the reality of God became more and more sharply focused in my life. After work I would go to midtown Manhattan, passing out tracts I had purchased and telling the prostitutes and other street people about Jesus. The more I read the Bible, the deeper my understanding of God's plan to redeem people became.

Three months after I made my decision to believe in Jesus, something tremendous happened. I was talking to a Christian couple, and they casually mentioned something about the other Jewish believers they knew. "Others?!?" I said. "You mean there are actually other Jewish people who believe the way I do?"

I couldn't wait to meet these other Jewish believers in Jesus; it was like "coming home." It was so good to meet people who understood some of the hardships of being Jewish and believing in Jesus. I began to see distinctions between Gentile culture and Christian theology. I was able to set aside certain things which had felt a bit strange and alien to me without setting aside my belief in Y'shua. I didn't have to begin each prayer with phrases like, "Our dear gracious heavenly father we come unto thee in prayer...."

As I met more and more Jewish believers, my understanding of Jesus as the Jewish Messiah also deepened. I studied the promises God made to our people and began to see how being Jewish gave me even more reason to trust Jesus. I also learned that negative reactions from Jewish friends and family were not based on the content of what I believed. They were based on the emotional supposition that it was not right for Jews to believe in Jesus because he is viewed as the god of the Gentiles, who have hated and persecuted us.

I wanted to use my "cause-oriented" zeal as well as my experience in writing and drama to work at dispelling these misunderstandings. My first idea was to travel in a converted school bus with a few of the other Jewish believers I had met and proclaim our message across the country. We often discussed such plans, but between the four of us, I think I was the only one who really expected anything to come of it.   I decided I would have to go about my plans in a more organized way.   That is how I came to work with Jews for Jesus.

All my life, I had wanted to "make a difference," to be part of the solution, not the problem.   Nursing had not been the road for me, neither had marching for peace.   As worthwhile as those endeavors were, they could only touch the symptoms, not the source of life's problems.   Our pains and our griefs come because we are living in a world gone crazy--a world torn apart by rebellion against our Creator.   Introducing others to Jesus is the best way that I can "make a difference"--because he alone can make *the* difference.

PAUL STEINER

*I gradually realized that I had an emotional stake in **not** believing in Jesus. I was more concerned with avoiding the conflict of becoming a Christian than with discovering the truth. This was not logical and it troubled me. Was I being hypocritical? One day I was talking to April on the telephone and discovered, to my surprise, that I believed Jesus is the Messiah.*

I like races. In fact, I ran the "Bay to Breakers" race on my wedding day. People tease me about it, but my wife, Jodee, was very understanding. She knows I like races because of the satisfaction I get from achieving goals. And besides, the Bay to Breakers race in San Francisco is only seven miles long. I ran in the morning and got married in the afternoon without much "sweat."

I began running in Seattle, back in 1977, just to get in shape for backpacking and mountain climbing. When I started to work at Boeing, one of my co-workers, a runner, said, "Hey Steiner, you said you run now and then, why don't you get out there and prove it?" It was a challenge I couldn't resist, and we ended up training and entering a marathon together. Running has been a hobby of mine ever since.

I'll never forget my first marathon--the Vancouver-British Columbia International Marathon. At the start, the sidelines were crowded; everyone was smiling and encouraging us to "go for it." My goal was to finish in under four hours, but mostly, I just wanted to finish! I started at an even pace and felt pretty good for the first 15 miles. I thought, "Wow, it's incredible that I can run this long without stopping. I feel great!" And it really is a fantastic feeling to run, say, two hours without stopping.

Then fatigue began to set in and I began to worry: "Do I have what it takes to finish a race? Did I use too much energy at the beginning?" I wondered how I would finish the race, if I would finish. I held back, slowed down. It was a cold, wet day and by the eighteenth mile, there were very few people left to cheer us on. My morale sank and I wondered what I was doing out there anyway. Just about every part of my body was hurting. I was soaked in hot sweat and cold rain. All I wanted was to sit down at the side of the road and give up. Something inside kept me going, but just barely.

Focus is a key ingredient to finishing any race. I lost my focus toward the end and started to walk. I only walked for a hundred yards or so, but after that, the rest of the race was a real struggle. I had to push harder than I thought possible to finish the last few miles, but I forced myself to run again and actually completed the race in three hours, fifty-six minutes and forty seconds. It didn't matter that I wasn't first. I crossed that finish line, my arms stretched up over my head, and I felt like I'd accomplished the greatest feat in the world.

I guess I've run about a half-dozen marathons since then. Once I knew I could make it to the finish, the races provided an opportunity to set higher goals for myself--to concentrate on strategy and pacing, and to push my finishing time lower and lower.

Regardless of the number of races run, there's always pain for the runner who wants to do well--and there is always a struggle to keep a grip on one's standards. Runners who've competed in far more races than I have tell me they wrestle with the same thoughts that have crossed my mind: "Why are you going so fast, why do you want to kill yourself?" Or, "You can slow down and still do okay." One is always tempted to take it easy, slow down, avoid the pain. That's human nature, and it doesn't only apply to running marathons. The discipline it takes to run a race is not unlike the discipline it takes to be married, to hold down a job, or even to live a life in accordance with one's belief in God.

If you're wondering where the part about Jesus comes in, this is where I tell you that I believe he is the Jewish Messiah. I never wanted to believe in him. I come from an Orthodox Jewish home and, frankly, I could've done without the pain it caused to believe something which my family regarded as some kind of treason. But the sense of commitment I have when I run a race is the same thing that keeps me going with Jesus--even when I'd rather take the easy way out. You want an explanation? Well, I'll tell you....

I was born in New York City in 1952, and raised in Cambria Heights, a small community about four blocks from the city line which separates Queens from Nassau County. Our neighborhood was about a 50/50 mixture of Jews and Gentiles, and the Gentiles were primarily Catholic. I have very strong memories of people being either Jewish or Catholic. I met most of my friends through the synagogue and we all went to the same public school as

224

well. I don't recall having any non-Jewish friends.

I remember dressing in my dark suit and going to the synagogue with my father each Saturday. Dad and I would walk up the center aisle to our seats near the front; I'd give my friends in the last row a backward glance and envy them for sitting together. The row of stained glass windows that lined our sanctuary would have been even prettier with the sun shining through, but there wasn't much light. Our synagogue was somewhat dim, with the musty scent of something damp which had never quite dried.

There was a reason why my friends could sit together in the back while my father and I made our way toward the front of the synagogue. My father is a Kohen; therefore I, too, am a Kohen. Kohens have a special role in the Orthodox service: we are the hereditary priests. There were only two families of Kohens in our synagogue, so our already elite families were even more highly regarded. There was always a sense of our being set apart in the synagogue; people knew we were Kohens and that was something special. Everyone expected that one day, when I was bar mitzvah, I would begin taking part in the service just as my father took part. And I must say, even if I missed sitting with my friends, it felt good being special and I was glad to be a Kohen.

After services, my mother prepared a lunch of cold salads, but she left one stove burner on throughout the Sabbath to warm the food she'd cooked the day before. My father said the blessings over the wine and bread before we ate. He would not use electricity or ride in a car on the Sabbath. My mother did not share his convictions, but Dad seemed to look the other way when she did things he considered "forbidden."

I grew to resent our strict religious lifestyle, which both my family and friends seemed to experience as nothing more than a set of regulations. I do have positive memories of holidays like Purim and *Simchas Torah*--the joyous celebrations, after all, were fun. I enjoyed the social aspects of the synagogue and had a number of good friends there. I was less appreciative of the rabbi and his sermons, which were weekly lectures on everything that was wrong with "young people today." I was not the only young person in the congregation who found that tiresome. I don't think our rabbi was particularly typical of Orthodox Judaism, but he did not contribute anything positive to a system with which I was growing increasingly disenchanted.

When I approached my 13th birthday, my father gave me a choice. I could either go to Israel or have a big party. All my friends had celebrated their 13th birthdays with a "big bash," and I had been looking forward to the day when it would be my turn. I'm afraid my dad was disappointed when I asked for the party, but I think he also knew it was a natural choice for a 13-year-old. I learned all the necessary rituals, including the laying of tefillin. This I did faithfully for about a year after I became bar mitzvah.

Concerning the laying of tefillin--I didn't especially want to do it; I just knew it was expected. It was a chore, like making my bed was a chore. I needed to lay tefillin to stay on good terms with my dad. Eventually, my father realized I was only doing it for his sake, and he began exerting less pressure on me to join him. I gradually eased out of performing the ritual altogether.

It began to bother me that people who professed to believe in keeping the Law would find loopholes and other ways to avoid the inconveniences. I watched people acting like Orthodox Jews in synagogue on Saturdays, and then saw them going out for Chinese food the next day. Some even had a set of dishes at home for non-kosher food. Others would park their car a couple of blocks away from the synagogue on the Sabbath so people could see them walking there instead of driving. Of course, for observant Jews, driving on the Sabbath was strictly forbidden, and eating non-kosher food anywhere is taboo. So all the little ways of sidestepping the restrictions really bothered me, not because they weren't keeping the Law--I didn't believe in it and never professed to. But I simply thought those who did believe, or said they did, should act on it and do what the Law says. I prided myself on being an analytical, logical person who exercised sound reasoning. It annoyed me when I saw people acting illogically, and in this case, I felt they were acting hypocritically. It seemed that religions were created by man and for man, and that any was as valid as another. Whatever "works best" for each individual was sufficient. I concluded that what would work best for me would be to reject the religious lifestyle altogether. I never rejected my Jewish heritage; just the religious rituals. I rarely thought about God; I didn't feel the need to. I felt I could handle life myself. If a problem arose, I could put all my efforts together to solve it somehow.

After high school, I went to Cornell University. I involved myself in routine rebellions common to my age and to the era of the early '70s. I guess I wasn't too rebellious, since I managed to make the dean's list. I earned an A.B. in chemistry, with a heavy emphasis on engineering as a minor.

After Cornell, I moved to Seattle. I spent the next five years teaching organic chemistry at the University of Washington while earning my Ph.D. That was a time of making choices and giving up the rebellion of my high school and undergraduate years. I was setting career goals, breaking bad habits, and feeling good about the person I saw myself becoming.

Toward the end of that "shaping up" time, I had help and encouragement from a friend and former student named April. I didn't know it, but she had become a Christian after she'd been my pupil and before we became friends. I did notice that she had become "more religious" than I remembered. God was a frequent topic of her conversations.

April didn't preach, she just mused over issues and asked questions like, "Why do people say 'God damn it' when they curse?" I always felt a little uncomfortable when she wanted to discuss such things. I listened politely because she was a good friend, and because I respected her, but I let her do most of the talking. I regarded these discussions as a minor imposition--part of what one "puts up with" for friendship's sake. When I did interact, it was usually to answer her questions. She would say, "Well, what do you think about that?" and she wasn't the type to settle for "Gee, I don't know." She always probed to see what I really thought.

These conversations were usually theoretical and not penetratingly personal, so I didn't find them too threatening. Once we were late for a Seattle Sonics play-off game because April was late from church and that was somewhat irritating, but I didn't make a big deal over it.

I became more and more absorbed in completing my thesis, the title of which was, "The synthesis of new and novel sulphur nitrogen compounds and nitrocompounds for use in peptide synthesis." Okay, so it doesn't sound especially interesting. When you're a scientist, you don't have to be interesting. You just have to be right! Anyway, my Ph.D. was in synthetic organic chemistry.

Meanwhile, April became more involved with her new-found faith. Later I discovered that she had been reluctant to tell me about it because of her sensitivity to my Jewishness and her fear of offending me. But shortly after I defended my dissertation, April fought down her fears and told me everything I never wanted to know about Jesus, and never would have thought to ask.

It happened on a sunny afternoon. We were sitting in my car. I was trying to listen and understand what April was saying, but as I sat staring out the window, I couldn't help thinking, "What kind of abnormal occurrence took place here? She used to be such a nice girl...has she really gone off the deep end?" By the end of our first conversation about Jesus, I was completely convinced there was no validity to April's beliefs. I considered myself an intellectual and a scientist. April, on the other hand, seemed to believe that fairy tales were real. She was telling me that Jesus was born of a virgin, did miracles and that he rose from the dead...incredible!

The next time we met, April brought along a Bible and a taped series from a book entitled *Evidence that Demands a Verdict*, by Josh McDowell. It was a wise choice, because evidence was precisely what I needed. The book begins with four chapters about the Bible, giving historical and archaeological evidence for its reliability. The next six chapters are about the person of Jesus: his claims, fulfillment of prophecy and resurrection. The last few chapters deal with more specifics on messianic prophecy, as well as touching on the author's own experience of faith. This analytical approach was an acceptable challenge.

As a scientist, I understood the proper methods of examining evidence to reach a conclusion. I carefully considered the case this book was making for the "Old Testament," and was convinced that our Scriptures were true, and should be taken literally.

I had always considered the Bible somewhat like a history book and assumed that as such, it would contain some truths as well as some inaccuracies. One of the things that convinced me it was more than a history book was learning how the Scriptures were transmitted from generation to generation: the painstaking care taken to be sure every letter, every vowel was identical to the previous copy. When the Dead Sea Scrolls were discovered, it was found that in content, they were basically identical to the Old Testament which is used today. There is also scientific evidence to substantiate many Old Testament accounts of events, such as the flood in Genesis. There is even thought to be evidence for Noah's ark. In addition, Old Testament predictions--for example, that the city of Tyre would be destroyed, every stone be torn down and tossed into the sea--came true. Such pieces of information taken separately don't prove the validity of the Old Testament as being an inspired work, but taken together, they give an overwhelming amount of evidence that is really more than circumstantial. Because I was Jewish, it was a small step of faith for me to take the evidence I saw and conclude that the Old Testament was both accurate and inspired by God.

That meant there is a God who wants us to know and obey him. I was mildly surprised to find myself thinking along such lines, but it was not too difficult to accept. It didn't contradict the two things I really valued: my Jewish roots and my scientific mindset.

Many people have misconceptions about scientists; they think because we study facts and formulas, we have no room for belief in God. The truth is, the more one learns about the complexities of the universe, the harder it is to believe that it came into being without a Creator. I found it took more commitment to less logic to deny God's existence than to accept it.

But when I began considering the case for the "New Testament," and Jesus as the answer to messianic prophecy, the barriers began to slam down. Normally, I am an achievement-oriented kind of guy. My hobbies have ranged from running marathon races to climbing to the top of Mount Kilimanjaro (the highest mountain in Africa). Yet, discovering if Jesus might be true was not the kind of adventure or achievement I wanted.

April continued to ask me what I thought of these mysteries and I always had an answer...but as I listened to my own answers, my logic began to appear convoluted even to me.

I found myself trying to twist what the Bible was saying so I wouldn't have to take it literally. Maybe the resurrection didn't really mean Jesus was raised from the dead in a literal sense. Maybe people just felt his presence, as one might feel the presence of an old friend just by walking into that person's house. The miracles might have a similar explanation; maybe Lazarus really hadn't died. Maybe the records and the medical practice in those days weren't as good as they are today and he was simply unconscious or very ill. He didn't come back from the grave, he just became healthier. I was reaching for anything to avoid the truth, but my answers really didn't make a whole lot of sense, even to me. I treated prophecies in a similar matter. I'd protest, "It doesn't say it refers to Jesus." I tried to interpret Isaiah 53 by saying the prophet wasn't even referring to the Messiah. When April turned to the New Testament, showing that Jesus was more than a mere man, I would try to direct the conversation elsewhere.

I gradually realized that I was behaving this way because I had an emotional stake in not believing in Jesus. I was more concerned with avoiding the conflict of becoming a Christian than with discovering the truth. This was not logical and it troubled me. Was I being hypocritical? One day I was talking to April on the telephone, and discovered, to my surprise, that I believed Jesus was the Messiah.

There was a point in our conversation when we were discussing biblical matters, as we had done in the past. By then, my answers were getting less convoluted and more truthful. And when April asked, "Why don't you believe in Jesus?" I heard myself tell her, "Well, I do." I think it was just at the point when I said "I do believe in Jesus" that I actually did.

In retrospect, I think the most convincing piece of evidence to me for the case of Jesus being the Messiah was the resurrection. I'd studied a bit about the Roman guards during that period, so I knew those soldiers were standing back to back, guarding that tomb with their lives. If anything happened, they would be killed. That was pretty convincing, plus Josh McDowell gives references for Jesus and the resurrection from other books besides the Bible. The empty tomb, I think, is what got me to believe.

I hadn't planned to believe; and when the fact of my belief came out in our telephone conversation, I felt a little bit frightened at what I had said. I was worried about the implications, especially the change in family relationships I knew would occur as a result of my new faith. I wasn't confused. I didn't know enough to be confused. I just knew what it would do to my family and that worried me.

Shortly after I became a believer, April went to Europe and I took a job in the San Francisco Bay Area. So basically, we went our separate ways but remained friends. At this point, my parents knew nothing about my new-found faith. I didn't start going to church until several months after I became a believer. I was in a new area and was not comfortable with the idea of walking into a church by myself. After living in the Bay Area for a couple of months, I decided to try a church April had suggested before she left for Europe. The church she had recommended was a little too far away; I was looking for some place closer and I didn't know where. I called the church April had suggested and they gave me the name of a church much closer to where I was living. It was "Chapel of the Good Shepherd," a small, non-denominational congregation. There were only 70 people in the whole church; nevertheless, I was amazed to find that there were three other Jewish believers in Jesus there. It didn't take them long to find out that I was a Jewish believer, too. One girl was going to Bible studies at the

Jews for Jesus headquarters, so I went with her and started meeting some of the people there. In fact, soon after I began attending that church, Jews for Jesus came and gave us a presentation called "Christ in the Passover."

I was impressed to see how those familiar things which had been said and done in my home each year actually pointed to Jesus. The mere fact that Jesus was celebrating Passover on the night he was betrayed was exciting to me--he was really one of us! It was interesting to see how the church's ritual "communion celebration" was taken right from Jesus' statement about the third cup--the cup of redemption. This helped me to see how some of the church's celebrations are not alien to their Jewish roots.

I saw new meaning in many of the things I had done as I was growing up, and it made me feel really good about being Jewish. I just sat there with my mouth hanging open during much of the presentation. I was so pleased to learn of the connection between my background and my faith in Jesus. Up until that point, I had thought, "I am a Christian now; I was a Jew before." There really was little connection between my "former" life and my "new" life. After hearing that presentation, I understood more about the depth of my identity. I was able to see that I'm still Jewish and Christian, and there is no need for me to separate the two. I felt proud to be Jewish and to be a Christian.

I still hadn't told my parents about my faith, but by then I was more active in my Christian life. Between going to church and getting more involved with Jews for Jesus, I felt I had to tell my parents. It was too big a part of my life to hide any longer; to do so, I felt, was being dishonest with them. So I wrote a letter to my parents explaining my faith. By then, I'd been a believer for about a year. It was very difficult. They were upset, just as I'd expected. Though it was discouraging, I still felt I'd done the right thing.

After all, the Creator of the Universe made promises to the people he created, promises in which the Jewish people, my people, figure prominently. God keeps his promises and offers his friendship and fellowship to any who put their faith in him. I experienced great joy in this discovery, and I knew I shouldn't keep it to myself.

Eventually I married one of the women on staff with Jews for Jesus--another Jewish believer--Jodee. As you know, I began our wedding day by running a race. Now we're in "the race" together, Jodee and I. It's not that we're rushing to get somewhere. We're just pressing on, two Jews, following Jesus, determined to hang in and go where he leads us.

SCOTT RUBIN

I'm recovering from heart transplant surgery. But I had a "change of heart" long before my surgery, when in November of 1979 I sat in a synagogue and admitted to God that I knew Jesus was the Messiah.

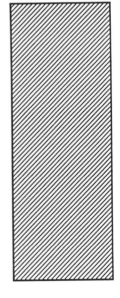

My father is a pediatrician with a private practice in Beverly Hills. My mother is his office manager. They are both Jewish, both born and raised in Chicago.

I was also born in Chicago--on May 9, 1957--but grew up in Southern California where I now live with my wife and two children. I am a corporate trust administrator, currently on a medical disability leave. You see, I'm recovering from heart transplant surgery. But I had a "change of heart" long before my surgery, when in November of 1979 I sat in a synagogue and admitted to God that I knew Jesus was the Messiah.

The first conversation I remember having with God was when I was 4 years old. Mom prepared my brother and me for a new addition to the family by telling us to ask God for another brother. I went outside, looked up at the sky, and dutifully asked the Almighty to please give me another brother. We even named my "brother-to-be" Mark, and I can't tell you how surprised I was when "Mark" turned out to be Dana Michelle!

I thought about God again when my great uncle died. My relatives said that he had gone to heaven to be with God. I wondered briefly what that would be like.

When I was 10 years old, I watched my grandmother become very ill with cancer. I pleaded with God to make her better, but she died anyway. I didn't think much more about God after that. In my youthful estimation, his batting average was rather poor.

My lack of interest in God did not affect my synagogue involvement. My memories of our synagogue stretch back as far as the third grade. We attended a Reform synagogue near our home, and I began going to Hebrew school there twice a week. I liked the classes and did well, receiving the academic award for my class year. Before Hebrew school, our family celebrations only included Hanukkah and Passover, but once my brother and I began Hebrew school, we observed all of the holidays to help us learn about our heritage. It was fun to build the booths for Sukkot, and I loved twirling *gragers* and biting into gooey-centered hamantaschen at Purim.

We also attended Sabbath services, but when a controversy arose over the rabbinic staff, ours was among the many families to leave.

We joined a large Conservative congregation in West Los Angeles, where I became bar mitzvah in 1970. It was a beautiful building, with impressive stained glass windows behind the bimah. The Torah scrolls were encased in glistening covers of elaborately worked silver and gold. (My parents still attend this synagogue for High Holiday services, though they rarely go to shul on the Sabbath anymore.) Most of the service was conducted in Hebrew, and I remember noticing that the majority of people didn't seem to know quite what it meant. I know my family didn't understand most of the prayers. Still, we found comfort in the synagogue because it was a tradition which provided an important sense of belonging.

After high school, I studied at Pomona College in Claremont, California. I took a course on "philosophy of religion," much of which was devoted to the Holocaust. By the end of that course I had concluded that God was vicious and capricious, a punisher of innocent people. I blamed God for all the world's evils and considered him unworthy of worship. A few Christians on campus tried to convince me otherwise, but they could not counter my accusations. As for my concept of the Messiah, it was completely unrelated to God. I imagined he would come when there was peace in the world; and if we wanted peace, I reasoned, we had better not rely on God to bring it.

I graduated from Pomona with a B.A. in economics and spent the next six months in the Army, training as a medical supply officer. Then I returned to Los Angeles, joined a reserve unit and immediately went on a two-week training drill.

That's where I met Captain Peterson, who was doing doctoral work at U.C.L.A. He asked me about Judaism and since I didn't want to show my ignorance, I answered as authoritatively as I could. When he asked me about the significance of the seven-branched candelabrum, I insisted that there was no such thing--that the candelabrum was supposed to have eight branches! In the midst of trying to answer his questions I realized I was being defensive because I didn't know about candelabra and ancient Jewish worship.

Then Captain Peterson asked, "In light of the prophets, why don't Jewish people believe that Jesus is the Messiah?" I could not use my standard argument against God and religion based on the suffering in the world because Captain Peterson had asked me a very specific question. It was not a question which could be answered based on evidence seen in the world around us. It was a question about the Jewish Bible.

I asked to which prophets he was referring, and he answered with passages from Isaiah, Jeremiah and Zechariah. It seemed pointless for me to continue bluffing. By this time, I had become curious and wanted to find out for myself what he was talking about. So I told Captain Peterson that I would look into it and then get back to him.

I returned to Los Angeles and went to a bookstore where I purchased a black, leatherbound Bible. I read through the prophecies Captain Peterson had mentioned and I read the Gospels. My training in economics had taught me to analyze people's actions based upon their incentives. I began analyzing the supposed resurrection of Jesus in that fashion.

Who would have had incentive to take his body? The guards? No, they would not purposely do something which would show they had failed at their post. The Jewish leaders? No, they wanted an end to the whole Jesus business. The disciples? They must have been severely depressed over the death of their teacher, but that would not have been cause for them to spend the rest of their lives following a lie. They certainly would not choose to die for a lie; yet they were martyred for their belief in Jesus. There was no body in that tomb and no incentive for taking it, if indeed it had been possible to get past the sentries, which seemed doubtful. Thousands of people reportedly saw Jesus alive after his death. I concluded that it was more logical to believe in the resurrection than not.

Here I was, a nice Jewish boy who had just reached the conclusion that Jesus had been raised from the dead. I didn't know what to do. I went for a walk with my father and told him what I was thinking. He raised objections to the resurrection and suggested various solutions to explain the missing body. I had already raised each of these objections in my own mind, so I answered each one and repeated the conclusions I had drawn.

When we got back to the house a terrible argument ensued and my father told me he wanted me out of his house. I had no choice but to leave, and as I thought through my alternatives, I decided to return to Claremont. That was where I had received my education, and as far as I was concerned, the issue of Jesus was a matter of learning an objective truth.

I began spending time with a local rabbi. I even took a class he was team-teaching with another rabbi for converts to Judasim because I wanted to make sure I understood the fundamentals of our religion. I also audited a secular class on biblical heritage at my old college campus. At the same time, I began participating in a Christian Bible study on the Gospel of John.

I was convinced, after two and a half months of comparative study, that Jesus was the Messiah. I wasn't sure how or even if that should affect my life. One Tuesday night, before the class for Jewish converts began, I asked the rabbi if he would open the auditorium of the synagogue for me. He asked me why, and I told him that I wanted to pray. He looked as though I had made a peculiar request, but he unlocked the doors for me.

I went to the front row of the synagogue and sat down. I simply told God that I believed Jesus was the Messiah, but that he would have to show me what that meant and what I needed to do next.

Two days later I was investigating an account as an auditor for a bank and met an employee there, a woman named Janice, who later became my wife. Janice had just given the bank her two weeks' notice, so if I'd delayed looking into the account, we never would have met.

I asked Janice out to lunch and somewhere in the conversation she mentioned her church. I told her that I was Jewish, but that I believed in Jesus. The assistant pastor at the church Janice attended happened to be a Jewish believer in Jesus, too. She introduced me to him, and over the next year or so I learned what it meant to know the Messiah. I found that God is concerned with our hearts. I had once thought the Messiah would come when there was peace in the world, but now I saw there could be no peace without him. There must be peace between God and his creation before his creation can be at peace with itself.

I was 22 years old when I accepted Jesus as my Messiah. Though I didn't know it at the time, it was the most important decision of my life. I discovered that through Jesus, I could have the intimacy with God that our ancestors wrote about in the Tanach. As I learned more about God, he became more and more important to me. Through recent troubles, I learned to prize my relationship with him above all else. And though I still cannot explain the evil in the world, I do know the goodness and mercy I've found in God.

By the time I was 28, I had a beautiful wife, twin sons, and a promising new job...everything was "going my way." My biggest complaint was the high cost of parking in downtown Los Angeles. In fact, I began taking the bus to work for that very reason.

I was detained at work one evening because of a conference call. When I hung up the phone I saw that I only had five minutes to reach my bus stop three full blocks away. With the L.A. bus system, I knew I'd be in for a long wait if I didn't make it. I was anxious to get home to Janice and our twin 14-month-old boys, so I sprinted the distance. I managed to catch the bus, but was unable to catch my breath. As I felt my heart pounding furiously, I chided myself for being out of shape.

I couldn't sleep that night because of the tightness in my chest. Within a few days, I had a dry cough and was terribly weak, especially in my arms. I had to use both hands just to carry my briefcase. That Friday, I went to an internist, where I was given a battery of tests. My problem was heart failure; a virus had seriously damaged my most vital muscle. I spent three weeks in the Cardiac Intensive Care Unit, then the doctors sent me home. They prescribed a year of bedrest, and then they would reevaluate the damage.

It only got worse after I went home. I couldn't keep food down and I was getting progressively weaker. I was readmitted to the hospital for more tests. The doctors gave me some drugs and sent me home again. Within a week, I was back in the hospital. I was dying. The doctors had to put me on the most powerful heart and kidney medication available in order to keep me alive.

On Saturday, July 27, my doctor told Janice to pack our bags. He wanted us ready to fly up to Stanford University Hospital in Palo Alto at a moment's notice. Stanford has the best heart transplant program in the world.

Hundreds of Christians were praying for me. People at my church were praying, the staff at Jews for Jesus were praying...and about a year's worth of red tape was cleared away in one day! Early Monday evening, my doctor told me I would be flown to Stanford by emergency air ambulance at 9 o'clock the next morning.

I had a steady stream of visitors that night. Their prayers and words of encouragement were a tremendous comfort. Avi Snyder, of the Los Angeles branch of Jews for Jesus, told me that I needed to decide now how I would handle this ordeal. I could grit my teeth and tough it out on my own, or I could focus every ounce of my attention on God and rely on his strength and wisdom to see me through. I decided on the latter.

I arrived at Stanford on Tuesday, and by Thursday my doctor told me that the only thing keeping my heart from stopping was the steady drip, drip, drip of the intravenous medication. They would try once more that night to take me off the medication, but it seemed likely that my only chance for survival would be a heart transplant. That would mean more examinations and two more doctors to determine whether or not I should be accepted as a transplant candidate.

I remembered the work God had already done in my heart, showing me that Jesus is the Messiah and bringing me into a personal relationship with him. I knew my heart was right with him spiritually. If he wanted to make my heart right physically, he would provide a way. I was ready to meet God, but I hoped for Janice and the boys' sake that God had another plan. And as I prayed, he gave me a calm sort of confidence that he would bring me through.

My doctor came back the next morning (Friday) to inform me that the attempt to take me off the medication had been unsuccessful. But he added the good news that more red tape had been dispensed with--that I had been accepted as a transplant candidate and given top priority because of the seriousness of my condition. Some people criticize doctors for "playing God," but I can't help thinking that God himself was with the doctors as they made their decisions.

By this time, there was a network of people praying for me all across the country. In addition to the people from the church I attended, and the staff at Jews for Jesus, my wife has relatives in churches all across the country, and even the Philippines, who were praying, too. All together, there must have been a thousand people asking God to heal me.

I called my parents and told them that I had been placed on the waiting list for a heart transplant and that they should fly up to see me right away--before I went into surgery. My parents replied that it could take a month or longer before a donor became available, and that they were coming up to see me on Sunday. I protested. I knew it usually took awhile before transplant candidates went into surgery, but I pointed out that a thousand people were praying for me and I was certain that something unusual was about to happen.

Saturday noon the nurses received a call: "Take Scott Rubin off food and water, there is a potential donor." Again, I called my parents and asked them to come right away. But they knew the score. A potential donor isn't the same as a donor. Everything has to be just right in order for the new heart to be considered compatible, and there are usually some false starts before the actual donor is found. Again, I pointed out that a thousand people were praying for me, and they should come immediately. They told me they still intended to wait until the following day.

At two o'clock that afternoon, the transplant surgeon came into my room to introduce himself to me. He announced that there was a 95.6% chance that I would be in surgery that evening. I asked him if it would be appropriate for me to call my parents and have them fly up, and he replied, "Absolutely!"

This time, I said to my parents, "Remember the thousand people who are praying for me? Well, I'm going into surgery in about 3 hours; I sure hope you can make it." My mother said she would hop in and out of the shower, dress in a jiffy, and they would be at the airport in no time at all. "Mom!" I said, "I don't care if you're a little sweaty. Forget about the shower!" She took the shower anyway, and they arrived at Stanford at 5:30. My surgery was running a little behind schedule, so we had about 15 minutes together.

I asked my mom and dad to promise that no matter how things turned out for me, they would carefully consider the evidence that Jesus is our Messiah. They only patted my arm and said, "We'll talk about it later, son."

I recovered from the surgery quickly. I was in the hospital for less than a month, and within 9 weeks, I was able to return to Los Angeles.

A miracle of science enables doctors to replace a heart that is dying with one that is healthy. But it is a miracle of God alone that can replace a heart that is dead by virtue of separation from him with a new heart that lives in communion with him. That is why the Messiah came--so that God could give us a new heart and a new life.

LAURA WERTHEIM

Laura Bing Wertheim was born in Eppersthausen, Germany, on October 15, 1930. Six years later, a ship called "The Manhattan" carried Laura and her family safely away from Nazi Germany and into the rush and roar of New York City. Her grandparents were not so fortunate. By the time they realized the terror that was upon their country, it was too late.... Laura would never forget the murder of her grandparents or the fact that they were killed because they were Jews.

Compared to Hitler's Germany, New York City was heaven. But that didn't mean we were living on "Easy Street." My mother took a job in a factory, pasting leather linings into handbags. She worked hard and kept on working at that same factory until she retired at the age of 65. My father took a job as a butcher in a wholesale house, cutting up meat until the day he retired. They both worked very hard to make the best life they could for the three of us.

I am so thankful that we came to this country when I was still young. It's a terrible thing to live in fear. Coming to America was like waking up from a terrible dream. It was easy for me to smile here, and I made friends quickly. Still, everything wasn't all roses--even though we were thousands of miles away from Hitler's Germany, there were still people who hated the Jews. I learned to stand up for myself and my people. The children at school who made the mistake of calling me a "dirty Jew" figured out in a hurry that I would rather use my fists than be bullied.

Of course, being Jewish meant more to me than defending myself and my people from being called nasty names by anti-Semites. My family attended an Orthodox shul. We didn't go on every Sabbath, but we went often enough to be considered a "religious" family. Yet, I never considered myself a particularly religious person. "Being religious" was just a small part of being Jewish. Being Jewish also meant we had a common history and we had ways of talking and relating and caring about the same things-- those things were more important to me than being religious.

I began praying to God when I was just a little girl, and I always knew he was there. I prayed to him when I wanted something good, something he could do for me. I never stopped to think that it might work the other way too--that God might want something from me. This attitude did not change as I grew into my teen years. Yet I continued to be active in the synagogue.

The synagogue was for social as well as religious purposes. Some people came to shul because they were devoted to Torah, but there were many who were not so religious, and they were as important a part of synagogue as those who were. For the younger people like me, going to shul was an opportunity to dress up, to flirt, and to meet future husbands and wives.

One Tuesday night, my mother and I were helping to serve cake and fruit to the men who had come to study the Torah. That's how I met Fred Wertheim. Fred didn't lose any time in trying to make a date with me--but I left the synagogue in a hurry to avoid saying yes. It didn't work though, because my mother, bless her heart, forgot to pack up some of her serving pieces and I had to go back and get them. When Fred saw that I'd come back, he asked me out again and he was so persistent that I finally gave in and agreed to see him.

I bought a pair of new, black alligator shoes for the occasion, low heeled to make sure I wouldn't be taller than Fred. I was just the right height, but the new soles were so slippery that as we walked down the steps en route to our first date, my feet slid right out from under me! Poor Freddy just looked at me there on the ground--I guess he was in shock. Then we both started to laugh. It was easy to feel relaxed around Fred, even in an embarrassing situation like that...but I wouldn't exactly say that he "swept me off my feet!" In fact, I came up with excuses when he tried to date me again. I remember being careful not to mention my sweet sixteen party to Freddy, because I hadn't invited him. Of course he eventually found out about it anyway. He felt bad, and I guess I did too...but I still wasn't interested in dating him.

One Saturday night I was going out with another fellow and lo and behold, who was coming up the street to pay a visit but Freddy. When he saw that I had other plans, he decided to stay and visit with my parents anyway. We left, my date and I, while Freddy made himself at home with my family.

It wasn't just any fellow who could feel at ease with a girl's parents, and eventually I recognized that Fred Wertheim was the man for me. That summer I worked as a mother's helper in Long Beach, Long Island. Fred came to visit me whenever he could, and when he couldn't, I would take the train into the city to see him instead. It was a schlepp, but I missed him so much when he didn't come...that's when I realized that I couldn't live without him. So in 1949, I asked him to marry me. Our wedding was on October 22--a week after my 19th birthday.

In our first few years together, Fred was a partner in a delicatessen business. He'd start work very early each morning and keep at it until 11 o'clock every night. Our older boy, Steven, was born on August 3, 1951. In 1956, Fred went to work for the U.S. Postal Service. His hours there were more reasonable and I was very happy that he was able to spend more time with Steve and me. In May of 1958, our younger boy, Robert, was born.

Freddy was at work when I went into labor, so a friend's husband offered to drive me to the hospital. But I was feeling very independent and figured I was strong enough to get there on my own. I called a cab, arranged for Fred to pick up Steven from school, and off to the hospital I went. That was just my style.

I was getting pretty much what I expected and wanted out of life. My loving husband was a good provider and a good father to our two beautiful boys. We lived in a pleasant neighborhood, Washington Heights, in Upper Manhattan. It was the kind of neighborhood where we all knew each other--we rejoiced over each other's births, bar mitzvahs and weddings--and comforted one another through the not-so-joyous times. The years went by without anything too unusual happening; I'd say we had an average share of joys and sorrows.

Then in 1975, Steven decided to move to California--California, the place some Easterners call "the land of fruits and nuts," and not because of all the farmland, either! Fred and I hated to see our oldest go, but what could we do? Steven really wasn't a boy any longer--he was a young man of 24 years. He was a good son who had shown respect for his parents, but he was also restless to leave New York. So off he went, and Fred and I comforted ourselves with the fact that our Steven was levelheaded. He would get a responsible job and he would certainly keep in touch with his mother and father.

As we expected, Steven got a good job right away; he went to work at a bank. He quickly settled into a comfortable apartment, began making new friends and, of course, he kept in touch with us. We were so pleased to hear that the managers of his new apartment were a middle-aged Jewish couple. We figured maybe they would introduce Steven to a nice Jewish girl. After all, it was about time for him to get married. With my own "babies" all grown up, the idea of having grandchildren appealed to me.

The nice middle-aged Jewish couple turned out to be a little out of the ordinary. In the first place, they were from England. Steve loved to listen to them talk because of their British accent. But there was another difference. They believed that Jesus was the Messiah and that he was for the Jewish people. Instead of introducing Steven to a nice Jewish girl, they introduced him to Baruch Goldstein--a nice Jewish guy--who also believed in Jesus!

We had raised Steven to have a strong sense of family commitment. He didn't like the idea of believing in Jesus because he knew the effect it would have on us, his parents. But Steve had inherited a curious and persistent nature from his father, and from me, he inherited a sociable, yet independent personality. He really liked Baruch and his wife, Marcia. After a while, Steven agreed to attend a Bible study held at their home in West Los Angeles. He intended to go just once, to be polite, but was surprised to find that the Bible study was very interesting...and so he went back.

Steven continued with that Bible study week after week. He read the Scriptures they were studying, and it began to make him very uncomfortable. He realized he had to make some choices. Either what these people believed about Jesus was true or it wasn't. And it suddenly seemed very important to our son that he find out which.

Steven kept studying and he asked God to help him make the right choice. And then it happened. Our son decided that he believed Jesus is the Jewish Messiah. I don't know who was angrier, Freddy or me. We were extremely upset and hurt. I almost wrote a letter to Steven informing him that we wanted nothing more to do with him. Our love for him kept us from doing anything so drastic, and now I'm so glad we didn't let our anger drive our son away. For even though we were 3,000 miles apart, we still felt close to one another. Yet, the anger was still there--no matter how much we loved Steve, it was there.

Childhood memories of those who called me names and made farfetched accusations about my people "killing Christ" crowded my mind. Even worse, I remembered the murder of my grandparents in Nazi Germany. As far as I was concerned, that was the kind of thing all of us Jews could expect from "the Christians." Fred had also emigrated from Germany, and he knew of the horrors of Nazi Germany firsthand. His family was still in Germany when their synagogue was destroyed in the dreadful Kristallnacht of 1938.

The Nazis began taking Jewish males who were 13 and older from Fred's village to "labor camps." Although Fred had been bar mitzvah just four months earlier, he was overlooked for the camps because he was small for his age. Soon entire families were being shipped off to the concentration camps, while Fred's family, for some mysterious reason, was spared. In May of 1941, their emigration number came up. They escaped from Nazi Germany and settled in the United States.

Two years later, Fred turned 18 and was drafted into the U.S. Army. After his basic training, he was sent to England and trained as a combat engineer. His division ended up taking part in the D-Day invasion, after which Freddy and his buddies continued to fight their way through Nazi-occupied territory. After crossing the Rhine River into Germany, they were captured by German soldiers. Fred still remembers how his captors discussed what they should do with the American soldiers. He was literally shaking, because he was the only American soldier who, unbeknown to the German soldiers, understood the language. He knew the soldiers were discussing plans to shoot them. They lined the men up, but changed their minds at the last moment and brought Fred and his buddies to Stalag 11B instead. They remained there as prisoners of war until 1945.

Fred came home from that harrowing experience with no doubt in his mind that God had spared his life time and time again. This gave him a strange sense of destiny which he did not understand, but which he believed God would some day make clear to him. That day was not to come until decades later.

Like me, Freddy equated Christianity with everything anti-Jewish. We always thought of the Nazis as Christians. So you can see why my husband was devastated when he learned that our oldest son had become "a Christian." After all he'd suffered, Fred felt his own flesh and blood had turned against him.

Meanwhile, Steven was trying to explain to us long-distance that his Jesus had nothing to do with the Nazi atrocities. He tried to tell us that these new beliefs did not mean he was turning his back on our people. But it was really impossible to reach an understanding over the telephone. One of us would get upset and the "discussion" would turn into an argument.

One day, Steven told us that Baruch Goldstein was going to be in New York and that he wanted to visit us. Fred agreed to see him; he told Steve, "I want to meet the man who did this to you and throw him off our terrace!" But when Baruch and Marcia rang our doorbell, instead of throwing them off our terrace as Freddy had threatened, we invited them into our apartment and offered them coffee and some danish pastry.

True, we were angry and frightened by our son's decision, but we were concerned first and foremost with his welfare. That concern made us want to understand what had happened. We asked the Goldsteins so many questions. After a while, Baruch began to answer our questions from the Jewish Bible. I was shocked at Freddy's response. He became so curious; it was like a light bulb was switched on from somewhere deep inside him. The Bible had never been very important to me, and it made me nervous to see my husband so interested.

Fred's curiosity was so strong that he began attending the Jews for Jesus Bible studies in New York. He would prepare for each lesson by reading the assigned portion of

Scripture. And on September 29, 1975, my husband became convinced that Jesus was his Messiah. It turned out that our younger son, Robert, had believed privately for some time, but would not speak of it openly until Fred's decision. With all the upset over Steven, Robert had wanted to avoid any more family commotion.

I did not take all this well. It wasn't so much Robert's decision that bothered me, but Fred's. I had gotten over the shock from Steven once I saw that he had not turned against our people. The Jewish believers in Jesus whom I'd met were nice people--not some strange new breed of anti-Semites. But with Fred, it was different. I resented the fact that my Freddy had made his relationship with God a priority. It's not that he was neglecting me; he was just as devoted a husband as ever. But somehow I just knew that his devotion to God was on a higher scale. I began to suspect that Freddy loved God even more than he loved me.

I'd always believed that God was somewhere "out there" for me. It had never occurred to me that I might be here for him. Yet my husband acted like that was how it should be--at least for him. He had dedicated his life to God. As ashamed as I am to admit it, I felt jealous.

I began going to the Bible studies on Tuesday nights with Fred and Robert, not because I wanted to, but because we were a family and we always went places together. Next, Fred wanted to start going to church on Sundays to learn more about the Bible. Oy vey! Each week, the three of us would sit together in the front row. Each week, I would cry.

I promised myself I would never accept Jesus, and to help keep my promise, I kept reminding myself of the crimes committed against the Jewish people in Jesus' name. But somehow the connection between Jesus and anti-Semitism seemed less and less believable. I held on tight to it though, because shaky as that connection was, it seemed to be the only thing that stood between me and a decision which I was determined not to make. The stubbornness I had shown in earlier years had been practiced to perfection!

One night we went to see a film called, "The Hiding Place." It was based on a true story about a woman who risked her life many times to hide Jews from the Nazis during WWII. The woman, Corrie ten Boom, was a Christian. I cried throughout the entire film; I was so moved to see how Corrie put her love for our people into action. The film showed me the difference between following Jesus' teachings and using his name as an excuse to hurt people. The barriers that kept me from accepting Jesus were starting to cave in.

Usually on Tuesday nights I would meet my husband and son at the Jews for Jesus Bible study. One Tuesday, I was working late and decided that I'd skip the Bible study and just go straight home when I finished. It ended up that my train took a different route, so I had to get off and transfer anyway. As long as I couldn't get straight home, I decided I might as well go to the Bible study after all.

The lesson was on Isaiah 53. I found myself listening very carefully. My old idea of a God who was there just to hand out whatever good things I might want suddenly seemed inappropriate. The reality of God's holiness was overwhelming. It made my jealousy of Fred's devotion seem small and silly. The fact that my own rebellion and willfulness stood between myself and the God of Israel was painfully clear. The fact that God loved me and had suffered the hurt and humilation of coming in flesh to redeem me made sense in light of the many Scriptures I'd heard over the past few months. That Tuesday night in December of 1975, I, Laura Wertheim, the "last holdout" in our immediate family, accepted Jesus as my Messiah.

Postscript: Eventually, Steven and Robert both met nice Jewish girls, each of whom believes in Jesus. Fred and I are now the proud grandparents of three grandsons and a granddaughter!

ZHAVA GLASER

I had been presumptuous as only a 16-year-old can be, expecting that the rabbi would learn from me how to believe in Jesus. Instead, he had

taken the time to tear apart every argument I had shown him. I was devastated....

There were bombs exploding all around our hospital in Buenos Aires, so my poor mother had to give birth in the middle of a blackout. The technicians had rigged some special lighting, so it was not totally dark when I made my way into the world on the first day of spring in Argentina--September 22, 1955, the day Peron was removed from office--the day our people were liberated.

My family lived in Argentina, but our roots were in Eastern Europe. My Jewish identity was based upon what we did as well as what we did not do. I knew we were Jewish because we went to synagogue, the one my father had helped to found. The pulpit was built from plain dark wood, and the ark behind it was made from the same. Dad had given what he could toward the purchase of the bimah. We sat on bare wooden benches, the men downstairs and the women upstairs. There were no such things as Reform and Conservative synagogues in Argentina.

I also knew we were Jewish because we celebrated Jewish holidays and we didn't go to church...and because my mother explained the difference between being Jewish and being Christian when I asked her why some of the children called me a "dirty Jew." She told me there were two kinds of people: Jews and Christians. She explained that some Christians don't like Jews because they believe untrue things about us. She also taught that one of the major differences between us was the fact that we Jews spent our money to help others, while Christians spent their money to build churches that had gold in them. She emphasized how that gold should have been used to feed people.

My father died of a heart attack when I was not quite 3 years old. I remember my mother explaining that Dad was in a lot of pain and God had taken him to heaven so he could stop suffering. Heaven was a beautiful place and Dad would be happy there. My first thoughts about God were that he must be very good. If God made my dad feel better, then God was my friend. When it rained, my mother told me that it was Dad, watering God's garden up in heaven. When we heard thunder, she'd put her arms around me and tell me not to be frightened; it was just Dad, fixing

God's car. It may sound silly, but it helped me feel that God was real and not so far away.

I had friends who weren't Jewish, so I assumed they were Christian--but I don't remember them saying anything to me about Jesus. I do remember that a Catholic girlfriend invited me to her church for the celebration of her "first communion." She told me she would be wearing a beautiful white dress and that it would be a very special day for her; she hoped I would come. I was curious, especially about the beautiful white dress, and was delighted when my mother gave me permission to go. The church was very ornate, just as my mother had described. I sat with another girlfriend and tried not to be conspicuous. I stood when they stood and knelt when they knelt, but I was very uncomfortable. When a priest wearing long robes offered me a strange round wafer I fled, terrified. I did not understand all these strange rituals and was afraid I might unintentionally do something to offend God. Throughout the rest of my childhood, whenever I passed a church, I ran past it instead of walking.

In elementary school, I became intrigued with astronomy. I read all the books I could find about the stars and the universe. I cried when I read about light years. To think that seeing the starlight was like looking into the past was overwhelming. After all, the light I was seeing had taken at least 27 years to reach earth, and for some of the really far away stars, it had taken the light millions of years to reach the earth! I suddenly felt very small. My concept of God's reality and his nearness was tempered with awe. I knew that he, as Creator, was even bigger than his vast creation. I wanted to know him, but wondered if it could really be possible for someone as small as me to know someone as big as God.

Meanwhile, my mother found that it is difficult for a widow to earn a living in Argentina. The United States was the land of promise, so that is where she decided to bring my sister and me. I was almost 9 when we left our brick house in Buenos Aires and moved to Los Angeles.

My mother always told me that I was a very good girl. She also told everbody else that I was a very good girl, so as far as I was concerned, I was a very good girl. I learned to get straight "As" in school because if I came home with anything less, my mother would look very hurt and say, "Am I doing something wrong?" So I tried hard to do the right thing, believing that I was quite the little angel my mother said I was, or if I wasn't, I soon would be. I hung around with the "in crowd" during junior high and high school, but was never comfortable at the parties they gave. Somehow, I felt I was different inside. I continued seeing my friends at school, but dropped the parties.

I was a candy striper in junior high. I would have wanted to be a doctor, only I couldn't stand the sight of blood! So I did my volunteer work in the library, taking books to the patients who were well enough to read. One day I saw a book titled, *The Greatest Story Ever Written*. The green cloth cover was so frayed that I figured even if it wasn't quite the greatest story ever written, it must still be pretty interesting since so many people had checked it out. I opened the book and saw it was filled with stories from the Tanach. Instead of bringing it to the patients, I took the book home for myself. I considered it a loan.

It was springtime. After school, on days when I wasn't at the hospital, I would lie beneath a tree on the hammock in our backyard and read. I don't remember what kind of tree it was, but it had sweet smelling white blossoms. And the book I had brought back from the hospital was spellbinding. I read about Abraham and how he talked to God and I thought, "Wow! I can talk to God!" When I read how God called Abraham, who answered, "Here am I," I paused for a moment to say, "Here am I" as well. I spent hours this way, reading Bible stories and talking to God.

The Greatest Story Ever Written made me hungry to read the real Bible, so I went to the public library and borrowed one. I was careful to put a rubber band around the "New Testament" so God wouldn't think I wanted to read the wrong part. Every two weeks I returned to the library to renew the Bible, until finally, I begged my mother for a

Bible of my own. She agreed, but since we didn't have much money, she took me down to a used book store. The only Bibles they had were the kind I'd been checking out of the library, containing both our Scriptures and the New Testament. I did not want anything to do with the New Testament because I knew it had pictures of Jesus in it, and it was against the Commandments to have pictures of gods. However, this was the only Bible available to me, and since my mother was willing to buy it, I took it.

The first thing I did when I got it home was remove what I considered the idolatrous pictures. I left the illustrations of Adam and Eve, Noah, Moses and Abraham in the Tanach. Then, without even looking, I flipped through the New Testament and tore out all the illustration pages. I could recognize them by touch because they were heavier than the other pages. I made a plain brown bookcover for my Bible because I didn't want to seem like a religious fanatic to my friends at school. I may have felt different inside, but like most teenagers, I didn't want to look different on the outside!

One day, I sent away for a book which was advertised in the TV Guide--it was about marijuana. I still considered myself "a very good girl," but although I wasn't taking drugs, I was curious. The ad made the book seem intriguing. The company promised to send it in a plain brown wrapper, which made it even more enticing. I received the book and was not impressed. After I ordered it, I began receiving regular issues of a religious magazine. They didn't look too interesting, so I simply stacked them in the attic.

A couple of years later (my sophomore year of high school) I went rummaging through the attic looking for something to read. It was a rainy day and I was bored. I came across the stack of magazines and began reading. I found the magazines very palatable; the articles talked about obeying the Ten Commandments and not worshipping false gods. At the same time, they introduced the idea that he might be the Messiah.

I wanted to know more about the group that published this magazine, so when I finished reading through my stack, I went to the library for further information. They seemed to have very few books about God there, so I just kept reading the Bible. I still didn't read the New Testament, just the prophecies in the Tanach that the magazines had suggested. The articles had claimed that Jesus fulfilled Jewish prophecies, and I decided I'd read those prophecies for myself. In doing so, I was beginning to think it might be true, but I still hadn't read the "fulfillment passages" in the New Testament.

One day, a group of Christians stood across the street from my high school and gave away miniature books which had "Holy Bible" printed on their red cover. They turned out to be excerpts from a book in the New Testament, the Book of Luke. It was only the first few chapters, describing how Jesus was born. I read the book and saw how it tied in with the prophecies I had been reading. But it was the prophecies themselves that convinced me.

The ninth chapter of the Book of Daniel was the key passage that led me to think Jesus was probably the Messiah. The magazine articles had claimed that according to that prophecy, the time for the Messiah had come and gone. Daniel's prophetic calendar of events pointed to Jesus as the one who appeared on the scene according to God's timetable. Daniel 9 indicates that the Messiah was to come before the Temple was destroyed. If Jesus was not the Messiah then there simply isn't going to be one. To me, it was a decision based on facts, a conclusion I'd drawn in my mind. Isaiah 53 was the chapter I could not read without feeling in my heart that Jesus was the Messiah.

Even though I now believed that Jesus was the Messiah, I didn't consider myself a Christian. The magazine I'd read never mentioned making a commitment, or what it should mean to me if Jesus really was the Messiah. So my search to know God better continued.

I became friends with a boy named Peter at my school, Fairfax High. Peter often met with a group of Christians during lunch to pray. The meeting was open to anyone who was interested, so one day, I decided to go. I was amazed to find this group of people talking to God. I knew immediately that they were speaking to the same God I had been speaking to, the God of Abraham, Isaac and Jacob. I'd never met anyone else who talked to him the way I did, and I was very excited.

Peter was friends with a man named Doug, who worked with The American Board of Missions to the Jews. Peter was sensitive and sympathetic to my doubts about becoming a Christian. He knew how to talk to me without making me feel defensive.

One night a group of us went to a Christian concert. Afterwards, Peter explained to me that the reason Jesus came to die and take the punishment for our sin was so that we could have an intimate relationship with God. He talked about being committed to God and turning to him for direction. I could come to God and ask his forgiveness based on what Jesus had done--just as the people of Israel had obtained forgiveness through the intercession of the High Priest and the sacrifice he made on Yom Kippur. I had not committed any earthshaking sins, but I knew I was not righteous enough to stand before the Holy One. I prayed that night and asked Jesus, my Messiah, to be central in my life. That was January 16, 1972.

My life really lit up; I immediately felt that God had heard me, that his promises were true, and finally had the communion with the God of the Universe which I 'd wanted for so long. My mother was alseep when I got home that night, but I was so excited, I couldn't wait until morning to tell her. I went right into her bedroom and said, "Ma! I'm a Christian!" My mother said I should go to bed and I'd feel better in the morning.

I couldn't sleep that night, and I didn't change my mind in the morning. I took the rubber band off my Bible, and the brown book cover came off, too. I began telling all of my friends at school about the Messiah. Many of them were also Jewish, and some even came to faith in Jesus as I had. I understood how hard it is for a Jewish person to overcome misunderstandings about Jesus and the New Testament, so I wanted to devote myself to telling my people about Jesus.

I especially wanted to tell the rabbi my good news. I figured if he could only realize who Jesus was, he would believe, too. So I went to Temple Israel in Hollywood. I couldn't get an appointment with the senior rabbi, but one of the younger rabbis set aside time to see me. He was in his mid-thirties I think, and his hair was a little longish for a rabbi. He wore wire-framed glasses and was very friendly. He sat and listened to me present the whole plan; I quoted a number of prophecies to show why I believed. I even quoted from the Zohar, an ancient rabbinic book, to show how our own books spoke about the Trinity.

After I was finished, the rabbi said to me, "You can't make a decision like this, you don't know enough about what it means to be Jewish." He went back to the original Hebrew (which I could not read for myself) and began telling me, "This is how it should be translated, and this is not what it really means." He also told me that no Jews today take the Zohar seriously. (He was right about the Zohar.) I had been presumptuous as only a 16-year-old can be, expecting that the rabbi would learn from me how to believe in Jesus. Instead, he had taken the time to tear apart every argument I had shown him. I was devastated.

It had taken me two years to become a Christian and, all at once, I really wondered about my decision. No church and no pastor could help me. I had to work out my problems with someone who was Jewish--someone who could discuss the rabbi's arguments with me. This was a couple of years before Jews for Jesus set up a branch in Los Angeles, but Doug knew a few Jewish believers, and he put me in contact with them. They took me under their wings; I reconstructed what the rabbi had told me and, they too, were able to go to the original language and discuss the texts with me. In some cases, they agreed with the rabbi that a certain passage was not speaking about Jesus. In other instances, they showed me how and why a passage might be translated one of two ways. But there were certain passages which were crystal-clear evidence for the messiahship of Jesus. These Jewish believers were able to point out weaknesses in the interpretations the rabbi had used to try to undermine my faith.

The text I remember most clearly was Isaiah 53. The rabbi had told me that the suffering servant described is

Israel. But the eighth verse reads, "He was taken from prison and from judgment, and who will declare His generation? For He was cut off from the land of the living; for the transgressions of My people He was stricken."

As my friends rightly pointed out, if the suffering servant is Israel, then who are "my people" mentioned in the eighth verse? Further, verse 9 goes on to say, "He had done no violence, Nor was any deceit in His mouth." If this refers to Israel, how do we explain the many judgments of the prophets found throughout the Tanach, strong judgments reprimanding Israel for her unfaithfulness and for following in the sinful ways of her pagan neighbors? If you read through our Jewish prophets, you'll quickly see that Israel was not the innocent lamb described by Isaiah.

One thing the rabbi did convince me of was that if I really wanted to persuade people that my message was true, I had better know what I was talking about. I didn't stop telling people about Jesus, but I began making plans for my future education. When I graduated from high school, I enrolled in a program that the University of Southern California offered in conjunction with Hebrew Union College. I majored in Jewish studies and Hebrew.

I also planned to spend a year in Israel between my freshman and sophomore years. My freshman year ended and I was all set to go to Israel, with my kibbutz assignment ready and my visa in order. Then Ma'alot happened; a number of children on a kibbutz were killed by terrorists. My mother said, "That's it, you're not going. It's too dangerous." I suppose I was old enough to have gone anyway, but I felt the right thing would be to honor my mother's wishes and not cause her any more anxiety than she was already undergoing because of my faith. I stayed in Southern California and earned my degree in Jewish studies and Hebrew, as planned. I learned modern as well as biblical Hebrew. I'm not a scholar, but I can translate and interpret Hebrew reasonably well, and I've taught a few classes for others desiring to learn Hebrew.

My first contact with Jews for Jesus was seeing their posters up at U.S.C. during the fall that I had planned on being in Israel. Next, I met one of their staff who had come to the campus to hand out pamphlets about Jesus. He invited me to come to their West Los Angeles Bible studies, and I felt right at home. Eventually, I met and married a Jew for Jesus who was studying at a nearby seminary.

My husband, Mitch, was brought up in a traditional Jewish home in New York City. He was 8 years old when he began attending an Orthodox Hebrew School; he studied Jewish culture, history and religion two hours a day, five days a week until he was bar mitzvah. Despite all the time spent in Hebrew school, Mitch never really had a personal relationship with God. Jewish religion is so intertwined with Jewish life that it's hard to tell where the culture ends and the religion begins. Mitch says that by the time he was 14, he took both for granted.

His experiences were a whole lot different from mine. While I was a (relatively) quiet and unrebellious teenager, my husband-to-be was getting involved in the counter-culture of the '60s. He and his friend, Efraim Goldstein, were very adventurous in their "quest for truth." They dropped out of college and hitchhiked across the country to see if the answers to life's questions could be found on the West Coast. Efraim was the first to come to faith in the Messiah. Mitch saw the changes in his friend's life, but did not want to admit that it could have anything to do with Jesus.

One night Mitch prayed and asked God to reveal himself. The same night he found a New Testament in a phone booth. He was shocked, but didn't have the same hesitation about reading it as I'd had. Reading about Jesus and seeing the changed lives of his closest friends--Jewish friends who believed in Jesus--convinced Mitch that Jesus really is the Messiah. He left the drugs and the "hippie" lifestyle and went back to school. By the time we met, he'd already finished his undergraduate work at Northeastern Bible College and was in the process of finishing his graduate degree at Talbot Theological Seminary.

Mitch and I were married under a *chupoh* by another Jewish believer in Jesus in December of 1975. In December of 1983 we had our first child, and in November of 1986 our second daughter was born. Miriam, our oldest, is just beginning to appreciate the holidays (especially Hanukkah!). Mitch and I do what we can to make sure our children know what it means to be Jewish...with Jesus, the Jewish Messiah at the center of our heritage and our faith.

DAVID CHANSKY

If you came to services at Ohev Yisrael, you would find men wearing yarmulkas. You would hear many of the same prayers chanted as are heard in synagogue. They are led by a cantor, who is also a Jewish believer in Y'shua. If you asked, you would discover that most of our people keep kosher kitchens, though those who don't are not looked down upon. Above all, you would find the message that no matter what is eaten or not eaten, whatever is worn and whichever liturgy is used, regardless of culture, tradition or style of worship, it is Y'shua, and Y'shua alone, who can make our hearts truly kosher.

It was bad enough that I had to think about Jesus when I was awake, but for him to invade my sleep was too much. I awoke soaked with sweat and a fear that my life could be turned upside down by this whole religion thing. I'd never had a supernatural experience prior to this; I certainly wasn't given to dreams and other eerie things that some people find appealing when it comes to the spiritual realm. So when I dreamed that Y'shua (Jesus) was telling me three things would happen to convince me that he was the Messiah, I decided to do the only logical thing--forget it! My first thought was to find a bar and get drunk, very drunk, which was easy to do in Alaska, but which was also uncharacteristic for me. I enjoyed having a few beers with the guys, but I was not the type to get drunk. However, I needed to forget about Jesus and drinking seemed to do the trick--temporarily.

Drinking was obviously a poor solution, but I wasn't ready to accept the radical implications of my dream. Whenever I thought about it, I reached for my wallet and pulled out my picture of Merle. Merle was my fiancee. We were to be married in just a few months. I'd look at her picture and I'd say, "Don't worry Merle, nothing's gonna happen." This helped remind me of what I had to look forward to and why I didn't want to mess up my life by believing in Jesus. My future was bright--and I didn't want him in it.

I was born in Boston, Massachusetts, on August 1, 1935, the son of an Orthodox Jewish butcher on Blue Hill Avenue in Roxbury. I attended the Otisfield Hebrew School from the time I was 5 years old (even before I was enrolled in public school) until I was 11. I continued my Jewish education at Maimonides Institute (a yeshiva) until I was 13.

I went to Hebrew school Sunday morning, as well as Monday, Tuesday, Wednesday and Thursday afternoons. We spent Friday afternoon preparing to go to evening services. We spent most of Saturday in shul as well. Then it was Sunday morning and back to Hebrew school. The regimen wasn't much fun for a young boy, and I can't honestly say that I enjoyed it. Between public school and Hebrew school, about all I had time for was dinner at 6, the Lone

Ranger at 7:30 and then I'd study until it was time for bed. We didn't have much time for playing ball and things like that. Still, I have fond memories of my youth, and especially of a family that was very closely knit.

I don't remember hearing an unkind word spoken in my home as I was growing up. I'm sure my father and mother must have argued from time to time, but my two sisters and I never heard a cross word between them. My father worked very hard. I rarely saw him except late at night, but I remember he'd always ask how my Hebrew school studies were going. It was important to him that I have a good Jewish education.

Just before my bar mitzvah, Dad took me aside and he said, "Now I'm gonna teach you how to put tefillin on, and the prayer shawl, so that after your bar mitzvah you can do it every morning." Dad was not in the habit of laying tefillin, but he wanted his son to do it.

I saw my bar mitzvah as the great "exodus" from hours and hours of "forced labor." I'm sad to say that now, but it was the typical attitude for most of the boys in my class. I didn't really have a zeal for God--I don't know that any of the boys in our Hebrew school or yeshiva did. What we did have, myself included, was a zeal for our religion and our people. My love for my Jewishness was very strong. When they would take out the Torah and carry it up and down the aisles each Shabbat I always had a tear in my eye and a bit of a lump in my throat. I found it very touching.

I didn't forsake the synagogue after my bar mitzvah, but my formal Jewish education stopped there. It was like stepping into a whole new world; there was so much more time for playing and socializing and "hanging out" after school. I spent a lot of time at the YMHA, the Young Men's Hebrew Association on Seaver Street. I especially liked basketball. I didn't get to play too often, but there's one game I'll never forget. Our team was winning, so they let me in at the beginning of the second half. I was so excited--I started dribbling down that court and I almost made a basket-- except my team tackled me because I was going the wrong way! In my excitement and zeal to win, I forgot they had switched baskets.

I have fond memories of the YMHA on Seaver Street, and a few grim memories as well. We met in a large stone building with a high wall and a big porch facing a park. One night, I was on the porch with some friends and suddenly, there was a huge crowd of kids across the park yelling at the top of their lungs, "Dirty Jew, Christ-killers! Dirty Jew, Christ-killers!" They stormed across the park, yelling and whooping themselves into a frenzy. I heard the crash of shattering glass; I don't know if the rocks were aimed at us or the windows, but my friends and I ducked behind that big stone wall. The whole thing lasted less than a minute, then the crowd of fifty to sixty kids disappeared back through the park and into the woods.

The neighborhoods in the Boston area were strictly defined and we were right on the border between a Jewish and a Gentile neighborhood. It wasn't unusual for non-Jews to come into our neighborhood and start fights...and there was always a racial epithet. They weren't big gangs like you might find in New York; they were little groups of guys who would come looking for any Jewish boy so they could give him a bloody nose. I was once the solitary Jewish boy they happened to find. They dragged me to a deserted field, tied my hands and feet and left me there. My family came looking for me, but it was a friend who finally found me. They simply took me home and nothing more was said about it. It was understood that these things were part of growing up Jewish in the 1940s.

Well, prejudice can quickly become a two-way street, and we didn't have such a high opinion of non-Jews. Most with whom we came in contact impressed us with their senseless hatred, so we assumed they were all like that. Years passed before I realized that many Gentiles don't hate Jews. I grew up thinking it was part of their heritage and duty. Gentiles hate us. Simple.

Another strange thing about the goyim was the fact that they ate the wrong food. My father was a kosher butcher, so I was very aware of what should and shouldn't be eaten. I recall going by a *traif* meat market and feeling repulsed by the meat I saw in the window. I knew it was no good because our meat was red and theirs was practically white. How could they eat pork? I thought, "No wonder they're like they are--look what they're eating!"

There was an exception. His name was Teddy Vinaux and he was the only Gentile in our club. It's not that he kept kosher, but as far as we were concerned, he was "one of the boys." In fact, we threatened to take our club out of the YMHA if they didn't let Teddy in. He fit in like one of us and he was treated like one of us, by "us" as well as by "them." One night Teddy and I were jumped by some boys wearing crosses as we were on our way to a club meeting. Teddy was getting pounded just like me, and he never tried to get off the hook by protesting that he wasn't Jewish. That sort of thing earned him our respect and affection.

In fact, when there was a big fire at my house, my parents sent me to sleep over at Teddy's house. Teddy was Catholic, and I must admit, the big crucifix overlooking my bed scared the life out of me--I'll never forget it. But Teddy was alright. He even went to synagogue with us once in a while. He was surprised to hear I'd never been in a church, and he invited me to come with him some time. One day I did; I actually stepped inside the door of St. Hugh's Church with Teddy Vinaux. There was incense burning, and no sooner had I smelled the peculiar odor and glanced around at all the statues than I told Teddy, "I gotta get outta here." He didn't realize that we considered the church a place of idolatry where no Jew should even set foot.

Most of my childhood memories tie in with my Jewish identity. There was one other thing that was very important to me as I was growing up: my dream of someday becoming a famous entertainer. In fact, my desire to go on the stage lasted into early adulthood.

My sisters took elocution lessons; that was the big thing back then. They'd get up and recite, and I would mimic them. At first it was just a way to annoy my big sisters, which was, after all, my brotherly duty. I soon found that I genuinely enjoyed reciting. I began practicing my imitations, mimicking such illustrious personalities as Donald Duck and Al Jolson. It was fun to make people laugh, so I began performing my "act" in front of audiences. In fact, I even got to perform on the radio. WMEX in Boston had a "newsboy broadcast" every Saturday--it was a talent contest sponsored by the Boston American Newspaper. I sold papers on the street corner when I was 11 years old, which upset my father, who felt that was "below my stature." At 11 years old, I was not overly concerned with "my stature." I was very enterprising and I liked selling papers, plus the fact that it qualified me to enter the talent show. I won the contest with my imitations; I had my picture in the paper and I was very proud of that. I put together a little comedy routine with my friend, Marshall; we won a couple of contests and appeared at various events in the Jewish community. My family would have me do my little *shtick* at weddings and so forth. I was a real "kosher ham," with a strong Jewish identity and aspirations of becoming a famous entertainer.

I graduated from high school and went into the service. I remember going to my rabbi and voicing concern over what I was to eat now that I was leaving home. My meals would obviously be prepared by people who were not concerned about the laws of kashrut. "Don't worry," my rabbi told me. "In the service, it's alright if you eat non-kosher. Otherwise you could starve to death." He was right about that!

I ate ham for the first time while in the Air Force. It was very difficult. It wasn't so much the thought of breaking the Law that bothered me; it was wondering what foul thing about ham had made God warn us against eating it. I put a piece of pork in my mouth once as a child, thought for a moment, then spit it out as I concluded, "I'm not going to be able to do this and live." In the service there wasn't much choice so I went ahead and ate the ham. If anyone saw me that first time, I'm sure they would have wondered from the grimace on my face what on earth I was chewing.

The change in menu was a tough adjustment, but I was in for a pleasant surprise as well. I made the delightful discovery that Teddy Vinaux had not been a freak of nature; there were actually many Gentiles out there who didn't hate Jews. Massachusetts had its own variety of anti-Semitism, at least when I was growing up. Things were a little different in other parts of the country. I went through three months of basic training at the Sampson Air Force Base in Geneva, New York, and it was a couple of guys from Salem, Massachusetts, who were constantly giving me grief. I remember their scowling faces and their typical greeting: "What do you say, *Jew*!" Then I began to meet guys from other parts of the country, Gentiles to whom my being Jewish meant absolutely nothing. Amazing...and very refreshing!

I went to radio school at Biloxi, Mississippi. Our class was scheduled to be stationed in Alabama after graduation. One night, I went to a movie where the air conditioning was so cold that after I left the theater, I promptly caught pneumonia. My stay in the hospital resulted in a postponed graduation. I had to finish with the class behind me, the class that was scheduled for Anchorage, Alaska. Servicemen are pretty quick about looking up certain statistics. We all knew that there were 3500 men to every woman in Alaska. I arrived there to find it cold and lonely, as expected. I thought of my friends having a great time back in Boston while I sat in the snow, doing security work. My duty had me working crazy hours, often from 12 at night to 7 in the morning.

After a year in Anchorage, I went home on furlough. I renewed my acquaintance with a high school sweetheart named Merle, and after I returned to Alaska, we maintained our relationship through the mail. How I looked forward to those letters! Eventually, Merle and I became engaged to be married. That took some of the chill out of being in Alaska.

The other thing which made life more bearable was that one of the guys, Ken Guthrie, put together a band. It was like a Spike Jones band; at first I just "played" an instrument, the clarinet. Our whole routine was done in pantomime, with various Spike Jones records backing us up. We did slapstick humor, using sight gags and puns, running onto the stage from the band or the side, using vaudeville-type humor.

We played at Fort Richardson in the officers' club and a local country club; in fact, we played almost every single bar all the way down to the "Last Chance," the final bar on the strip before you hit the base. We would go from one club or bar to the next, all the way down the strip on Fourth Avenue. They paid us for the shows we did, and I saw my childhood dreams of becoming an entertainer coming true. Guthrie lost interest after a while and I took over for about six months, thoroughly enjoying the work. I saw it as a serious opportunity to develop my career; especially after someone "in the business" told us we had talent.

A booking agent from Hollywood named Lou Cohen came up with a troupe to do one of the Bob Hope type shows they put on for servicemen. He saw our act, came up afterwards and actually offered us a Hollywood contract! He suggested we appear on various T.V. shows, doing guest spots. He also offered to fix us up with night club dates; I remember his words, "You'll get going and you'll have a great career on the stage." I was thrilled.

Not everything in Alaska was such a thrill, however. The band and the letters from Merle were bright spots in what otherwise would have been a pretty miserable two years. One of the worst things about Alaska was a group of tough guys who were big and mean and enjoyed picking on anyone else who wasn't. There was an Italian guy in our barracks from Pittsburgh, Pennsylvania, by the name of Al Tosi. Al was a phenomenal guy, a clean-living guy. He wouldn't go out with the guys drinking, but he wasn't a "holier-than-thou" type either. He was just a very down-to-earth, well-adjusted, happy person. And these tough guys would persecute him like you wouldn't believe.

Al merited their displeasure merely by politely declining invitations to go drinking, and by reading his Bible and praying before he went to bed. He didn't pray out loud, nor was he flaunting his religion. He just wasn't ashamed to do what he thought was right. These guys didn't like it a bit. They were very vulgar, very childish; they labelled him "fairy" and "fruitcake" and they didn't let up. Once they took him to a place called Eastchester Flats. It's a very notorious place outside of Anchorage, Alaska, where the "bad boys" had their fun. Four guys held Al while someone opened his mouth and poured the liquor down his throat. They roughed him up a little, then brought him back to the barracks, hopelessly drunk.

I had been up there a year, so it was my job to keep peace in the barracks. I was what they called "barracks chief." As such, I had my own little room. I figured the only way I could keep peace was to pull Al out of the barracks. The only alternative to having him in the barracks was putting him in my room, and that's exactly what I did. My sister tells me to this day, "That was your big mistake."

Al was a Christian. He wasn't a "Christian" like the ones I'd known; the ones from my childhood who wore big crosses around their necks, crosses that banged against your nose every time you got tackled. Al wasn't that kind.

He amazed me with his great respect for Judaism. I was floored when he asked, "Would I be able to go to the synagogue with you?" I used to lead the services on Friday nights. We had a rabbi who would visit once a month; he had the whole territory to cover so he was like a circuit rabbi. (I say "territory" because Alaska wasn't even a state when I was there.) So I led the services the other three weeks of the month. Al wanted to go to shul with me, so I said, "Sure. Why not? Come." He came, and after we got back, he asked me a number of questions.

The questions had a depth to them which was beyond my understanding. He asked about the Temple and the sacrifices. In retrospect, I'm sure he was trying to get me thinking about Jesus, but he was also genuinely interested in my point of view. I told him, "Wait a minute. You're asking me questions that I don't know how to answer. I'd have to look into it before we discuss it further." I remembered one of our rabbis once said, "Someday, *Ha'Shem* will restore the Temple." I didn't know what that meant. I knew there had been a Temple in Jerusalem. I knew we had sacrificed animals until the Temple was destroyed. We never dealt much with what the sacrifices meant, why God required them, whether or not he stopped requiring them, and if so, why.

Al knew the Jewish Bible better than I did. I'd had what was considered "a good Jewish education." I'd read through the five books of Moses in Hebrew school; we'd translated many portions of it from Hebrew into English. I continued to translate from the Torah in yeshiva. Yet, we didn't progress to content. Al knew content; he knew the message. He could relate parts of the synagogue service to his knowledge of the Bible. And his knowledge extended beyond the first five books. Mine didn't. The Torah was always our main focus; we didn't hear much about the prophets. Sometimes we would read from the Psalms, but we regarded them more as prayers than as God's Word. We heard stories about Daniel, but I wasn't familiar with the prophet's place in the Tanach.

Al didn't take advantage of that to start talking about Jesus. He wasn't trying to force or wheedle me into anything. He simply asked, "Would you go to church with me?" I answered without hesitation, "No." Al looked surprised.

"I went to synagogue with you," he remarked. I got a little terse at that point.

"I didn't know that we were trading off." Al shrugged and didn't press the issue. Later, I thought about it and felt a little silly. What would it hurt for me to go once and see what it was like? It wasn't as though Christianity was a contagious illness. So I went.

It was my turn to be surprised. I'd expected to see pictures of Jesus on the walls and statues everywhere. Instead, we walked into a very plain building--no pictures, no statues. The lesson was about Daniel, my Daniel, the Jewish prophet. I was impressed. After it was over I met the minister, we talked, then Al and I went home.

After that, Al began asking me more questions from the Jewish Bible. Suddenly, it seemed like the whole barracks was getting involved in our discussion. Alaska is a strange place. You could go to the cafeteria and get a meal just about any hour of the day or night. We didn't have regular schedules. Some of us worked from 12 to 7 in the morning, so we'd go down to the cafeteria for coffee and breakfast at 7 and often stay there until noon.

Religion is like politics; everybody wants to throw his opinion into the ring. With all this talk, I took inventory and realized I was lacking in knowledge. When I went into the service, it was customary to provide all the Jewish recruits with two books. They gave us a siddur (a prayer book), and they also gave us what they called "Excerpts from the Holy Scriptures." I'd read from the excerpts occasionally, but now I decided that what I needed was a whole Bible, a Jewish Bible to study.

Al went to his chaplain's office and got a Bible for me. I thumbed through it and thought, "Yeah, Genesis, that's my book, Exodus, uh huh...." I kept flipping through until I got to "Saint Matthew." I thought, "Wait a minute. He's not one of the guys I know!" Al had given me a Bible with a New Testament in it. He was standing right there and I told him, "I just wanted to study my Bible. This is not mine." I calmly ripped the New Testament out of the Bible and handed it to Al, who stood aghast. He must have wondered if lightning would strike me from heaven.

I began studying the Scriptures. I decided, "For once in my life, I'm going to show the Christians what Judaism is about." I'd recite for Al, *"Shema Yisrael Adonai Elohenu, Adonai echad*: Hear O Israel, the Lord our God is one." I'd explain that we Jews don't have three gods, we only have one. Al insisted that Christians also believed in only one God, and we'd have great discussions and debates. I was getting to know my Bible pretty well.

Yet, there were questions arising from the Jewish prophets which I was unable to answer, Scriptures mentioning the Messiah. Daniel the ninth chapter, for example: "And after the sixty-two weeks Messiah shall be cut off." In Hebrew, that means cut off in death. After the Messiah was thus cut off, according to Daniel, a prince would come and destroy the city of Jerusalem and the Temple.

Al would ask me, "What Messiah was that, who was to die?" I didn't know. And Daniel wasn't the only problem. There was Isaiah. "Who has believed our report?...He is despised and rejected...He has borne our griefs and carried our sorrows; yet we esteemed Him stricken, smitten by God, and afflicted. But he was wounded for our transgressions, He was bruised for our iniquities...He was cut off from the land of the living; for the transgressions of My people He was stricken." I thought to myself, "Jesus, it sounds like Jesus." I didn't know who else it could be. But I knew who would: the rabbi.

I needed an appointment with the rabbi. I called and he said, "I don't know if I can see you this trip." I told him, "You've got to see me." So he did. I went to his office and I opened up to the fifty-third chapter of Isaiah. I read it out loud. I said, "Rabbi, I want to ask you a question. Who is this?" Without hesitating, he replied, "Well, it isn't Jesus."

I thought, "Oh, great. Just what I needed to hear. He's afraid it might be Jesus, too. " His response left a deep impression. I hadn't even mentioned Jesus, yet his name was the first thing out of the rabbi's mouth. I feared there might be something to it, after all.

I said, "I didn't ask you who it isn't. I asked who it is." No answer. It occurred to me, "What if Jesus was the Messiah?" I didn't even want to think about it. "Jesus" was a hateful and a hated word to me. I couldn't even say his name out loud.

I left the rabbi's office distraught, but I came to one conclusion. I resolved to close this Bible, just put it aside, and concentrate on my band. I still wanted a career in show business, and I figured that concentrating on that would provide a good distraction as well as a productive use of my time.

It turned out that I was past the point of whether it mattered if the book was open or shut. I couldn't rid myself of the questions and fears that crowded my mind. Frankly, my problem was not even spiritual, at least, not that I was aware. The trouble was this Jesus; I grew up disliking him immensely because of all the black eyes and bloody noses I associated with his name. The possibility that he could be the Messiah--that we might have been wrong about him--I did not know how to handle it. I didn't see it as a simple question: believing in Jesus versus not believing. I saw it as a choice between the beauty of my Jewish home life and the non-Jewish lifestyles I had seen as a child and did not especially admire. For him to be the Messiah seemed to mean the collapse of my whole world. I had a deep, intense Jewish identity. If "they" were right about Jesus, where did that leave us? It was a humiliating and sickening thought.

I wanted to get away from all these discussions. I volunteered for a special assignment doing some high-level security work. They put me in a little room with two other men, one of whom was my friend, Al. I came in and he and the other guy were arguing religion. They were talking about Jesus. I thought, "What is going on? I can't get away from this. Now I can't even get out of this room." Our work was very intense but sporadic; there was a lot of waiting time when we were still on duty and couldn't leave. While we were waiting, they'd talk about Jesus. I'd volunteered for the job and I was stuck with it--and them.

The one guy was involved in studying the Bible with a friend who lived off base. He invited me to his friend's house for dinner and an informal Bible discussion afterwards. Anyone who has eaten in a military mess hall knows that it can be pretty bad. The mess halls in Alaska are no different, except maybe they're worse. When the weather froze up, we would eat dry barrelled beef, day after day after day. Salty, dry barrelled beef was one of the most awful tasting things I ever had to put in my mouth.

I thought, "Even if I have to get an earful of religion, it would be worth it to get a stomachful of decent food!" So I went. There were some others there and they were talking about religion. No one was bothering me; they were debating among themselves, this bunch of Gentiles, some of whom believed in the Trinity and some of whom did not. It didn't seem so bad, so I accepted subsequent invitations to go back. One night as they were debating after supper, one of the Bible teachers said, "C'mon, let's go to the kitchen and have a cup of coffee." We sat down with some coffee and he proceeded to tell me, "You know, you shouldn't be bothering with that debate in there. You should be trying to find out whether or not Jesus is the Messiah."

I told him, "I really don't want to talk about whether Jesus is the Messiah." Still, I found myself involved in another discussion about him.

This man (his name was Smith) opened his Bible and said, "I want to read something that you might find interesting." Then he read the passage I mentioned before, from the ninth chapter of Daniel, verses 24 through 27.

He said, "Tell me something. Who is the Messiah that was supposed to come before the destruction of the Temple in Jerusalem?"

I replied, "Look, I've been through this I don't know how many times with other Christians and I don't know. That doesn't prove it was Jesus."

He said, "Well you're going to have to face something. Regardless of who Jesus is, either a messiah came before the Temple was destroyed, or you might as well take the Jewish Bible and throw it out the window. If it doesn't tell the truth, what good is it?"

That set off alarms inside me. As an Orthodox Jew I was taught that every word in there was the Word of God--maybe I didn't understand it, maybe I didn't have comprehension, but I still believed it was God's Word. I could not disregard or throw it out. I said, "You know, Mr. Smith, I appreciate the dinner, but you're not going to see me again. If you ever do, it'll be because I believe in Jesus, and that's not going to happen."

A few days later I had a very strange experience. I finished work at 7 a.m. I didn't stop to have coffee or breakfast or anything else. I went straight to bed and had the weirdest dream of my life. In that dream, I was rising up in the air; I was going up and up. Then there was a layer of clouds, and in my dream I was walking on top of these clouds.

There was a man. He put his hand on my shoulder and said, "You are going to leave everything and follow me because I have called you." I looked into his eyes and knew without being told: it was Jesus. He didn't say who he was; I just looked in his eyes and knew. He told me three things were going to happen to me, and that when each of these things happened, I would know he was revealing himself to me. After he said this, I began falling. There was an island beneath me, and when I hit the island I woke up, drenched in perspiration.

I took a shower and then I went into Anchorage to the "Last Chance" where I proceeded to get drunk, something that I never, ever did. But this dream had me so scared that I went and had too much to drink just so I wouldn't have to think about it.

I tried and even managed to forget my dream...for a while. Then things began happening. The first prediction was that a specific sergeant in our company would become a corporal. I knew of no problems with this particular sergeant, so I wasn't worried. One night as I was working the late shift, someone walked into the room. I looked up and did a double-take. It was the very sergeant mentioned in my dream, and he only had two stripes on his shirt. I tried to talk to him, but he wouldn't even acknowledge me; he just walked away. I remembered my dream, and I literally felt like I was going to faint.

Next chance I got, I went into the coffee room and found another sergeant. I told him whom I'd just seen and asked what had happened. I was told, "He was court-martialed for a very serious offense; they took three stripes away from him and now he's a corporal." The offense they busted that sergeant for was rather personal, and I would have had no way of knowing about it. It came as a complete shock. In my dream, Y'shua (Jesus) had said, "When you see this, you'll know I have spoken to you." I didn't want to know. I didn't want to know at all.

The second prediction in the dream was that I would be attacked by a large man and I would call on God, who would protect me. I didn't understand it; I didn't expect it to happen. I convinced myself that our sergeant's demotion was a fluke. A week later, I was taking a shower, and a man built like a bull came into the shower. He looked around to see if anyone else was there, he looked at me, and he had bad things on his mind. You'll remember I said there were about 3500 men for every woman in Anchorage. This brought out both the best and the worst in men. Some lost all sense of perspective--they developed a prison mentality and did things that maybe, later on, they regretted. I knew people were engaging in homosexuality, but no one had ever approached me.

This huge man began making suggestions, and it didn't matter to him that I declined his offer. When he came at me all I could do was think, "God, help me!" And immediately, I heard the door open. The guy backed off, a couple of men came in and my would-be rapist said, "You say one word buddy, and you're dead." Then he left, and, I might add, he never bothered me again.

I was so relieved, and so grateful to God for hearing my "prayer." I don't know what shook me up the most, the event itself or the fact that in my dream, Y'shua had predicted it.

The third prediction was "I will show myself to you visibly and you will know that I am the Messiah." Not likely. The first two things could be explained naturally. It was disturbing that they happened to fit into my dream, but coincidences happen. I was not afraid of bumping into Jesus in Anchorage, Alaska.

A week after the shower incident, Al Tosi said "Hey, Dave, there's a picture playing on base that you might want to see; it's called 'Day of Triumph.' It's about the life of Jesus and it'll give you a flavor of who he was."

I said, "Buddy, I don't want to see that movie; you can keep it. Don't talk to me about it. I'm not studying with you anymore." (Those weren't my exact words, but I wouldn't want them in print.) Here I had done this guy a favor by taking him in, and what did I get? I got troubles like I'd never had in my life, that's what I got. When the guys asked me to join them for a few drinks in Anchorage, I figured it was as good an alternative as any to seeing that dumb movie.

The bars in Anchorage are open 24 hours a day. They close for half an hour now and then just for cleaning purposes, but generally, there was always a convenient place open to get a drink. That evening, for one reason or another, we couldn't get served--and we tried about four different places. We finally drove to a store instead. We bought some beer and smuggled it into the barracks. The guys decided we might as well have a card game to go along with the beer.

I only had sixty days left to serve in Alaska. Just sixty days and I would go back to the States, back to my girl, back to get married. When you got down to sixty days, you were referred to as a "short-timer." They put a little pin on your shirt, and you would write 60, 59, 58 and so forth. I was trying to save money for my forthcoming marriage. I'd lost enough playing cards, and I felt I couldn't afford to lose any more and still get married. I don't think I've ever won a game of cards in my life and I knew I wasn't likely to win that night. So when I saw them getting out the cards, I decided I'd better stay out of it.

I heard an announcement that the last bus leaving for the base was out at the gate. (Our barracks were about four miles off of the main base, which was where the movie was playing.) I looked at the cards and I looked at the beer and I looked at everybody sitting around. Then I looked out at the gate where that bus was sitting, and I still don't know why I did it, but the next thing I knew, I was sitting in the back of that bus. I was headed for the base theater to see the movie Al had told me about...and that's a fact.

The movie had already begun when I slipped into the theater. Like Al said, it was about the life of Jesus. I had never read the New Testament, so I knew very little about Jesus. This wasn't a Hollywood picture and it wasn't particularly professionally done. I wasn't impressed. Toward the end of the film, the man who portrayed Jesus was standing on a hill. He was talking to the disciples and then he spread his arms out and said, "Come unto me all you who are laboring and heavy laden. Take my yoke upon you and learn of me and you will find rest." I heard those words and saw the movie screen begin to shimmer. If you've ever had an old-fashioned radiator in your window, it was the same kind of wavering as you'd see when the heat goes on. At first I thought it might be eyestrain. I shut my eyes for a moment, and when I opened them, the face of the man portraying Jesus had changed. It was no longer the face of the actor; it was the face of the man in my dream. He looked straight into my eyes and his arms were outstretched to me. I knew that this Jesus was not who I'd grown up thinking he was. He was Jewish, like me. He was foretold in my Bible. I couldn't deny him any longer. I closed my eyes again and I said, "God of Abraham, Isaac and Jacob, I don't know what this means, but I do believe that Jesus is the Messiah."

I walked back to the barracks instead of taking the bus. It was three or four miles from the movie theater to the outskirts of the base and another four miles to the barracks. All the way back I prayed and asked God what to do. I didn't know exactly what had happened. I just knew my life would never be the same. That was in August, 1955.

I wrote home about my decision. I felt that would be better than waiting till I got back to spring it on everyone. I got a letter from my sisters saying, "Don't come home!" The next day I got another letter from them telling me, "Do come home, we'll talk about it." It turned out that after the first letter, they spoke to the family doctor. He warned them not to make premature judgments. He said, "Maybe something happened to him up there. Tell him to come home; maybe we can help."

Next, I got a letter from Merle's father saying that I was not to call his daughter when I came home. He didn't want to ever see my face again, and he threatened to kill me if I ever came near Merle. I'm sure he would not have carried out his threat, but he was angry enough to put it in writing.

When I got home, my sister's husband, Irving, took me to the rebbe, who was a friend of his. The rebbe looked at me and he said, "How could you believe in that bastard? How could you believe in Jesus?" I looked in his eyes and it was like my whole world was coming to an end.

Our family doctor tried to talk to me as a father; both my parents had been dead for some time. The doctor said to me, "Look. You were in that God-forsaken place for two years, and it's crazy up there. Maybe something happened to your mind. So before you go telling everybody that you believe all this *mishegoss*, please, just go into the hospital for some tests. We want to be sure that you're mentally all right." He and my sisters were so concerned and so sincere, and they put it in such a way that I felt obligated. Merle, my fiancee came down and she said that she'd stick by me. So I allowed them to talk me into going to the hospital, just for some routine tests. After all, if it made them feel better, what could it hurt?

I was there for over a week without so much as one doctor coming to see me. I was in a ward with certified insane people who were acting out their illnesses like people do in a mental hospital. I finally got to see a doctor, a Jewish psychiatrist. The first thing out of his mouth was, "You know, I am a camp survivor." (The word "Holocaust" hadn't yet come into common usage, but I knew that was what he was talking about.) He said, "I was a camp survivor and we didn't have a choice. But here in America, you have a choice. What could make a Jewish boy feel he has to believe in Jesus?"

I thought, "Oh great. Here is the doctor who's supposed to examine me and he's looking at me through his own scars." I was very frightened. I had no liberty to leave until someone decided I should leave. It was a military hospital, Chelsea Naval Hospital, and one could go in voluntarily, but as I discovered, one could not simply volunteer to go home.

There was a little room with an "American Red Cross" sign on the door. I walked into the room and I gave my serial number to the lady at the desk. I told her what had happened, and I told her I was concerned that my entire leave would be wasted. I asked her to contact my next base. Three days later, thanks to the Red Cross, I was released. I went home, packed my duffel bag and left. I did not talk to my family for one year after that. Despite all the show of concern, I felt they had manipulated and betrayed me. My engagement to Merle did not survive the ordeal.

San Antonio was my next base. I stayed there a year and a half, and saved just about enough money for the trip back to Boston. I came back and stayed with one of my sisters for a while. Even though she tried to accept me back as family, she couldn't bring herself to do it. She said, "I just can't handle it. You're going to have to leave. You'll have to find a new life on your own. I have two daughters to raise, and I don't want you around. I can't risk the possibility of you talking to them about Jesus." My other sister said I could stay with her until I got settled, but that did not work out either.

The "crime" was believing in Jesus--but from the punishment, one would have thought it had been child molesting. It was very painful. I loved my family and I never wanted to be separated from them, but as much as I hated being an outcast, I couldn't pay the price for their acceptance. The more I learned about Jesus, the more I understood that because of him, I was reconciled to God. His message was one of peace and hope. How I wished my sisters could understand that. No matter how much I wanted peace in the family, God had to come first in my life. He is the Creator. He is righteous. He is deserving of my obedience.

I tried going away for a while; I moved to Worcester. But I grew lonely for my family, so I went back to try once more for reconciliation. Once more, I was told I was not welcome.

I went to the Blue Hills to pray because I knew it was quiet and peaceful there, and I didn't know what else to do. As I was praying, God comforted me. He planted a thought in my mind and that thought was, "There's $300 waiting for you in the mail. You will begin a new life." I never doubted that it was true. I'd been so upset that I left my sister's house without a thought about my mail. I went back to her home and she said, "I told you, I don't want you here." I replied, "I just want my mail and you can't keep that from me." She gave me a stack of letters.

I went to the corner drugstore and bought a cup of coffee to go. I sat in the car and opened my mail. Sure enough, there was a letter from the Commonwealth of Massachusetts, and it said "For Honorable Service to the United States, and to the Commonwealth of Massachusetts, we award you as an honorably discharged veteran $300." I went out, rented a room and got a job. That was in 1957.

The job was at the Carter Children's Clothes outlet in Needham, Massachusetts. And the "room" I rented was actually a screened-in porch. The landlady said, "It'll just be for a little while until one of my boarders leaves." I found a church in Boston called Tremont Temple, a church with a real concern for Jewish people. They displayed pamphlets in their Information Center on Tremont Street in Boston-- people came there to relax from their big city journeys--it was a nice, quiet atmosphere where visitors could sit and read if they wanted to. Many of the pamphlets were especially geared for Jewish people. I remember lying in bed on the porch, reading these tracts by the light of an Eveready flashlight...until a boarder finally left and then I had a real room.

Time passed and I kept studying the Bible, learning more about Jesus and what it meant to trust and follow him. I met and married a woman named Carol. We had a son. This helped take some of the sting out of the loss of my family, although nothing could wipe away all the pain of that rejection. I began going to Friday night meetings at a Jewish mission called Israel's Remnant. There I met Al Brickner, a Jewish believer who studied the Bible with me and did much to encourage me in my faith.

An experience in 1960 helped set the stage for a major struggle I was to have years later. That experience was with a man whose name was Morris Baker. Morris was a Jewish man who had been brought up by a Methodist minister. And when the Methodist minister retired, he confided in Morris that during the last years of his life, he didn't really believe in the gospel. He said that he'd only continued because of monetary considerations, retirement and so forth. Morris was devastated. He felt he had been robbed of his youth. He became very angry and bitter and decided to embrace the Judaism he felt he'd been deprived of as a child.

Morris came to a meeting of Israel's Remnant, and he began denouncing what we believed. It was a rude thing to do and he was asked to leave. When he left, I followed.

When I first became a believer, all I heard from the Jewish establishment was, "You're doing a terrible thing. You've betrayed us." Nobody had ever opened a Bible to try to prove his point. I was fascinated by Morris because he'd tried to tear down our faith by actually using his Bible. I decided to meet with him to see what he had to say.

Morris had contempt for all authority figures. He said, "Christian interpretation is just garbage. They don't even know their Bibles!"

I asked, "Why don't the rabbis?"

"Ah, the rabbis," he sneered. "What do you expect from them? They're professional religionists!" Morris put me in touch with a man in Israel by the name of Mordechai Alfandari who wrote to me and put forth some arguments. Between the two of them, they managed to plant some real doubts in my mind.

I was troubled, but I finally just put my doubts on the shelf, and decided that there would be answers forthcoming if I prayed and continued to study. I was not going to throw out everything I believed because I didn't have answers to a few questions that were brought forth by these predecessors of today's anti-missionary movement.

I continued believing in Jesus, and continued studying the Scriptures, though I did so on my own, not formally. We moved away from the Boston area and I became involved with a church which accords leadership to lay members. In 1968 they ordained me as a minister, though, as I said, my theological training had been through my own private studies.

Six years passed, and in 1974 I hit a low point. My wife believed in Jesus, but her relationship with God had lost much of its vitality. I was a minister at a church where people seemed to come more to punch a time clock than to worship. I'm not sure if most of the people there really believed in Jesus or if they had just been raised in a church and were merely in the habit of going there on Sunday mornings. There were a few ministers besides myself attempting to inject some life into the church, but after a couple of years, they left and I felt very much alone.

On top of this, throughout the 17 years of my Christian life, I never really dealt with a deep identity problem which had troubled me. I missed my Jewishness. I missed it terribly. I knew that Jesus loved the Jewish people and that I was not doing anything to betray my people by believing in him. But I missed being with Jewish people in Jewish settings. I had known a few Jewish believers in Israel's

Remnant, but it was not the same as being in a community of Jewish people. On top of this, I felt like a failure as a minister; I wasn't doing anything to touch people's hearts in this church. I was very discouraged. I withdrew from the church and I withdrew from ministry.

I decided this would be a good time for me to address some of the doubts I'd put on the "back burner" since communication with Baker and Alfandari. I didn't deny that Jesus was the Messiah, I just felt I needed to grapple with my doubts. I spent hours and hours studying the Bible, and reading traditional Jewish as well as Christian commentaries. I wasn't going to church--I was keeping to myself. It was during this period that I received a phone call from a girl in New York.

She told me that she had met Mordechai Alfandari in Israel, and that he sent his greetings. I told her I hadn't been in touch with Mordechai for years. It didn't matter. What she really wanted to say was that she had been a "Jew for Jesus" in Miami, Florida, and how a visit from a Rebbetzin Jungreis had shown her the light. She went to a Jewish retreat, had an experience with Ha'Shem, and returned to Judaism.

Then this girl put Esther Jungreis on the phone, and I must say, she is one charismatic lady. She said to me so earnestly, "David, I believe you've been struggling." It so happened that I had been. She said, "The trouble is, you never saw real Jewishness. I want to challenge you. I'll pay for you to come up to New York. Come to a weekend retreat, a Jewish retreat, and I guarantee that by the time you leave, you'll see that Jesus is not the Messiah."

I talked to my wife, and she didn't have any problems with my going. She believed in Jesus, but at this point, he was not central in her life. I thought I'd go up there and maybe have an opportunity to tell these people about Jesus-- maybe it would liven up my own spiritual life. I didn't realize that given my "spiritual slump," the weekend would result in something quite different than what I'd planned.

I went on the retreat and I met Esther Jungreis and her father. Her father was a very lovely man who spoke gently to me. "David," he said, "you've become like a leaf on a tree. The leaf looks at the birds and wants to fly from the tree. But you know, David, God meant birds to fly, not leaves. So, if the leaf comes away from the tree, he can fly for a little while, but suddenly he finds he's on the ground. He becomes very dry and brown. That's how I see you--you flew for a little while with the birds, but you're supposed to be a leaf on a tree." Then he patted my cheek and he said, "David, come back, we need you. We need you on the tree."

Well, the analogy may not make a whole lot of sense if you press it, but I was moved by his manner, which was gentle and very knowing. The children came up to him during the Sabbath dinner; they would climb into his lap to give him a kiss, and he would put his hand on their forehead and say a blessing. I was very touched by this genuineness of expression in a Jewish context.

There was dancing after dinner. They were having a marvelous time, singing and dancing before God, praising him. I could not believe the liveliness of their religious expression. I'd heard of *Chasidim*, but I had never been around them, so that Friday night was quite a shock. We went to the Sabbath service the following morning in the synagogue, and that was more like the routine Orthodox services that I was accustomed to from my youth. People more or less went through the motions--something like the church I'd resigned from.

After the Sabbath was over, Rebbetzin Jungreis started speaking to me about Jesus. She pointed out a passage from the Book of Deuteronomy where God warns that he will drive those who do not obey the Law into all nations, and there they will serve gods of wood and stone that they have not known. She said, "David, how do you think your forefathers got to Russia and from Russia to America? Do you think it's because they obeyed Ha'Shem? No, David, it's not because they obeyed him, it's because they disobeyed him. They were driven into the nations, and that is how you found Jesus. He is just one of the gods of the nations." I had been so bombarded by the emotions of the weekend; I was not altogether convinced that she was wrong.

She said, "I want to challenge you to obey the Torah and live a Torah-observant life. If you will obey God in this way, Jesus will fall away from your life and you will reject him."

I decided to take her up on that challenge. To immerse myself in a more Jewish lifestyle was very appealing. I wanted to learn more about this Jewishness which seemed so new and alive. I decided to live an "observant" life and see if what they were telling me was true. If my belief in Jesus did not survive this test, then perhaps it was not valid.

I went back to my wife and son. I koshered my home and began observing the Sabbath, as well as the dietary laws. My wife, Carol, was not Jewish but she knew the heartaches I'd had over missing my Jewish identity, so she was very sympathetic. In fact, she rather enjoyed it.

Carol would come with me once a month to spend the Sabbath with the Jungreis family. They tried to convert her to Judaism, but Carol told them very bluntly, "To become a Jew would be the most wonderful thing in the world to me. I love the philosophy of Judaism, I love everything about it. There's only one problem: what do I do with the man from Galilee? I know he's the Messiah, and it's just out of the question for me to ever say he isn't." She was sincere in her admiration of Judaism. She even told me privately, "If it wasn't for Jesus, I could really identify with this." Carol knew I was reevaluating Christianity, and we were both determined to respect one another's views on whether Jesus was or wasn't the Messiah. We had been married for a long time; we had a commitment to each other and whatever was decided, we would see it through together.

I went through a time of very seriously doubting my faith. I read all the books written to persuade Jews that Jesus is not for us. For six months or so, I leaned toward thinking that I'd made a mistake to believe in him. I told the rabbi about my experiences in Alaska because I could not deny the reality of what had happened to me there and how Jesus had made himself known to me. The rabbi said I had been deceived by false gods. He claimed to have more discernment over these things than ordinary people. In fact, the rabbi, and in Esther Jungreis's case, the rebbetzin, claimed more authority in interpreting personal events as well as Scripture than most Christian ministers I know.

In their circles, rabbinic understandings of Torah are totally at the discretion of whichever rabbi is in authority over you. In the *Pirke Avot*, (the Ethics of the Fathers) in the Talmud, it says one is responsible to obey the edicts of one's own rabbi. If your rabbi's edicts contradict the edicts of the rabbi down the street, you must observe the edicts of your rabbi. Here was my big problem with the Jungreises. I did not want man's authority. I wanted God's authority, which I felt would come to me through the Scriptures. I told the rebbetzin I needed an understanding from the *written* Word of God why I should obey the rabbi. That was all I wanted. I said, "If you can hook up the Talmud with the written Bible, where the written Bible gives you authority in my life, we'll talk." She and her husband really tried, but their "proof" was never satisfying to me. Once when I questioned her interpretation of Scripture, Rebbetzin Jungreis actually put her hand over my mouth and said, "Do you know you're speaking blasphemy against Ha'Shem!?" To her, my questioning her authority was blasphemy. This didn't seem quite "kosher" to me, but I was still confused, still questioning, and still very much attracted by the "Jewish experience" which these people provided.

During that time, I'm afraid I hurt many people. They felt I had betrayed the faith and they expected me to cause others to do the same. Part of their expectation was my own fault and part of it was due to the fact that I was being used. I was trying to deal with my life and my questions, and as I see it in retrospect, Rebbetzin Jungreis was trying to make me into a trophy. She wanted me to be a shining example of a Jew who had given up believing in Jesus to make this dramatic "return" to Judaism. She took a picture of me and without my permission, she gave it to her right-hand man, an editor for a large newspaper on Long Island. The picture went out all over the country. The caption said something about me as a Jew who had been a Christian minister for many years, then renounced it to come back to Judaism. At that point, I had not reached a definite conclusion about

Jesus. I had not made any definitive statement, nor had I given anyone permission to make such a statement on my behalf. However, I was still confused, still searching, and though I found less and less reason to trust this woman personally, I was not ready to discount all she was saying. So I let it go, and that was a mistake. Some people felt I was a traitor, but others, like Al Brickner, stuck with me. Al once said, "No matter what you're saying, I know the Lord's got his hand on you; he's not going to let you go." Another friend said, "I don't care what's coming out of your lips; I've known you too long; I know that Jesus is in your heart, and he'll bring you through this."

After about six months of this "new life" I was miserable. For the first two or three months, the excitement of my change in lifestyle actually did distract my thoughts from Jesus. Carol and I enjoyed our monthly weekend retreats, and the Friday night services were always an emotional shot in the arm. But after a while, I realized that things weren't happening like I'd been told they would. I was doing all I could to be an observant Jew, yet I began to think about Jesus again. He did not "fall away from me," and keeping kosher was not a substitute for the relationship I'd had with him. The emotional satisfaction of Friday night was just that...emotional. It was like getting a battery recharged, but there was no substance to keep me going throughout the rest of the week. Everything seemed to center on the rules, the regulations, and a few charismatic personalities who were in authority. What had seemed like a genuine experience with God turned out to be the same emotional high that any number of religions offer. I was not finding the peace that had been promised me. There was no assurance that I was doing the right thing, as there had been when I'd accepted Jesus so many years before. It wasn't working. What they told me just was not working.

I decided I had better reach a conclusion about what was true and what wasn't. I continued keeping kosher, but I dropped away from the synagogue as well as from my Christian friends. I picked up my Bible and I began to pray. Whether or not this isolation was the wisest thing is open to debate, but I did spend several months honestly searching and willing to hear from God either way. And he was very gracious in leading me through.

During this time, Carol was hospitalized. It was very serious. She'd been ill before, with a kidney condition she'd struggled with for many years.

While Carol was in the hospital, and I was just beginning to fit the pieces of my faith back together, Rebbetzin Jungreis called. I hadn't been in touch with her for quite a while. She was going to Israel, and wanted me to come, too. She said, "Look, David. Rabbi Akiva was 40 years old when he converted and became the great man that he was. You're almost 40 years old; I believe Ha'Shem has called you. You should come to Israel to fulfill your destiny." She wanted me to go into the yeshiva and study to become a rabbi. I could be used in a "mighty way" to convince Jewish believers in Jesus that they had been deceived.

I said to her, "Look, Rebbetzin. I'm still looking for answers and I wouldn't make a move like that unless I was sure. Besides, you know my wife has been sick. She's in the hospital now. There's no way I could leave her and go to Israel with you. And even if Carol was well, I'd have to borrow the money to go and do it."

And this is how she answered me: "You should borrow the money and do anything you have to do. I believe God is saying to you, go to Israel, go into the yeshiva. Now is your chance."

I said to her, "What do I do with my wife who's in the hospital? I have a 16-year-old boy...What do I do, leave? And he comes home from high school to an empty house; his mother is in the hospital and he doesn't know where his father is?" I said, "Are you telling me that this is what God wants me to do?"

She said, "Absolutely. I think you need to forsake your Gentile wife; you've given her the opportunity to convert and she has refused." She talked about Ezra and Nehemiah and quoted Bible verses that say, "Put away your foreign wives."

I listened to her and I said, "I want to make sure I'm not misunderstanding you. You're telling me to leave my wife?"

She replied, "That's what the prophets told our forefathers, to leave their foreign wives. God told Abraham to give his wife bread and some water and send her away. And that's exactly what you should do."

I said, "God told Abraham, not Rebbetzin Jungreis. And it would take God himself, not you, to convince me that I should abandon my family. I have a job and a home here, which perhaps I could leave. But I also have a wife who is sick; I have a child who is 16 and who needs me. What you're suggesting seems crude to me as well as cruel. I have been studying and looking for answers. I have also been looking for a genuineness in you that I have not seen. I see a lot of dancing before God in your way, but the genuineness of the love of God, I have not seen. You'll not hear from me again." I hung up the telephone, and neither of us ever contacted the other again.

I felt the truths I had believed for so many years coming back to me in strength. Within a few months, I had reached the conclusion that Jesus is the Messiah and I needed to follow him, whatever the cost. I did a lot of apologizing: to God as well as to people whom I'd alienated or confused with my problems. I learned that whatever mistakes one may make, if he or she really desires to know the truth and will search the Scriptures and humbly seek God in prayer, he will reveal himself. When I submitted myself to God and was truly willing to go either way if he and he alone showed me, he began putting my faith back together. Even the doubts that had been sown by Baker and Alfandari were being answered as I searched the Scriptures.

I would not say my disillusionment with Esther Jungreis is what solidified my faith in Jesus. However, part of the reason I was susceptible to doubting my faith in Jesus was that it seemed to preclude my Jewish identity. I missed that part of myself so much. I drifted farther and farther from faith in Jesus in my pursuit of the emotional and experience-oriented religion her movement offered. When I recognized the "ends-justify-the-means" mentality, I no longer found what they had to offer appealing. These people seemed obsessed in their zeal to "win back" Jewish converts. They knew how to make a person feel important and needed. But they didn't know how to offer the reality of a relationship with God, because they didn't know his Messiah, Y'shua.

Many young Jews are being sold on the "goods" that because they grew up Reform and Conservative, they've never tasted real Jewish life. So they meet someone with a strong personality who takes an interest in them, and on weekends they dance and they praise God in a very charismatic way. There's no question that there is an emotional quality that is just vital. The problem is that emotions come and go. Only God's Word never fails and is always the same, no matter if you're high or low.

Even when I had such strong doubts about Y'shua, he did not turn his back on me. The commitment I'd made to him in Alaska was real, and even more, the promises he made to those who have truly trusted in him are real. Y'shua said, "My sheep hear my voice and I know them, and they follow me; and I give eternal life to them, and they shall never perish, and no one shall snatch them out of my hand" (John 10:26, 27).

I came from this most difficult time in my life with much more than answers to the questions which had troubled me. It was a blessing that God gave me the answers to those questions through my study of Scripture. But more than that, I came away from my experience with the solidity of a real relationship with Y'shua, which nothing can shake. I am no longer an objective person when it comes to him. It's difficult explaining that to people who have never made that degree of commitment to anyone or anything. God has answered my deepest questions, and I'm no longer open to discussing any possibility that Y'shua is not the Messiah. God sealed my heart on that issue.

There have been some repercussions from my time of doubting, but God has an interesting way of turning things around. Back in the late '60s, when I was corresponding with Alfandari, we had a written dialogue regarding the fifty-third chapter of Isaiah and whether or not it referred to Y'shua. At that point, I was already exploring the possibility that perhaps it didn't, and I did a written study expressing some doubts. Alfandari had a tract made of my study, and presented it to me as a gift. In 1974 I showed the tract to some of the people who were so eager to "win me back into the fold."

In 1986, over ten years after I had reaffirmed my faith in Jesus, a man by the name of Larry Levey, who knows full well that I do believe in Y'shua, got hold of that tract. He reproduced it without my permission and distributed the tract (with my name on it), in an unsolicited mailing to Jewish believers in Jesus nationwide. Levey knew the tract represented some of my thoughts from over a decade ago. If he was capable of disproving the claims of Y'shua, he wouldn't need to dig up my long-since resolved doubts. As far as I'm concerned, it was a manipulative attempt to undermine Y'shua's credibility, and the credibility of my commitment to him. Yet it was also an encouragement. The fact is, more and more Jewish people are turning to the Messiah. Even the most questionable attempts to discourage us from believing are evidence that Y'shua's claims are far too significant to be ignored.

I suppose Levey meant to discourage me when he said, "You know, this is the best thing that was ever written to prove that Jesus isn't the Messiah of Isaiah 53." Poor Larry. What he and his cohorts fail to see is that if my tract was the best thing written, their case against Jesus is truly weak. I'm the one who wrote the tract, so I'm obviously acquainted with the arguments...and in the end, they weren't strong enough to keep me from Y'shua. In fact, I told Levey I could easily write another tract refuting each and every doubt that I'd had over a decade ago--but he didn't seem too interested in that idea.

It actually took me a while to get "back on my feet" spiritually after my time of doubting. My resolve and renewed commitment to Y'shua did not mean my life was suddenly filled with happiness, nor did all problems disappear. Things were difficult. My wife, who had been sickly for many years, died. The grief was hard for my son and me to bear. In addition, I had many fences to mend, and trust to rebuild in a number of relationships. Through it all, God comforted me and I was assured of his forgiveness.

I involved myself in a church which was very helpful in my period of recovering both from Carol's death as well as my whole experience of faith crises. I became a Sunday school teacher at this church and as I regained the strength of my convictions, I was asked to tell the story of how I came to faith to various Christian groups. That's how I met Glenna.

Glenna taught a Bible study for a group of Christians at the National Right to Work, in the Education Department. She met with a group of Christians there every Tuesday afternoon at lunch, and I was asked to come and speak to them.

Glenna had a great love for Jewish people. A friend of hers had gone to Israel, and when she returned, she just immersed herself in Jewish things. This friend, who was also a Christian, was so enthusiastic about Israel that Glenna became very interested in what was happening among Jewish people. When she met me in 1978, she began asking me about Jewish things. My reply was, "Why so interested?"

She was surprised, because she assumed that next to Jesus, being Jewish would be a major focus in my life. After my experience with the Jungreises, it wasn't. Glenna asked me, "Haven't you been to Beth Messiah?" Beth Messiah is a congregation of Jewish believers in Y'shua who worship in a Jewish context, using much of the synagogue liturgy, yet affirming faith in Jesus as the Messiah.

I said, "No. I'm not even interested in going to Beth Messiah." I thought the Messianic movement was a flukey thing, a way to attract Jews to Christ. I had made a great many judgments about it without much knowledge, and with no firsthand experience. Glenna practically had to twist my arm to get me to visit Beth Messiah. I finally went, but I wasn't especially interested. Then a Jewish believer in Y'shua challenged me to study the Book of Acts in the New Testament, because he claimed I would find that being Jewish and being a Christian need not be mutually exclusive. I started studying, and began to recognize for the first time just how Jewish the Messiah's first followers were. They'd had no problem being Jewish and following Y'shua.

I was still troubled because I knew that according to the New Testament, forgiveness for sin came through Jesus, not through keeping any of the laws. I did not want to involve myself in anything that would seem to undermine the sufficiency of what Jesus had done. I brought my questions to another Jewish believer in Jesus who said, "Dave, God never meant the Law to give life. The Law was to point out sin, the Law was to show us what God's mind is on certain issues. It never was meant to give life, unless you obey it like Jesus did, perfectly. Even before the Messiah came, people were not saved by the Law, but through their faith and obedience to God."

When I first accepted Y'shua as Messiah, I was told by well-meaning Christians that I could no longer maintain that I was Jewish. It was only through my desire to please God that I, with great sadness, threw away my tallis and tefillin and no longer observed my holidays. For many years after becoming a believer in Y'shua, when the holidays (especially Rosh Hashanah, Yom Kippur and Passover) rolled around, a deep pain within reminded me of what I had given up.

When, in more recent years, I became aware of the fact that Y'shua never rejected his Jewishness (he worshipped in a synagogue and he observed the Jewish festivals), I realized there was no need for me to forsake those things which the Messiah himself affirmed. The joy of my identity as a Jew was restored, as there was finally a coming together of my Jewishness and my faith in Jesus.

It's interesting to think about the story Rebbetzin Jungreis's father told me that first Sabbath I spent with them--the story about the leaf wanting to depart from the tree to fly with the birds. It appealed to me because it was such a Jewish thing to sit and hear a rabbi telling a story. But you know, there was another rabbi who told a story about a tree. His name was Rabbi Saul (also known as Paul), a Jewish believer in Y'shua. He told his tree story to Gentiles. You can read about it in the eleventh chapter of the Book of Romans.

In this story, there was a cultivated olive tree. Some of the branches were broken off, and wild olive branches were grafted in. Rabbi Saul warned the Gentiles, whom he equated with the wild olive branches, not to boast against the cultivated branches, whom he equated with Jews. He admonished them to remember that it was the root of the olive tree which supported both. Anticipating their response, he continued, "You will say then, 'Branches were broken off that I might be grafted in.' Well said. Because of unbelief they were broken off, and you stand by faith. Do not be haughty, but fear. For if God did not spare the natural branches, He may not spare you either...And they also, if they do not continue in unbelief, will be grafted in, for God is able to graft them in again."

I have returned to Judaism. True, it was not the return that opposers of Y'shua were hoping I would make. But I have been grafted back into the tree planted by our God when he made that first promise to Abraham. The fact that so many Gentiles have accepted the Messiah and were grafted into our tree shows God's goodness, and I am glad. The fact that our Messiah came for Jews and Gentiles affirms my Jewish identity, for God promised Abraham that we would be a light to the nations.

In late 1978 Glenna and I were married. I watch, with great satisfaction as our three children grow, embracing faith in Y'shua as the Messiah and their Jewish identity. It is as natural for Joshua, Elicia and Jeremy to say the *borachas* each Sabbath as it is for them to tell how God answered a prayer through Y'shua. That is who they are. In fact my 7-year-old, Joshua, just can't understand how someone can be Jewish and not believe in Y'shua! I have much joy in the knowledge that my fulfilled Jewishness will be passed on to future generations.

In 1980, I gave up my business (an advertising agency) to begin building a messianic congregation in the Washington, D.C. area. My visits to Beth Messiah had awakened in me a real hunger to be part of such a congregation. I happened to be meeting weekly for Bible studies with one man who started inviting his friends. As more and more people began coming on Friday nights, I realized the same sense of "coming home" as I'd felt at Beth Messiah was beginning to develop. I started Ohev Yisrael as a congregation of nine people. Now, seven years later, 140 attend our services, 115 of whom are members of the congregation. We are a group of people who have found that the God of Israel is just as real today as he ever was, and that we can have a vital relationship with him through the Messiah, Y'shua.

CONTINUATIONS
OF THE
CASE

Maybe you noticed, each of the preceding accounts is different, yet there are certain issues that are common to several. For example, many people expressed hesitation over reading the "New Testament," as well as surprise upon discovering that it is a Jewish book after all. Another point mentioned in many of the "testimonies" is the ninth chapter from the Book of Daniel in the Hebrew Scriptures, which many found convincing in the case for Y'shua's messiahship. Also repeated was the problem of "Christian" anti-Semitism and the fear that belief in Y'shua would be seen as joining the persecutors of the Jewish people.

Those three subjects will each be addressed in the following articles, written by Jewish believers in the Messiah. They will add depth to your understanding of the accounts you have just read.

"The Jewishness of the New Testament" was written by Al Brickner, a minister and professional counselor. He received degrees in theology and counseling from Gordon Conwell Theological Seminary.

"The Messianic Timetable according to Daniel the Prophet" was written by Arnold G. Fruchtenbaum. Dr. Fruchtenbaum received his Ph.D. from New York University by initiating a new branch of theological studies called "Israelology." He is the founder and leader of Ariel Ministries, a Bible-teaching ministry which specializes in the area of messianic studies.

"Christian Anti-Semitism?" was written by Barry Leventhal, who was co-captain for the Bruins when U.C.L.A. won the Rose Bowl in 1966. He went on to receive his Th.M. (master of theology) and his doctorate from Dallas Theological Seminary for a thesis on anti-Semitism.

The Jewishness of the New Testament
by Al Brickner

What does the New Testament teach? For whom was it written? What kind of men wrote it? What about its alleged "anti-Semitic" passages?

Little-known Facts About a Widely-read Book

Rabbi Isaac Lichtenstein was curious when he observed one of the teachers in his school reading a book printed in German. After asking the teacher what he was reading, the book was passed to him. He leafed casually through the pages until his eye fell upon the name, "Jesus Christ." Realizing that the little book was a New Testament, he sternly rebuked the teacher for having it in his possession. He furiously cast the book across the room. It fell behind some other books on a shelf and lay forgotten for nearly 30 years.

An outbreak of intense anti-Jewish persecution arose some years later in Rabbi Lichtenstein's native Hungary, and he was not surprised that the attacks were carried on in the name of Christianity. In the midst of the pogroms, he was startled to read the writings of men who, in the name of Christ, sternly denounced the anti-Semites and defended the Jews. Among these were prominent figures such as the honored biblical scholar Franz Delitzsch, professor at the University of Leipzig. He was intrigued by statements which spoke of the message of Christ as one of love and life to all people.

At this time, the little New Testament, flung in anger into a dusty corner years ago, was found. For the aging rabbi it had been a closed and hated book which he thought to be the source of venom aimed at his people. *Was it really what he had supposed it to be?* He opened its pages and began to read.

Rabbi Lichtenstein later wrote in "Two Letters: or What I Really Wish," describing the experience which flowed from his reading of the New Testament:

I had thought the New Testament to be impure, a source of pride, of overweening selfishness, of hatred, of the worst kind of violence, but as I opened it, I felt myself peculiarly and wonderfully taken possession of. A sudden glory, a light, flashed through my soul. I looked for thorns and gathered roses; I discovered pearls instead of pebbles; instead of hatred, love; instead of vengeance, forgiveness; instead of bondage, freedom; instead of pride, humility; instead of enmity, conciliation; instead of death, life, salvation, resurrection, heavenly treasure.

A Closed Book

The story of Rabbi Lichtenstein is true. It epitomizes two poles of experience that Jewish people have had so far as the New Testament is concerned. For the majority, the New Testament is a closed and unfamiliar book because it is identified with the age-long persecution of the Jewish people in the name of Christianity. Because most Jews believe that the New Testament promotes anti-Semitism, they think there could be nothing in it which could sustain Jewish life and values.

Thus, the common Jewish assessment of the New Testament is formed by a preconditioned impression. In many ways, Jewish experience seems to support this assessment. However, the majority of the Jewish people do not feel inclined to verify the assessment by an investigation of the New Testament itself.

The Message is Jewish

Yet there is a growing number of Jews, who, like Rabbi Lichtenstein, have been prompted, for one reason or another, to investigate seriously what the New Testament actually contains. This writer is among them. *We have come to recognize through careful investigation that the New Testament is something different than we had first supposed.*

First of all, we have discovered that its authorship and cultural background are Jewish. The beginning scenes of the New Testament are centered in the land of Israel at the time of the Second Temple. Even as the focus widens from the original setting, the action takes place primarily among Jewish communities in the Diaspora. The New Testament writers, with perhaps the exception of Luke, are all Jews. The early apostles and followers of Jesus are also Jewish.

Fulfillment of the Jewish Hope

The basic theme of the New Testament is uniquely a Jewish one: the fulfillment of the messianic hope. This expectation was peculiarly the possession of Israel. An early passage in the Gospel of Matthew portrays Gentile wise men recognizing that the promised deliverer is to be "King of the Jews." In the early stages of the spread of the good news about the Messiah, it is only Jews and those Gentiles who are under the influence of Judaism who are prepared to receive and understand the message about the advent of the long-expected Redeemer. The primary centers for the initial preaching of the message are the synagogues in the communities of the Diaspora.

In page after page of the New Testament, by direct quote, by free paraphrase, and by allusion, there is one primary literary treasure that is invested with supreme authority: the Hebrew Scriptures. When Jesus or the New Testament preachers intone, "It is written," or "Thus saith the Lord," they rest upon Jewish Holy Writ as the final court of appeal. Jesus challenges the religious teachers with "You search the Scriptures...it is these that bear witness of Me" (John 5:39). Peter proclaims to the Jewish throng: "And likewise, all the prophets who have spoken, from Samuel and his successors onward, also announced these days" (Acts 3:24). The initial New Testament proclamations are laced with passages from Moses and the prophets, indicating that what is taking place is the fulfillment of the Jewish hope.

When one investigates the general content of the New Testament, if he is somewhat acquainted with the Hebrew Scriptures, he will find himself in familiar territory. Angelic communications remind one of the experiences of Abraham, Isaac, Jacob, Moses, Joshua and many other ancient Hebrews. Supernatural births recall the nativity of the patriarch, Isaac. Miracles represent God's confirming activity as he reveals himself, even as they did in the days of the patriarchs, Moses, the prophets and the kings of Israel. They are not capricious acts of arbitrary power, as in pagan mythology, but they bear profound moral connections through which God trains his people in the ways of faith. Also, as in the Hebrew Scriptures, there is prophetic activity and inspired preaching when the Spirit of God enables men to speak his message. None of these occurrences are strange to the spiritual life and heritage of Israel.

The great themes of the New Testament are the same as those of the Hebrew Scriptures: God's holiness, righteousness and mercy; man's alienation and estrangement from God through disobedience; God's seeking love, forgiveness and reconciliation. There are also the great themes of faith, sacrifice, redemption, hope, love, peace, joy, the ultimate triumph of God's Kingdom and his judgment and reward. One can read and compare them. There is nothing presented in the former which is not unfolded in the latter. Only the perspective differs. In the Old Covenant, the emphasis is upon promise and in the New Covenant the emphasis is upon fulfillment. The one stresses preparation and the other consummation.

A Suffering Messiah

At this point, some might object that there are themes central to the New Testament which are non-Jewish. Many contend that the idea of a suffering, dying and resurrected Messiah who is at the same time divine is alien to Jewish belief. It is supposedly traced to pagan Egyptian and Greek sources. In addition, it is alleged that the manner in which the New Testament traces the rise and spread of the messianic community remolds it into a Gentile phenomenon, ripping it from the Jewish context.

The ancient rabbis wrestled with evidence in the Tanach that Messiah was both to suffer and die and to reign as a triumphant and glorious king. Because of this problem, they developed the idea that there would be two messiahs: Ben Joseph who would suffer and die, and Ben

David who would triumph and reign. In the Talmud (Sukkah 52, a and b) there is the suggestion that the passage in Zechariah 12:10, which speaks of a pierced one, gave rise to this explanation.

In the *Musaf* service for the Day of Atonement, there is an ancient prayer which refers to *Mashiach Tzidkenu* (Messiah our Righteousness) as one who is "wounded for our transgressions."

The concept of a suffering and dying Messiah is not strange to Jewish lore.

While the resurrection of the Messiah, as declared in the New Testament, seemed to take everyone by surprise, there are passages in Holy Writ which are seen as promising Messiah's resurrection. Psalm 16:10 declares that God will not abandon his Holy One to the grave. Isaiah 53:10,12 portrays the Lord as prolonging the days of the Suffering Servant and causing God's good pleasure to prosper in his hand because he has willingly poured out his soul unto death.

There are passages in the prophetic writings which give evidence that the Messiah is to be divine. In Isaiah 9:6, the Messianic King is called by the awesome names: *Wonderful Counselor; Mighty God; Eternal Father; Prince of Peace.* In Jeremiah 23:6, the Righteous Branch that is to be raised to David is given the name, "The Lord Our Righteousness." In Micah 5:2, where there is the announcement of Messiah's birthplace, he is spoken of as coming from eternity. In Daniel 7:13-14, Messiah is seen coming in the clouds of heaven and receiving an eternal dominion over all peoples. The rabbis who developed the mystical lore, such as that contained in the Zohar, observing these and other passages, speculated that the Messiah was to be divine.

Though Jesus himself declared that "salvation is of the Jews" (John 4:22), he also declared that other sheep which are not of the Jewish fold would also be added to the flock of the messianic Shepherd (John 10:16). This vision is not strange to Jewish expectation. God declared through Isaiah (Isaiah 49:6) that Messiah would be a light to the Gentiles and his salvation would spread to the ends of the earth.

Isaiah 60:1-3 proclaims that Gentiles shall come to the light that spreads from Israel through the Messiah.

So the New Testament vision is not a Gentile aberration. It is rather the vision of the ancient Hebrew prophets who proclaimed that God would bring the Gentiles into the blessings of Israel through the Messiah.

In all of these ways, we Jews who have been prompted to investigate the New Testament carefully have come to recognize its basically Jewish character. But we have also discovered something else. THOSE PASSAGES WHICH ALLEGEDLY PROMOTE ANTI-JEWISH SENTIMENT, UPON CLOSER INVESTIGATION, ARE NOT REALLY ANTI-JEWISH AT ALL.

Family Dispute

There is conflict in the New Testament over the messianic claims of Jesus, but it is mainly conflict between Jews who accept those claims and Jews who do not. In other words, it is a family dispute. When one looks closely at the ways in which the term, "the Jews," is used, especially in the Gospel of John as well as in some other New Testament writings, it can be seen that it is often used to represent the coalition among the Jewish leadership that had purposed to oppose Jesus. In those passages where this conflict is in view, the term refers to these opposed leaders. The New Testament reveals that Jesus was so popular with the people that his opposers had to operate in secret. This indicates clearly that the term, "the Jews," did not refer to the general populace.

Certain harsh statements pronounced by Jesus and the New Testament preachers are not vindictive but prophetic rebukes, in the same vein as the words of Isaiah when he calls Israel "offspring of evildoers, sons who act corruptly!" (Isaiah 1:4). Though anti-Semites who professed to be Christians have used these seemingly harsh statements as a pretext to persecute Jews, they did so in contradiction to the express teachings of Jesus and the apostles.

Jesus wept over Jerusalem and lamented her coming destruction at the hands of the Romans, which he announced prophetically (Matthew 23:37-39). He taught his followers to love those who opposed them and to pray for those who shamefully treated them (Matthew 5:43-46). The writings of Paul are often cited to show the anti-Semitic nature of the New Testament. *How can this be in light of the fact that Paul taught Gentile believers at Rome that, though many Jews opposed the Gospel, they were loved by God for the sake of the forefathers* (Romans 11:28)? Believers are not to be boastful or arrogant against the natural branches (the Jewish people), but they are to make them envious of the messianic blessings by showing them compassion and kindness (Romans 11:11-12, 17, 30-31). Jesus taught that only the merciful were to receive mercy, only the forgiving could expect forgiveness and that love would be the hallmark of his true disciples.

Is It True?

We see nothing in the New Testament that is non-Jewish or anti-Jewish. It is, to the contrary, woven with the warp and woof of Jewish hope and prophetic promise. If one can accept the revelation of Moses and the prophets with utter seriousness, there should be nothing really strange in the New Testament. The real challenge of the New Testament, as we see it, is not about Jewishness, but about faith. It is not a question of, "Is it Jewish?" We believe that careful investigation will verify its Jewishness. The real question is, "Is it true?" That, as we have stated, is really a question of faith and it holds a challenge for all people, Jew and Gentile alike.

Scripture quotations are taken from the Standard American Edition of the Revised Version of the Bible (a.k.a. American Standard Version), 1901, Thomas Nelson & Sons.

The Messianic Timetable According to Daniel the Prophet

by Arnold G. Fruchtenbaum

More than any other book of the Hebrew Scriptures, the writings of the Prophet Daniel confront us with evidence of the time of Messiah's coming--evidence that many people would rather not see. But it is there and cannot be ignored.

That Daniel was indeed a prophet is well substantiated. He accurately prophesied the rise of the Medo-Persian, Greek and Roman empires even at a time when the Babylonian Empire, which preceded them all, was at its height. He accurately predicted the fortunes, conflicts, wars and conspiracies of the two kingdoms of Syria and Egypt between the fracturing of the Greek Empire and the conquest by Rome. He prophesied the role of the Maccabees during this period. It is Daniel's detailed accuracy in his prophecies that has caused many critics to try to give a late date to the Book of Daniel, although no evidence has been discovered that would negate the book's composition at the time that it claims to have been written. At the very latest, the book was completed around 530 B.C.E.

The purpose of this article is to discuss in some detail verses 24-27 of Daniel chapter nine. However, it will be wise to survey the entire chapter in order to see what engendered the prophecy of when Messiah would come.

The Background--Daniel 9:1-2

The date for Daniel's prophecy is "the first year of Darius," which means that it occurred in the year 539 B.C.E., about 66 or 67 years after the Jews initially went into exile to Babylonia.

It was on this occasion, Daniel stated, that he was studying the Scriptures; and from these Scriptures he came to understand that the number of years for the completion of the desolations of Jerusalem were almost over, since the duration was to be 70 years. Daniel mentioned that he was studying "books," and we can see for one that he had been studying the writings of Jeremiah; the lives of Jeremiah and Daniel did overlap to some extent. On two occasions (Jeremiah 25:10-14, 29:10-14) Jeremiah predicted that the captivity and desolation of Jerusalem would last 70 years. What other books Daniel may have been studying we cannot know with certainty. But there are some strong possibilities that he also studied the Book of Isaiah, since Isaiah actually named Cyrus as the one who would permit the Jews to return (Isaiah 44:28-45:1). Furthermore, there are other writings in Moses and the Prophets that spelled out some specific conditions for the establishment of the messianic kingdom, and Daniel may have looked at some of these as well (Leviticus 26:40-43, I Kings 8:46-53, Jeremiah 3:12-18, Hosea 5:15-6:3). These passages emphasize that Israel as a nation must repent and confess sin prior to the establishment of any kingdom of the Messiah.

Reckoning the 70 years from the year 605 (when the Jews went into exile) would bring the end of the 70 years to 536 B.C.E. Daniel realized that the captivity had only about three years to go.

But Daniel not only expected the captivity to end after 70 years, he also expected a final termination of any possibility of future desolations for Jerusalem. He had acted as if the messianic kingdom were about to occur: since the Word of God was to be established on the basis of prayer, he prayed; and realizing that the prerequisite was the confession of national sin, he confessed the sins of Israel.

Daniel's Prayer--Daniel 9:3-19

Daniel's detailed prayer can be divided into two portions. The first (verses 3-14) is the confession of sin. Daniel acknowledged both sin and guilt, which had been incurred in two ways--first by disobedience to the Law of Moses, and second by disobedience to the prophets who came after Moses. Daniel neither denied the sin of his nation nor his own sin, and by the use of the pronoun "we," Daniel fully identified with all Jewish people in their sins. He did not see sin as merely a bad habit, but as something ingrained in the people that had brought on divine judgment. This disobedience to both the Law and the Prophets caused Israel "confusion of face," an idiom meaning a sense of shame. It also resulted in the need for forgiveness. Here Daniel confessed that to God belong forgiveness and mercy, and that forgiveness was needed. Daniel concluded the first part of his prayer by describing the punishment for sin and guilt. That punishment, captivity in Babylon, confirmed the words of the prophets who had predicted it and confirmed the Law of Moses, which taught that divine judgment would come as a result of disobedience.

The second part of the prayer (verses 15-19) is a plea for mercy. Daniel made his plea on the basis of righteousness--not Israel's, but God's righteousness. He also pleaded for mercy on the basis of God's grace, for Israel did not merit mercy; but the grace of God was (and is) able to extend it anyway. Furthermore, the righteousness of God required him to fulfill his promises, and therefore he should do so at the end of the 70-year period. The conclusion of Daniel's prayer is very dramatic: "O Lord, hearken and do; defer not, for thine own sake, O my God; because thy city and thy people are called by thy name."

The Arrival of Gabriel--Daniel 9:20-23

Then, while Daniel was presenting his supplications, he was interrupted. He apparently had intended to say more, when Gabriel arrived. The interruption came by the touch of the angel's hand, "about the time of the evening oblation." This refers to the daily, regular evening sacrifice that was offered while the Temple stood. Although it had not been practiced for seven decades, Daniel showed his longing for the return from captivity and for the rebuilding of the Temple by remembering the sacrifice.

Gabriel told Daniel that the purpose of his visit was (1) to correct Daniel's misunderstanding concerning when the messianic kingdom would be set up and (2) to present God's revelation, which contained a timetable for Messiah's coming.

The Decree of the 70 Sevens--Daniel 9:24a

Gabriel's prophecy to Daniel began with the words, "Seventy sevens are decreed upon thy people and upon thy holy city...."

Many English versions have translated the phrase to read "seventy weeks." But this translation is not totally accurate and has caused some confusion about the meaning of the passage. Most Jews know the Hebrew for "weeks" because of the observance of the Feast of Weeks, and that Hebrew word is *shavuot*. However, the word that appears in the Hebrew text is *shavuim*, which means "sevens." The word refers to a "seven" of anything, and the context determines the content of the seven.

Here it is obvious Daniel had been thinking in terms of years--specifically the 70 years of captivity. Daniel had assumed that the captivity would end after 70 years and that the kingdom would be established after 70 years. But here Gabriel was using a play upon words in the Hebrew text, pointing out that insofar as Messiah's kingdom was concerned, it was not "70 years," but "70 sevens of years," a total of 490 years (70 times seven).

This period of 490 years had been "decreed" over the Jewish people and over the holy city of Jerusalem. The Hebrew word translated "decreed" literally means "to cut off" or "to determine." In chapters 2, 7 and 8, God revealed to Daniel the course of future world history in which Gentiles would have a dominant role over the Jewish people. This lengthy period, which began with the Babylonian Empire to continue until the establishment of Messiah's kingdom, is for that reason often referred to as the "Times of the Gentiles." Now the prophet was told that a total of 490 years was to be "cut out" of the Times of the Gentiles, and a 490-year period had been "determined" or "decreed" for the accomplishment of the final restoration of Israel and the establishment of Messiah's kingdom.

The focus of the program of the 70 sevens was "thy people and...thy holy city." The "people" were Daniel's people, the Jewish people, and the city was Daniel's city,

Jerusalem. Though he had spent the vast majority of his life in the city of Babylon, Jerusalem was still Daniel's city. For Jews, whether they are in the land or outside the land, their city is always Jerusalem and not any other.

The Purpose of the 70 Sevens--Daniel 9:24b

Daniel was next told by Gabriel that the 70 sevens are to accomplish six purposes. The first is to finish transgression. The Hebrew word translated "to finish" means "to restrain firmly," "to restrain completely" or "to bring to completion." The Hebrew word translated "transgression" is a very strong word for sin and more literally means "to rebel." The Hebrew text has this word with the definite article so literally it means "the transgression," or "the rebellion." The point is that some specific act of rebellion is finally going to be completely restrained and brought to an end. This act of rebellion or transgression is to come under complete control so that it will no longer flourish. Israel's apostasy is now to be firmly restrained, in keeping with a similar prediction in Isaiah 59:20.

The second purpose of the 70 sevens is to make an end of sins. The Hebrew word translated "to make an end" literally means "to seal up" or "to shut up in prison." It means to be securely kept, locked up, not allowed to roam at random. The Hebrew word translated as "sins" literally means "to miss the mark." It refers to sins of daily life, rather than to one specific sin. Even these sins are to be put to an end and taken away. This, too, is quite in keeping with predictions by the prophets that proclaim that in the messianic kingdom, sinning would cease from Israel (Isaiah 27:9, Ezekiel 36:25-27, 37:23, Jeremiah 31:31-34).

The third purpose is to make reconciliation for iniquity. The Hebrew word translated "to make reconciliation" is *kaphar*, which has the same root meaning as the word *kippur*, as in Yom Kippur. The word "kaphar" literally means "to make atonement." The third purpose, then, is to make atonement in some way for iniquity. In fact, it is by means of this atonement that the first two purposes will also be accomplished, that of finishing the transgression

315

and making an end of sins. The word translated "iniquity" refers to inward sin. This has sometimes been referred to as the sin nature, or perhaps a more common term among Jewish people would by *yetzer ha'ra*, "the evil inclination."

The fourth purpose of the 70 sevens is to bring in everlasting righteousness. More literally this could be translated "to bring in an age of righteousness," since the Hebrew "olam" is better translated as "age" rather than as "everlasting." This age of righteousness is to be the messianic kingdom spoken of in the Prophets (Isaiah 1:26, 11:2-5, 32:17, Jeremiah 23:5-6, 33:15-18). It is this very age that Daniel had been expecting to see established after the 70 years of captivity, but now he is told that that will only be after the 490-year period.

The fifth purpose is to seal up vision and prophecy. Here Daniel used a word which means "to shut up." So "to seal up" means to cause a cessation or to completely fulfill. Thus, vision and prophecy are to be completely fulfilled. "Vision" is a reference to oral prophecy, while "prophecy" refers to written prophecy. Both oral and written prophecy will cease with the final fulfillment of all revelations.

The final purpose of the 70 sevens is to anoint the most holy. A better translation here would be "to anoint a most holy place." This is a reference to the Jewish Temple which is to be rebuilt when Messiah comes. It refers to the same Temple that Daniel's contemporary, Ezekiel, described in great detail (Ezekiel 40-48).

The Start of the 70 Sevens--Daniel 9:25a

Daniel was clearly told when the 70 sevens would begin their countdown. Gabriel said, "Know therefore and discern, that from the going forth of the commandment to restore and to build Jerusalem...." The 70 sevens would begin with a decree involving the rebuilding of the city of Jerusalem. Not everything in Persian chronology is as clear as we would like to have it, and there are still some gaps in our knowledge of history. But from what biblical and historical records we do have, there are four possible answers to the question of which decree the passage refers to.

One is the decree of Cyrus, issued somewhere between

538-536 B.C.E., which concerned the rebuilding of the Temple (2 Chronicles 36:22-23, Ezra 1:1-4, 6:1-5) and of the city of Jerusalem (Isaiah 44:28, 45:13). Another option is the decree of Darius Hystaspes (Ezra 6:6-12), issued in the year 521 B.C.E.; it was a reaffirmation of the decree of Cyrus. A third possibility is the decree of Artaxerxes to Ezra (Ezra 7:11-26) issued in 458 B.C.E., which contained permission to proceed with the Temple service. The last option is the decree of Artaxerxes to Nehemiah (Nehemiah 2:1-8), issued in the year 444 B.C.E. This decree specifically concerned the rebuilding of the walls around Jerusalem. Of these four possibilities, only the first and fourth are valid in fulfilling the wording Gabriel gave to Daniel. It goes beyond the purpose of this article to deal with the various arguments of either option, but one thing is certain: by the year 444 B.C.E., the countdown of the 70 sevens had begun.

The First 69 Sevens--Daniel 9:25b

The 70 sevens are divided into three separate units-- seven sevens, 62 sevens and one seven. During the first time period (49 years) Jerusalem would be "built again, with street and moat, even in troublous times." The second block of time (62 sevens, a total of 434 years) immediately followed the first for a total of 69 sevens or 483 years.

It is at this point that we are told what the ending point is of the 69 sevens: "unto Messiah the Prince." As clearly as Daniel could have stated it, he taught that 483 years after the decree to rebuild Jerusalem had been issued, Messiah would be here on earth.

The obvious conclusion is this: If Messiah was not on earth 483 years after a decree was issued to rebuild Jerusalem, then Daniel was a false prophet and his book has no business being in the Hebrew Scriptures. But if Daniel was correct and his prophecy was fulfilled, then who was the Messiah of whom he spoke?

The Events Between the 69th and 70th Seven-- Daniel 9:26

Whereas the second subdivision of the 70 sevens was

to immediately follow the first, the third subdivision was not immediately to follow the second. Daniel pointed out (in verse 26) that three things would occur after this second subdivision and before the third one.

Stepping back in time and looking ahead from Daniel's perspective in verse 26, we see first that "the Messiah shall be cut off and shall have nothing." The Hebrew word translated "cut off" is the common word used in the Mosaic Law and simply means "to be killed." The implication of the term is that the Messiah would not only be killed, but he would die a penal death by execution. The Hebrew expression translated "and shall have nothing" has two meanings. It may mean "nothingness," emphasizing Messiah's state at death. It can also be translated "but not for himself," and the meaning would then be that he died for others rather than for himself, a substitutionary death. The latter meaning would be much more consistent with what the Prophets had to say about the reason for Messiah's death (e.g. Isaiah 53:1-12). The first three purposes of the 70 sevens--to finish transgression, to make an end of sins, to make reconciliation for iniquity--have to be accomplished by an atonement. The Law of Moses decreed that atonement is made by blood (Leviticus 17:11). It appears that Messiah's death "not for himself" but for others would be the means by which Israel's transgression, sins and iniquity would be atoned for. The point of this phrase is that between the end of the second subdivision (the 69th seven) and before the start of the 70th seven, Messiah would be killed and would die a penal, substitutionary death.

Secondly, during this interim period it would also happen that "the people of the prince that shall come shall destroy the city and the sanctuary; and the end thereof shall be with a flood...." The city and the Temple that were to be rebuilt because of the decree by which the 70 sevens began would not be destroyed. So sometime after the Messiah was cut off, Jerusalem and the Temple would suffer another destruction. Our knowledge of history during this period is extremely clear: the people responsible for this deed were the Romans, and Jerusalem and the Temple were destroyed in the year 70 C.E. Based upon this verse, it is also clear that the Messiah should have both come and died prior to the year 70 C.E. If such an event did not take place, then Daniel was a false prophet. If such an event did occur, then the question must be answered, who was that Messiah who was killed before 70 C.E.?

The third thing to take note of would be, "and even unto the end shall be war; desolations are determined." For the remainder of the interval between the 69th seven and the 70th seven, the land would be characterized by war, and its resulting condition would be desolation. All this would set the stage for the final, or 70th, seven.

The 70th Seven--Daniel 9:27

From where we stand in time today, the last seven years of Daniel's prophecy are still prophetic, still future, but it is with their conclusion that all six purposes of verse 24 will reach their fulfillment. The verse's main points are as follows: First, the 70th seven will begin only with the signing of a seven-year covenant or treaty between Israel and a major Gentile political leader. Second, in the middle of that period, that is, after 3 1/2 years, this Gentile leader will break his treaty with Israel and cause a cessation of the sacrificial system. The implication here is that by this time a Temple in Jerusalem will have been rebuilt again and the sacrificial system of Moses reinstituted, but then will be forcefully ceased. Thirdly, the result of the breaking of this covenant is that the temple will now be abominated. The "abomination" refers to an image or an idol. As it was in the days of Antiochus Epiphanes, so it will be again in the future when a Gentile ruler will abominate the Temple by means of idolatry. Fourth, the abomination is to be followed by wrath and desolation, persecution and warfare, for the remaining half of the 70th seven (the final 3 1/2 years). This is similar to the trials and tribulations the rabbis spoke of as preparation for the establishment of the messianic kingdom. These terrible days were referred to as "the footsteps of the Messiah." But once those days have run their course, the last three things predicted in verse 24 will occur; after this period the age of righteousness will be brought in, in which the most holy place will be anointed and every vision and prophecy be fulfilled. At this point the messianic kingdom for which the prophet Daniel yearned will be set up.

Obviously, the messianic kingdom requires the Messiah to rule as king. This means the Messiah will come after the 70th seven.

Yet earlier Daniel stated that the Messiah would come and be killed after the 69th seven. This would appear to be a contradiction unless Daniel was speaking of two comings of the Messiah. The first time was to be after the 69th seven, when he would die a penal, substitutionary death for the sins of Israel and accomplish the first three purposes listed in verse 24. The second time was to be after the 70th seven (still future), when he will establish the messianic kingdom and accomplish the last three things of verse 24. There is also an important implication here that should not be missed. The Messiah would be killed after his first coming. Yet he would be alive at his second coming. The implication is that the Messiah would be resurrected from the dead after he was killed.

Conclusions

This dramatic prophecy features certain things in very clear and unmistakable terms. First, the Messiah was to be on earth 483 years after the decree to rebuild Jerusalem. Second, after his appearance on earth he was to be killed, not for his own sins, but rather for those of others; and the death he would die was to be the death of the penalty of the law. Third, the death of the Messiah had to come sometime before Jerusalem and the Temple were destroyed again, which occurred in the year 70 C.E. Fourth, some time after the destruction of Jerusalem and the Temple, and following a long period of warfare, the 70th seven will commence, and once that has run its course, Messiah's kingdom and age of righteousness will be established. For that to occur, the implication is that the Messiah who was killed would return again.

But who is this Messiah? One man fulfills all that is required in this passage. Jesus of Nazareth was born into the Jewish world and proclaimed his messiahship 483 years after the decree to rebuild and restore Jerusalem was issued. In the year 30 C.E., Jesus was executed by crucifixion. Daniel indicated that he would be cut off, not for himself, but rather for others. Isaiah 53 also prophesied the death of the Messiah, pointing out that he would die a substitutionary death on behalf of his people Israel. The teaching of the New Covenant is that Jesus died a penal death by taking upon himself the penalty of the Law as a substitute for his people. In keeping with Daniel 9:24, he died for the purpose of making an atonement for sins. Three days after his death, he was resurrected. Finally, the New Covenant proclaims the fact that he will someday return to set up his kingdom and the age of righteousness. If Daniel was right, then Messiah came and died prior to the year 70 C.E. If Daniel was right, then there are no other options for who the Messiah is, but Jesus of Nazareth. If Daniel was right, this Jesus is destined to return and to set up the messianic kingdom.

Scripture quotations are taken from the Standard American Edition of the Revised Version of the Bible (a.k.a. American Standard Version), 1901, Thomas Nelson & Sons.

Christian Anti-Semitism?

by Barry Leventhal

Anti-Semitism is both illogical and irrational. Its bitter fruit stems from psychological, political and religious roots. Whatever the causes, this scourge has plagued humanity for centuries. Although the term anti-Semitism was only recently coined in 1879 by the German agitator, Wilhelm Marr, it was soon applied to all forms of hostility toward Jews throughout history.[1] Its genesis and genealogy go back hundreds of years before the common era. So-called Christian anti-Semitism is antedated by hatred of Jews among ancients. One authoritative Jewish source accurately reflects these anti-Semitic beginnings, "Anti-Jewish prejudice appeared in antiquity mainly in countries which later became part of the Roman Empire. Refusal by the Jews to accept the imperially sanctioned cult in any form was regarded by Rome as a refusal to recognize the authority of the state, and the rejection of rules then universally held sacred."[2] The Jewish people could only allow themselves to worship the one, true, invisible God. Caesar was lord--no other was tolerated, especially an unseen One. The first recorded outbreaks of anti-Semitism as a national policy date back to around 1550 B.C.E. Interestingly, the Bible records the historical incident. The first chapter of the Book of Exodus credits the Egyptians with the infamous distinction of beginning national anti-Semitism. Their irrational fear that our people would outgrow and eventually outnumber them led them to the conclusion that the Hebrews would take over their mighty empire. This ancient episode has a very modern ring to it!

Who Is Really Responsible?

Although anti-Semitism goes back to ancient history, its greatest impetus came as a result of the accusation that the Jews committed deicide, the killing of God by the crucifixion of Christ. It was vehemently asserted that the sole guilt for the death of Jesus Christ must lie with the Jews.

Maintaining the guilt of the Jews, the church, primarily composed of Gentiles by this time, sought to "repay" the guilty party, a "repayment" enacted in the name of Christ and for the glory of God. But is it really true that our people bear the sole guilt for the death of Jesus? Have the stinging cries of "Christ-killer" been justified down through the centuries? The New Testament portion of the Bible is our major source of information for the events surrounding the death of Jesus. Where does the New Testament actually place the burden of guilt? Who is really responsible for the death of Jesus Christ?

The following disciples of Jesus recorded the names of those parties whom God holds responsible for the death of the Messiah:

For truly in this city there were gathered together against Thy holy servant Jesus, whom Thou didst anoint, both Herod and Pontius Pilate, along with the Gentiles and the peoples of Israel, to do whatever Thy hand and Thy purpose predestined to occur.

Acts 4:27-28

It is obvious that the Jews alone were not responsible for the crucifixion of Jesus. The Roman government, through the decisions of her governing authorities, Herod and Pontius Pilate, bears a portion of the guilt. It is worthy to note that the Roman historian Tacitus, writing in his Roman Annals (written between C.E. 115 and 117), mentions that Christ "was executed by sentence of the procurator Pontius Pilate in the reign of Tiberius" (Annals, XV. 44). He does not mention Jewish responsibility for the death of Christ. The historical account in Acts also states that the Gentiles share in the guilt of Jesus' death, and "the peoples of Israel," as well. The first-century Jewish historian Josephus also records a more balanced responsibility between Pilate and the Jews of the first century (Antiquities of the Jews, XVII. 3). Peter, one of the early Jewish believers, says that the first-century Jews crucified Jesus "in ignorance" (Acts 3:17).

But without removing human responsibility, it is obvious that God himself determined that the Messiah must die. Whatever the Romans, the Gentiles, or the peoples of Israel did in the first century, they fulfilled whatever the hand and purpose of God predestined (Acts 4:28). It was divine imperative, the Messiah of Israel must die in order to become the Savior of the world. Isaiah, the prince of our Jewish prophets, predicted such a voluntary death some 700 years before the coming of Jesus the Messiah (Isa. 52:13-53:12). It was the Lord who "caused the iniquity of us all to fall on Him" (Isa. 53:6). It pleased the Lord "to crush Him, putting Him to grief" (Isa. 53:10). Isaiah prophesied that the Messiah would go to his death willingly, "Like a lamb that is led to slaughter, and like a sheep that is silent before its shearers, so He did not open His mouth" (Isa. 53:7).

Jesus himself made this quite clear when he said, "I lay down My life that I may take it again. No one has taken it away from Me, but I lay it down on My own initiative. I have authority to lay it down, and I have authority to take it up again" (John 10:17-18). The death of Jesus was not the helpless, morbid charade of a demented first-century Jewish carpenter. It was God's greatest display of mercy and grace for a guilty human race. Jesus died voluntarily for humanity and it is all humanity that must bear the collective guilt for that death. But this guilt is removed from anyone, Jew or Gentile, when he receives the Messiah and his free gift of forgiveness and eternal life.

While admitting that some of those who professed Christ were responsible for the wholesale persecution of the Jewish people, it does not necessarily follow that they were consistent with biblical teaching on this point. In fact, they demonstrated utter inconsistency with that which they supposedly professed. This can be seen in at least three major areas.

Forgiveness--Not Revenge!

First, anti-Semitism is totally inconsistent with the stated attitude of Jesus toward the Jews. To believe that Jesus is the Messiah or Christ and then not reflect his attitude toward the Jewish people is the height of hypocrisy, let alone a fallacious inconsistency. Jesus was born a Jew, he lived as a Jew, and he died a Jew, by his choice. Even his resurrection was molded after Jewish expectation. He lived in the midst of his Jewish people and he loved them with a love unparalleled in the annals of Jewish history. Even when it became apparent that a large number of his people had rejected his messianic claims, Jesus wept over a city that not only missed his arrival, but also a city that would come under the Roman destruction in the very near future. Jerusalem the golden, would become Jerusalem the ruin (Luke 19:37-44).

Even in his hour of death, he prayed, "Father, forgive them; for they do not know what they are doing" (Luke 23:34). His dying heart desired forgiveness, not revenge! Is it any wonder that Jesus told his disciples that love would be the one undeniable evidence that they had been with him (John 13:34-35)? He commanded them, "Love your enemies, and pray for those who persecute you" (Matt. 5:44). One can argue against a doctrine and fight against a cause, but when love is felt, the message is heard! The early Jewish believers were known for many things, but none more forcibly than their undying love for their Messiah and their Jewish kinsmen. It is utterly inconsistent to despise those who are so dearly loved by Jesus himself. Prejudice must fade in the dawn of his love.

Second, anti-Semitism is absolutely inconsistent with the attitude and teaching of the apostles, the early Jewish leaders of the Christian church. They were not only loyal Jews who had come to believe that Jesus was the Jewish Messiah, but they also wrote the documents of the New Testament. They knew Jesus personally and willingly died as martyrs rather than renounce him. The Apostle Paul, more than any other, carried the good news of the Jewish Messiah to the farthest corners of the earth. And yet, wherever he traveled, he never bypassed the Jews; he always went to them first. God's program begins with the Jews (Romans 1:16). Paul's greatest sorrow was that many of his kinsmen had rejected their Messiah. This great apostle's love for his Jewish people was so intense that he was willing, if it were possible, to surrender his own salvation and suffer the eternal judgment of God if they would only come back to Jesus as the Jewish Messiah. "I have great sorrow and unceasing grief in my heart. For I could wish that I myself were accursed, separated from the Messiah for the sake of my brethren, my kinsmen according to the flesh" (Romans 9:2-3). His prayers were constantly rising before the throne of God on their behalf: "My heart's desire and my prayer to God for them is their salvation" (Romans 10:1).

Paul realized that Israel's future was anchored in her great heritage. The Jewish people "are beloved for the sake of the fathers" (Romans 11:28). God's covenant promises to Abraham, Isaac and Jacob are not broken and irretrievably cast aside. The promises stand firm and secure. Like Jesus before him, Paul foresaw a day in the distant future when Israel would experience all of the messianic blessings, that glorious day when the nations would turn to Jesus as the Messiah of Israel and the Savior of the world (Romans 11:25-29). The apostles would have been appalled at the centuries of anti-Semitic hatred. It is absolutely inconsistent with not only their love and concern for the Jews, but also with their hope for Israel and her future

Third, anti-Semitism is utterly inconsistent with the Old Testament portion of the Bible, the only authoritative book of the earliest church. The Jewish Scriptures formed the basis for the early Christian community. Deny these Scriptures, and the foundation of their Christian faith disintegrates. Even when the New Testament documents were completed, the believers still embraced the Jewish Scriptures alongside of them, totally equal in authority and teachings.

One of the most significant passages in the Jewish Scriptures, a passage to which the early church undoubtedly adhered (see Galatians 3:8), is Genesis 12:1-3. God called Abraham to follow him to a place that he would show him. He gave to Abraham certain personal, national and universal promises. One of these promises contained a clause against anti-Semitism. God said to Abraham, "And I will bless those who bless you, and the one who curses you I will curse" (Genesis 12:3). God committed himself without reservation to preserving Abraham and his posterity. And his intention to preserve and bless them is expressed in this phrase. The way an individual or a nation treated Abraham and his people would determine the way God would treat them. Blessing the Jews brought God's blessing and cursing them brought God's condemnation.

This stipulation against anti-Semitism has proved out through both biblical and secular history to this very day. All the great powers, individual or corporate, who attempted to exterminate the Jews, fell sooner or later by the same divine stroke of justice, whether it was Assyria or Babylon of the ancient world or Spain or Germany of the modern world. The divine promise stood secure and inviolate, for God himself had declared it. And this same principle still stands secure and inviolate today, as it always will. The promise reflects the character and nature of the promise-giver, who is truthful and unchanging. To believe in Christ is to believe in Christ's Bible. And to believe in his Bible is to believe in God's covenant with Abraham, the father of the Hebrew people. Any attack on God's covenant people is an attack on the God of the covenant, which is antithetical to belief in Christ. For he said, "You shall love the Lord your God with all your heart, and with all your soul. and with all your mind," and "You shall love your neighbor as yourself" (Matt. 22:34-40). Those guilty of such an attack show by their fruits that they don't follow Christ at all.

Believing in Christ does not produce anti-Semitism It may have been the convenient scapegoat for some, perhaps for many. For prejudice runs deep in the core of men's experience. But belief in Christ is not the cause of anti-Semitism. In fact, one Jewish source claims that modern anti-Semitism is not religiously motivated at all, "Modern anti-Semitism is thus built on racial, not religious foundations and the adoption of the prevailing faith no longer provides an escape route for persecuted Jews."[3] For a professing Christian to side with the anti-Semite is to side not only against the Jewish apostles who penned the Christian New Testament, and against the Jewish Messiah who inspired the Christian New Testament, but it also invites the sternest judgment from the God of Abraham, Isaac and Jacob. To court God's judgment doesn't seem very rational or logical.

ENDNOTES

1 Wigoder, Geoffrey, ed., "Anti-Semitism," Encyclopedic Dictionary of Judaica (New York: Leon Amiel Publisher, 1974), p. 33.

2 Ibid., pp. 33-34.

3 Werblosky, R.J. and Wigoder, Geoffrey, eds., "Anti-Semitism," The Encyclopedia of the Jewish Religion (New York: Holt, Rinehart and Winston, Inc., 1965), p. 34.

Conclusion

They were brothers. They looked alike. But they weren't twins.

One was brilliant. His mind seemed able to cut through almost any problem. Not only that, he was artistically talented. Whether through fine art, photography, music, or dance, his work always showed that he knew and could do what was truly beautiful. Friendly and compassionate, with a wide circle of friends, this one never seemed lonely. He was the older of the two.

The younger brother was, well, just ordinary. Now it's no tragedy to be just ordinary, unless you happen to have an older brother who beams with such a brilliant light that his brightness seems to put you in a shadow. The younger brother was smart enough to solve most of the same problems; it just took him a little longer. He, too, could write poetry, take pictures, paint, sing and dance. He was actually quite gifted in some areas, and even when he didn't excel, he still did reasonably well...until he compared himself to his brother. Then his poetry, his painting, his music, his everything all seemed to pale under his brother's brilliance.

It was hard for the younger to live in the same town with his brother, so he moved away. Older brother rose to receive praise and acclaim far beyond the borders of their home town. Eventually, there was no place where the younger brother could go to escape comparison, for his older brother was known everywhere. The younger brother changed his name, grew a beard to cover his face, and tried to forget from whence he came. He nearly succeeded in forgetting his true identity after his parents died, for he no longer had an obligation to visit his old home town.

Then he became seriously ill. The lady at the hospital admissions office asked that somber question, "In case of...who is the next of kin to be notified?" The younger brother had never married, never had children; his "next of kin" was his older brother, now an acclaimed and famous statesman. He hesitated, then told the lady the name of his brother. She couldn't believe it. He drew a long breath and said that it was true. He explained that he had changed his name years earlier. When she heard his real name and carefully examined his face, she saw enough resemblance to convince her that he was telling the truth.

The sick man was admitted, and his condition worsened. The doctors felt someone should be notified, for even if the man recovered, he would not be able to care for himself. They sent a telegram to the celebrated brother, who upon hearing the grave news cancelled important matters of state to come to the side of the younger brother. Upon his arrival, the younger brother was able to talk and chuckle, smile, and almost cry at things he hadn't talked or even thought of for a long time: their home town, their parents, the people they knew together. And the younger brother realized that for decades he had been running to escape from the person who would have been his best friend-- someone who really valued and appreciated him.

So far as coming home from the hospital, there was no question about it. He would be moved by air ambulance and have the best medical care. His brother the statesman would cut back his busy schedule and see to that. To be sure, this attentiveness sweetened the life of the younger brother, but it was a bitter sweetness. Now he knew that all those years--as a boy, as a young man, as a mature adult--he had deprived himself of what could have been his greatest joy--being the brother of a great man, and being brightened by the presence of a brilliant light.

Y'shua is that older brother. Jesus is our relative, our Kinsman-Redeemer, who wants to claim us as his family.

Yet for some, the very mention of his name causes revulsion. Wherever we Jews go we're reminded of him, whether it's a place called Trinity Square, or a person called Hans Christian Andersen. Most Jews would prefer to hear "Happy Holiday," but people keep slipping and saying "Merry Christmas," instead. These are all constant reminders of that elder brother from whom we would like to escape.

Perhaps it's difficult to see Y'shua as the older brother, when you regard Abraham as the father of our faith. After all, Abraham lived 1800 years before the babe was born in Bethlehem. Yet it was Jesus himself who told a crowd, "before Abraham was, I am." He was not only stating that he existed before Abraham, but by using that portion of the Ineffable Name, "I am that I am," he was saying that he always existed. The prophet Micah, in predicting the birth of the Messiah some 700 years before the event took place, said that the Messiah was to be born in Bethlehem...and that "his goings forth have been from of old, from everlasting" (Micah 5:2). This older brother is not only preexistent, but self-existent, and he has created all which does exist.

Some insist, "Jesus is the Gentile god," or "Jesus is not for the Jews." What so few of our Jewish people seem to realize is that even the name "Christ" involves an essential teaching of the Jewish religion. When Maimonides compiled the Thirteen Articles of Faith, he said, "I believe with perfect faith in the coming of the Christ (Messiah), and though he tarry I will pray for him." That's right, the common word "Christ" is from the Greek *Cristos*, which is a translation of a Hebrew word meaning "anointed." It is taken directly from the word "Mashiach."

Christian theologians recognize that if Christianity is anything other than Jewish, then it is not truly Christian. Some deny that the name "Christ" and "Christian" are Jewish in their origins. That is like an Israeli denying that an American Jew is Jewish because he lives in a "foreign" country. The fact that Gentiles (non-Jews) believe in Jesus Christ cannot reach back in time and change the fact that he is Jewish, or that he is for Jews.

It wasn't the Gentiles--followers of Zeus, or Ahura Mazda--who were awaiting the coming of a Messiah who would be a prophet, priest, and king, God's truly anointed one. No, from the beginning it was the Jewish people who hoped for a Christ, an "anointed." It was the Jewish prophets who promulgated a belief in the Jewish Messiah.

In Hebrew thought, "anointed" is a metaphor of appointment or the designation and consecration of a person to do a particular task. There's absolutely no corollary in any of the Gentile religions, unless those religions borrowed from Judaism.

It might be argued that modern Christendom is merely derivative of the original Jewish revelation, and that Christianity has so drastically departed from its Jewish roots that it is no longer true to its beginnings. It must then also be admitted that Judaism has departed even more from the original revelation. In fact, modern-day Judaism is not merely alienated from biblical Judaism, it's alienated from the Judaism of 100 years ago! This can be seen by reading the contents of any prayer book (siddur). The siddur constantly deals with themes of sin and salvation, redemption and revelation, the sovereignty of God, and the obligation of man to obey. The prayer book of 100 years ago was filled with praise for a Creator and a Sustainer. Today, many rabbis ignore the religion of their great-grandfathers, and formulate more palatable ideas, which are conveyed not as their own opinion, but as what "Judaism teaches." To many Jews today, God is a remote notion, and man in this life is ever and all important.

If changes in Judaism make it difficult to recognize the Jewishness of Y'shua, depictions of him in art as the blue-eyed, blond-bearded person seated in repose further suggest the idea that Jesus was from the Gentiles and for the Gentiles. In fact, one could almost say he looks more like a bearded lady from the very feminine features depicted...but most women I know would object to being characterized by the extreme passivity in which he's portrayed. The Jewish Messiah was a man of action, a commander, a king, a leader; a judge like Joshua; a ruler like Moses; a manly poet like King David. He was also gentle, sensitive, wise, compassionate and loving. The Messiah is so much more than any artist has ever been able to depict or any prophet has been able to describe. Only Jesus lived up to that role.

Jesus' teachings were Jewish, and the manner in which he taught was Jewish. When he said that he was the Messiah, he was speaking to the hearts of people who believed that a Messiah would come. As Messiah, he was a prophet, and a priest, and a king. Like the prophets before him, Y'shua spoke outside the established religious channels. As a priest, the sacrifice he offered was outside of the established sanctuary. As a king, he gathered citizens, not only from Israel, but from what was commonly understood to be "the nations."

Jesus was "the outsider" to Jews. And he was "the outsider" to Gentiles as well. He spoke lovingly to the Jewish people. It's true, some of his words were harsh, but not nearly as harsh as the words of the ancient prophets. Y'shua condemned sin, but he never condemned the sinner. He invited those sinners to come to him, to come to God. He gave them hope and courage when society rejected them. He granted forgiveness freely to those who recognized their need, but to those who cloaked themselves in the robes of self-righteousness and sanctimoniously sought to confound rather than elicit truth, he spoke sternly.

Jesus was a Jew. He was recognized as a Jew, and he certainly was for the Jewish people. Before the formation of the body of knowledge that was necessary when the atonement was accomplished, he sent his Jewish disciples out, and commissioned them to go only to "the lost sheep of the house of Israel." And when a Syro-Phoenician woman came to him, asking him to heal her, he pointed out that he was a Jew and had come for the Jews. Yet her faith reached past that barrier, her faith crawled over the wall, that she might touch him...and she received the healing she desired. According to God's plan, the Messiah is what the prophet promised--a light to the Gentiles. Our Messiah, the Jewish Messiah, is to be the Messiah of all people.

No matter how hard we might try to forget our "older brother," we are flesh of his flesh and bone of his bone, and we cannot disown him without alienating ourselves from our own Jewish identity. Jesus taught the themes and topics which are Jewish concerns today, especially what is now called "Zionism" or the restoration of Israel--the Kingdom of God. He taught how to deal with people redemptively in day-to-day relationships, how to grapple with persecution, how to transcend the trials of life. While we grope for guidance and answers and truth, he stands there, patiently, waiting.

Have you ever seen that bumper sticker: "If you can't find God, who is it that is lost?" In a sense, Y'shua, Jesus, came to call Jews home to the God of Abraham, Isaac, and

Jacob. Jesus was for Jews. He honored the Jews. He upheld the revealed Jewish religion. He commanded kindness toward the Jewish people. He wept over Jerusalem as he anticipated the destruction of the holy city. And when he was angry, he was angry because the Jewish Temple had been defiled, and the Jewish God had been defied. His zeal was for Jewish things, but even more, for Jewish people to know and love the God of Israel.

Jesus not only was for the Jews, but since Jesus still exists, he *is* for the Jews (as well as all people) today. For us to turn our backs on him, the most celebrated Jew in all of history, is a paradox. It is puzzling that somehow, what he showed as love is interpreted as hate. And that which was given to be eternal truth, has become, in the minds of some people, an historical lie. What Y'shua demonstrated was the apex of Jewishness; yet it is characteristically thought to be Gentile. We Jews have lost that which is most Jewish: our own Messiah, Jesus. He is that older brother who is seeking us, wanting to enrich our lives, imploring us to be reconciled to him. Jesus is for Jews, so we are Jews for him.

Glossary

Alef-Bet: the Hebrew alphabet; one of the first things a Jewish child learns as part of his or her religious instruction.

Bar Mitzvah: "son of commandment." In the Jewish religion, 13 is the age of accountability. This "rite of passage" is marked by a public reading from the Torah, often followed by a big celebration.

Bimah: the synagogue pulpit, or place of judgment.

Borachas: blessings.

Chasidim: "pious ones," followers of Chasidism. This movement was founded by the Baal Shem Tov (1700-1760) and emphasizes a more emotional religious expression than is traditionally practiced by most Jews. Chasidim are also distinct in their personal loyalty to the *tzadik,* or spiritual leader.

Cheder: literally "room," as in one-room school. Cheder is the Jewish elementary school, privately owned as opposed to the Talmud-Torah, which is a community-supported religious school. Probably the most prevalent elementary Jewish education is acquired via the congregational schools, i.e. parochial schools connected with the synagogue. Though each of these three methods of Jewish education is distinct, many people use the word "cheder" when referring to any one of the three.

Chupoh: what every Jewish mother wants her son or daughter to stand under—the wedding canopy. It symbolizes a tent which the bride and groom are to enter upon their nuptials. The square cloth cover (sometimes very ornate) is held up with four poles.

Coconut shy: what every Jewish mother doesn't want for her son or daughter to be—the indirect target of an attack meant for somebody else. Derived from a game where the player throws a ball, aiming to hit a coconut. If the player misses the target, that which is hit becomes the coconut shy.

Fleishedik or *fleishig:* one of three divisions of food which has been categorized for the purpose of keeping kosher. Fleishig is meat, *milchig* is dairy and *pareve* is neutral.

Frum: very religious, observant of Jewish law.

Goy: literally "nation," it is a term which means one who belongs to another nation, i.e. a non-Jew (plural: goyim).

Gragers: a delight for children and a test of endurance for adults. They are noisemakers which are used on the eve of Purim. As the Scroll of Esther is read, it is traditional to cheer whenever the name of Mordechai is read and to "boo" and twirl gragers whenever wicked Haman's name is read. The gragers make a loud rattling sound which is used to blot out Haman's name whenever the villain's name is pronounced.

Haggadah: literally "the narrative" or "story." This is the book (or in some cases, condensed booklet) which gives the order of service for the Passover celebration. The Haggadah tells the story of how God brought Israel out from slavery in Egypt. Included are narratives, songs, psalms and other prayers to commemorate freedom and praise the Almighty for his mighty acts of redemption.

Hamantaschen: high-calorie reminders of how our people were rescued from wicked Haman's plot on Purim. They are three-cornered pastries or cookies with prune, poppy seed or apricot filling. They represent the three-cornered hat of Haman, whose defeat in destroying our people is cause for celebration. They also represent the diet many of us will have to go on after Purim.

338

Ha'Shem: "The Name," a way of referring to God which particularly points out his holiness, for his name is too sacred to be pronounced.

Kashrut: system of discerning forbidden and permitted foods according to the dietary laws of the Torah and Talmud. This includes draining of blood, separation of meat and milk, abstinence from diseased or improperly slaughtered animals as well as abstinence from prohibited animals.

Kiddush: "sanctification," a benediction which is said over a cup of wine to sanctify Sabbaths and holidays.

Kippa: head covering (see "yarmulka").

Kol Nidre: literally "all vows," Kol Nidre is the prayer of repentance which is traditionally chanted just before sunset on the eve of Yom Kippur (the Day of Atonement).

Lerner: teacher.

Lubavich: a small town in the Eastern Ukraine where a branch of Chasidim known as "Chabad" was centered in 1897. Followers of the Chabad movement today are still associated with the town; the term "Lubavich Chasidism" or "Lubavicher" has reference to Chabad.

Megilla: the scroll; often used to refer to the Scroll of Esther, which is traditionally read in the synagogue on the eve of Purim (see "grager").

Menorah: the nine-branched candelabrum used at Hannukah is commonly referred to as a menorah, although a more accurate description for it would be "chanukiah." Menorah is actually the word for a candelabrum consisting of six or eight branches, which is used in the synagogue. The original temple menorah had seven branches, but the use of seven branches is avoided today, that we might draw a distinction between worship today and worship when the Temple was still in existence.

Mezuzah: a parchment scroll attached to the doorpost of a Jewish home and, in ultra-observant families, on all the doorways within the home. On the parchment are written the words from Deuteronomy 6:4-11 and Deuteronomy 11:13-21, affirming the oneness of God. The scroll is encased in metal or wood.

Mishegoss: what your mother tells you if you say you don't want to get married—or worse yet, if you're married and you tell her you don't want to have children—craziness!

Mishpochah: what you should have if your head is not filled with mishegoss—family!

Nachas: what you'll get when someone in your mishpochah becomes a doctor or lawyer: the pleasure or satisfaction usually derived from enjoying the accomplishments or happiness of those who are close to us.

Nudge: a little push, but it's only for your own good!

Purim: Jewish holiday to commemorate God's preservation of our people, and the heroic foiling of a plan to destroy us. The origins of this holiday are found in the Book of Esther.

Pushka: collection box used for charitable donations.

Schlepp: the trip your mother will make for you, no matter how long it takes, so you shouldn't go hungry, cold, or suffer in any other way because she didn't travel the two hundred miles to bring you whatever it was you left at her house the last time you visited (like half her refrigerator, or the sweater you've been trying to ditch since Aunt Grizelda gave it to you on your bar mitzvah). To schlepp means to drag or travel an inconveniently long distance.

Schlocky: the way you shouldn't look if you want your mother to have nachas. Schlocky means sloppy or in poor taste or poor quality.

Schmaltz: for cooking purposes, schmaltz is fat used instead of butter or mayonaise. Can also mean dripping with sentiment as in the schmaltziest farewell ever given.

Shabbat: Sabbath.

Shabbat Shalom: "Sabbath Peace," an appropriate Jewish greeting from sundown Friday evening to sundown Saturday evening.

Shema: passage of Scripture from Deuteronomy (6:4-11). It is chanted as one of the most important of all Jewish prayers. It affirms the sovereignty and oneness of God.

Shmatte: what a woman who wants to impress you will call the evening gown she's wearing when you complement her— "Oh, this old shmatte?" (rag)

Shmues: small talk, chit-chat.

Shockle: a shuffle or little dance done at prayer.

Shtick: a word with many uses, including a bit of a theatrical act, professional or otherwise. For example: "Enough with the crying shtick. You turn the tears on and off like your eyes would be a water faucet."

Shul: synagogue.

Siddur: prayer book. The siddur contains prayers arranged in a traditional order for daily worship as well as for specified occasions, both public and private.

Sukkot: tabernacles. This is an eight-day holiday of thanksgiving for the harvest.

Tallis: prayer shawl worn over the outer garment by Jewish men for morning prayer, excepting certain holidays when it is worn in the afternoon, or as in the case of Yom Kippur, throughout services all day.

Tenach: the Hebrew Scriptures. Each of the three consonants signifies one of the three divisions of the Bible: "T" for Torah (the first five books) "N" for Neviim (the prophets) and "CH" for Chesuvim (all the other writings).

Tefillin: Scriptures inscribed on parchment which are encased in small leather boxes to be strapped on the arm and head for prayer. Two of the Scriptures on the parchment are from Exodus (Exodus 13:1-10 and Exodus 13:11-16) and the other two are from Deuteronomy (Deuteronomy 6:4-9 and Deuteronomy 11:13-20). The ritual of strapping the tefillin on for prayer is referred to as "laying tefillin," or "putting on tefillin." It is done in accordance with Exodus 13:9, "And it shall be for a sign upon thy hand and for a frontlet between thine eyes." The ritual is to be performed each morning, excepting Sabbaths and holidays.

Traif (terefah): food which is forbidden according to the dietary laws. Most pizza and Chinese food are definitely traif.

Tsuris: troubles or woes, like you shouldn't have.

Tzimmes: holiday food traditionally eaten at Passover. Nobody makes it the same, so it's hard to define. My mother makes it with carrots, yams, prunes, and turnips. Everything should be cooked long enough so that it is a hodge-podge of blended flavors. Some people add stew meat. Sometimes "tzimmes" is used to mean "fuss." When my mother thinks someone is going on long about something, she'll say, "Why are they making such a big tzimmes out of nothing?"

X: there are no words in Hebrew or Yiddish that begin with this sound.

Yarmulka: skullcap. If you are not Jewish, please know that this should not be referred to as "one of those little beanies." It is worn by religious Jewish men and is meant to signify man's humility before God.

Yichus: genealogy, bloodline, family tree. If you come from a good family, you've got yichus. A good family is usually one which is noted for a scholarly and charitable lifestyle.

Yiddishkeit: Jewishness; Jewish tradition, culture or "flavor."

Suggested Reading

If you don't yet believe in Jesus but want more information, the following books might be helpful:

Benhayim, Menahem. *Jews, Gentiles and the New Testament.* Jerusalem: Yanetz Press, 1985. An examination of many charges levelled by critics of the New Testament, both Jewish and Gentile, against its alleged anti-Semitism.

Fruchtenbaum, Arnold G. *Jesus Was a Jew.* Nashville: Broadman Press, 1974. Written to show the relationship of Jesus to the Jewish people; how Jesus fit into his own Jewish society and how Jesus is still for Jewish people today.

Frydland, Rachmiel. *When Being Jewish Was A Crime.* Nashville: Thomas Nelson Publishers, 1978. This story of a Polish Jew who came to faith in Y'shua during the Nazi occupation dispells the myth that Jews become Christians to avoid persecution.

Habermans, Gary R. *Ancient Evidence for the Life of Jesus.* Nashville: Thomas Nelson Publishers, 1984. A concise presentation of the evidence for the resurrection of Jesus.

Kac, Arthur. *The Messiahship of Jesus.* Chicago: Moody Press, 1963. A compilation of quotes and excerpts from books, pamphlets and articles by Jews, past and present-- some believers, some not--to authenticate the claims that Jesus is the Messiah of Israel.

Katz, Arthur. *Ben Israel.* Plainfield, NJ: Logos International, 1970. A candid presentation of a secular agnostic American-Jewish radical's odyssey to faith in Israel's Messiah.

Lewis, C.S. *Mere Christianity.* New York: Macmillan Publishing, Inc., 1964. An articulate and erudite apologetic for Christianity.

Lockyer, Herbert. *All the Messianic Prophecies of the Bible.* Grand Rapids: Zondervan, 1973. Lists passages pointing to the Messiah.

McDowell, Josh. *Evidence That Demands a Verdict,* Vol. 1. San Bernardino, CA: Campus Crusade for Christ, Inc., 1972. A study of the reliability of Scriptures and their implications as regard Jesus.

McDowell, Josh. *The Resurrection Factor.* San Bernardino, CA: Here's Life Publishers, Inc., 1981. A scholarly and readable presentation of evidence from non-biblical sources that Jesus lived a sinless life, died on a Roman cross and was resurrected.

Morrison, Frank. *Who Moved the Stone?* Downers Grove, IL: Inter-Varsity Press, 1958 (orig. publ. 1930). An examination of the resurrection of Jesus by a lawyer who started out to disprove it and became convinced that it happened.

Rosen, Moishe. *Y'shua.* Chicago: Moody Press, 1982. An argument for the messiahship of Jesus for Jewish people who are interested in examining the claims of the New Testament against the background of the Hebrew Scriptures and rabbinic writings.

Roth, Sid. *Something for Nothing.* Plainfield, NJ: Logos International, 1976. Sid Roth thought the power of wealth and the occult could satisfy, but he paid a high price to experience their destructive power, until he met Jesus.

Schaeffer Edith. *Christianity is Jewish.* Wheaton, IL: Tyndale House, 1977. Traces the continuity of faith from the Old Covenant to the New.

Telchin, Stan. *Betrayed!* Lincoln, VA: Chosen Books, 1981. The dramatic story of a Jewish father who set out to prove to his daughter that Jesus is not the Messiah, and proved to himself the exact oppposite.

If you're Jewish and you've become a believer in Y'shua, the following helps are available:

Bruce, F.F. *New Testament History.* Garden City, NY: Anchor Books, Doubleday & Co., 1972. Helps the reader of the New Testament to see the books in the historical setting in which the events took place and the books themselves were written.

Buksbazen, Victor. *The Gospel in the Feasts of Israel.* Philadelphia: Spearhead Press, 1954. Explains how the Jewish festivals pointed to the coming of Jesus and his ministry as Messiah.

Douglas, J. D. ed. *The New Bible Dictionary.* Grand Rapids: Eerdmans, 1962. A thorough one-volume reference book about the people, places and subjects found in the Bible.

Edersheim, Alfred. *Old Testament Bible History.* Grand Rapids: Eerdmans, 1972. An excellent work on the history of Israel in the Old Testament by a Jewish-Christian scholar.

Fruchtenbaum, Arnold G. *Hebrew Christianity --It's Theology, History and Philosophy.* Washington, D.C.: Canon Press, 1974. An introduction to the modern Hebrew-Christian movement.

Glaser, Mitch and Zhava. *The Fall Feasts of Israel.* Chicago: Moody Press, 1987. An in-depth study of the origins, traditions and messianic implications of Rosh Hashanah, Yom Kippur, and Sukkot.

Growth Book. San Francisco: Jews for Jesus, 1983. A 34-page booklet to help new Jewish believers in Jesus become oriented in their faith as well as understand how family and friends might respond to their belief in Jesus.

Juster, Daniel C. *Jewishness and Jesus.* Downers Grove, IL: InterVarsity Press, 1977. Dan Juster, leader of the Union of the Messianic Jewish Congregations in the United States, has given the perspective of Jesus in his Jewish setting.

Little, Paul. *Know Why You Believe.* Wheaton, IL: Scripture Press, 1970. Helps the lay person understand the reasonableness of our faith in Jesus.

Mears, Henrietta C. *What the Bible Is All About.* Glendale, CA: Regal Books-Gospel Light Publishers, 1974. An excellent "book-by-book" introduction to the Bible for beginners.

Rosen, Moishe and Ceil. *Christ in the Passover.* Chicago: Moody Press, 1978. An explanation of the Jewish Passover feast as it was celebrated and fulfilled by Jesus at the Last Supper.

Schaeffer, Edith. *Christianity is Jewish.* Wheaton, IL: Tyndale House, 1977. (See first heading.)

Sire, James W. *Scripture Twisting.* Downers Grove, IL: Inter-Varsity Press, 1980. A look at how "cult" groups misuse the Scriptures, what we can learn from this, and how we can keep from going astray ourselves.

If you're not Jewish but are a believer in Jesus who wants to find out more about how Jesus is for Jews, the following might help:

DeRidder, Richard R. *God Has Not Rejected His People.* Grand Rapids: Baker Book House, 1977. Affirms God's continuing covenant relationship with Israel, and the need for Jews to be introduced to Jesus.

Edersheim, Alfred. *The Life and Times of Jesus the Messiah.* Grand Rapids: Eerdmans, 1971. An excellent, detailed study of the Jewish background of the life and ministry of Jesus.

Hagner, Donald A. *The Jewish Reclamation of Jesus.* Grand Rapids: Zondervan, 1984. An analysis and critique of the modern Jewish study of Jesus. Also includes a historical survey of the Jewish views of Jesus.

Jocz, Jakob. *The Jewish People and Jesus Christ.* London: SPCK, 1962. Scholarly and intriguing study of the relationship between Christians, the gospel message and the Jewish people.

Jocz, Jakob. *The Jewish People and Jesus Christ after Auschwitz.* Grand Rapids: Baker Book House, 1981. An updated continuation of the previous book.

Kac, Arthur. *The Messianic Hope.* Grand Rapids: Baker Book House, 1975. An analytical look at the mission of Jesus of Nazareth in the light of the messianic expectations of the Old Testament and post-biblical Jewish teaching about Messiah, resurrection and life after death.

Kac, Arthur. *The Spiritual Dilemma of the Jewish People.* Chicago: Moody Press, 1963. An excellent analysis by a Jewish Christian of the factors at the heart of the present Jewish spiritual plight.

For more information write:
Jews for Jesus
60 Haight Street
San Francisco, CA 94102-5895